The Decline of Empires

How Britain and Russia lost their grip over India, Persia and Afghanistan

For Simon, who helped me get it done.

The Decline of Empires

Heather A Campbell

Pen & Sword
MILITARY

AN IMPRINT OF PEN & SWORD BOOKS LTD.
YORKSHIRE - PHILADELPHIA

First published in Great Britain in 2022 by
Pen & Sword Military
An imprint of
Pen & Sword Books Ltd
Yorkshire – Philadelphia

ISBN 9781526775801

Printed and bound in the UK by CPI Group (UK) Ltd, Croydon, CRO 4YY

Pen & Sword Books Ltd includes the Imprints of Atlas, Archaeology, Aviation,
Discovery, Family History, Fiction, History, Maritime, Military, Military
Classics, Politics, Select, Airworld, Frontline Publishing, Leo Cooper, Remember
When, Seaforth Publishing, The Praetorian Press, Wharncliffe Local History,
Wharncliffe Transport, Wharncliffe True Crime and White Owl.

For a complete list of Pen & Sword titles please contact
PEN & SWORD BOOKS LTD
47 Church Street, Barnsley, South Yorkshire, S70 2AS, England
E-mail: enquiries@pen-and-sword.co.uk
Website: www.pen-and-sword.co.uk

Or

PEN AND SWORD BOOKS
1950 Lawrence Rd, Havertown, PA 19083, USA
E-mail: Uspen-and-sword@casematepublishers.com
Website: www,penandswordbooks.com

Contents

Introduction   vii

Chapter 1:   Curzon, Russia and the Great Game   1

Chapter 2:   The Iron Hand and the Velvet Glove, 1918–1919   22

Chapter 3:   A Nice State of Affairs, 1920   48

Chapter 4:   Making Friends, 1921   76

Chapter 5:   A Gigantic Drum, 1922–1923   102

                 The End of An Epoch   128

Notes   137

Bibliography   189

Index   207

Introduction

The East will help us to conquer the West. Let us turn our faces towards Asia.
Vladimir Lenin[1]

It is the prestige and the wealth arising from her Asiatic position that are the foundation stones of the British Empire.
George Nathaniel Curzon[2]

This work was conceived while researching the little-known case of the 26 Baku Commissars – the execution of a number of members of the Azerbaijani Baku Commune on the night of 18 September 1918 outside the city of Krasnovodsk. In the context of the First World War and the Russian civil war, the murder of a few men might not appear very significant. But the incident quickly became a *cause célèbre* for Russia's new rulers, who blamed the British for the act.[3] Essentially, the case of the 26 Commissars was a small but distinct example of just how important this region of the world has always been to Anglo-Russian relations. Indeed, it was only because a British contingent had been in Baku to defend the area from Turkish encroachment that Britain was in a position to be accused of executing the Commissars.[4] It was such considerations which led to one of the founding questions of the work at hand – how did Britain's foreign policy towards South Asia affect its relationship with Soviet Russia?

The importance of Asia to Anglo-Russian relations has certainly been recognised by historians of the pre-1917 period, and the Great Game is a well-established area of historical research. It is in Asia that Britain and Russia battled for supremacy in the nineteenth and early twentieth centuries; where adventure and intrigue were sought by some of the most colourful characters of history; and where Rudyard Kipling found his inspiration for *Kim*. Contemporaries of the post-Russian revolution period also recognised the continued importance of this region of the world, as the above quote from Lenin shows. As a number of scholars have demonstrated, the Bolsheviks were keenly aware of the benefits of spreading revolution among the discontented Asian masses.[5] An 'Appeal to the Working Moslems of Russia and the East' was among the first declarations made by the party upon seizing power, for example,[6] while at the founding of the Comintern in 1919, there was an awareness that the 'colonial question' needed to be addressed.[7] And, as the chances of revolution breaking out in Europe faded in the years after 1917, so the Bolshevik regime looked increasingly to southern Asia to deliver them from isolation.[8]

Given the state of Asia in the period after the First World War, it is unsurprising that Lenin and his comrades looked keenly at the revolutionary potential there. Nationalist fervour, combined with a resentment against Western imperialism, had been growing among the populations of Asia for some time, and after 1918 would only increase in potency, while Muslim discontent (also apparent before the First World War) was inflamed by the involvement of Turkey in the conflict. Great Asian leaders such as Mahatma Gandhi, Reza Khan and Kemal Ataturk would harness these feelings to initiate mass popular movements within their respective countries, and everywhere in the region the oppressed would start pushing back against their domineering rulers. For Britain, this heady combination of nationalism and pan-Islamism was to provide a particular set of difficulties; for the Bolsheviks, it appeared a perfect opportunity.

For Britain, the complexity of the situation in Asia after the war is exemplified by the creation of the Anglo-Persian Agreement in 1919. The brain-child of Lord George Nathaniel Curzon, this diplomatic arrangement between Britain and Persia was designed to create a stable and secure buffer zone between Soviet Russia and India. British money and expertise was to be used to reform Persia's financial and military structures, which would ultimately protect that country from potential Russian advances from the north. Britain's fear of Bolshevism taking hold in Persia (and subsequently the rest of southern Asia) was a seemingly crucial motivator in the creation of this agreement: anti-Bolshevik rhetoric fills the pages of the Foreign Office files of this time. And yet, what also emerges from these documents is a complex debate on Britain's Persian policy. Some British officials could not decide who they were more afraid of: Lenin's newly formed government or a re-constituted imperial Russia. More important, however, is the vigorous opposition which the Government of India had to the creation of the Anglo-Persian Agreement. While London was busy worrying about the catastrophe to be wrought on the world should Bolshevism infiltrate Persia, Delhi was unafraid. Instead, the viceroy and his men were adamant that it was the growth of pan-Islamism and Asian nationalism which Britain should be concentrating on, not Bolshevism. They believed that the agreement was likely to inflame nationalist and Muslim feeling and therefore advocated a less intrusive policy towards Persia. But what made the Indian government view things differently to the Home government?[9] And if the whole point of the Anglo-Persian Agreement was to protect India, why were the protests of the Indian government ignored?

This disagreement between the Home and the Indian government over foreign policy was not restricted to Persia. Comparing the internal government debates on that country with what was said about Afghanistan is even more illuminating. One would think that with India being in such close proximity to Afghanistan, London would largely follow Delhi's lead (especially given that the Indian government had been administering Afghanistan's foreign relations since 1880). What is evident from the archives, however, is that similar debates which were occurring over Persia were being repeated when it came to Afghanistan. Again, there was a propensity for the Home government to emphasise the threat of Bolshevism taking hold in Afghanistan, while the Indian government was continuously pre-occupied with pan-Islamist and nationalist agitation. What also quickly becomes apparent from studying the numerous telegrams, letters and memorandum which flew between departments and across continents, is that there were some within the British government who seemed highly reluctant to accept that the international scene may have changed after 1914. Much of Delhi's time appeared to be spent trying to convince London of the empire's limitations in the post-war world. By 1922, the progress of events in Russia, South Asia and within Britain itself would conspire finally to show the Home government the error of its ways. Little by little through the early 1920s London would be forced to adapt its policies towards Tehran, Kabul and Moscow, until by 1923 things would stand much closer to what the Indian government had advocated in 1918.

The Foreign Office

The creation of British foreign policy in the twentieth century was a complex business. While it may be presumed that the foreign secretary is always responsible for the direction of foreign policy, many have argued that in the post-First World War period the Foreign Office lost its privileged position within the British government. The idea that 'the Foreign Office lacked the influence over British foreign policy that it had exercised before the outbreak of the Great War' is commonplace in the historiography of this topic.[10] Others have taken this further and argued that the Foreign Office was all but ignored until the mid-1920s.[11] The exclusion of Arthur Balfour (Foreign Secretary from December 1916 until October 1919) from Lloyd George's War Cabinet is one such example of the Foreign Office being edged out of government decision-making.[12] Even following the conclusion of the conflict, Balfour did not make an effort to exert his position: during the Paris Peace Conference, Curzon complained that Balfour 'did not know, was not told, and was as a rule too careless to inquire, what was going on'.[13]

In 1919, contemporaries hoped that Curzon's arrival at the Foreign Office would stem its loss of influence. Yet clashes between Curzon and Lloyd George were commonplace, the prime minister feeling particular animus towards his foreign secretary, teasing him publicly on his pompous manner.[14] However, more troublesome for the Foreign Office than this personality clash was Lloyd George's inherent dislike of traditional diplomacy in general. Believing that 'diplomatists were invented simply to waste time' the prime minister was happy to evade the Foreign Office when it came to matters of foreign affairs as frequently as he could get away with.[15] Indeed, Lloyd George's distrust of the officials of the Foreign Office was demonstrated by his creation of the Prime Minister's Secretariat, otherwise known as the notorious 'Garden Suburb' – staff housed in a number of huts in the garden of No. 10 whose responsibilities appeared to be everything from drafting Lloyd George's speeches to making special enquiries on his behalf.[16] By giving men such as his private secretary, Philip Kerr, such a wide remit, the prime minister effectively circumvented the Foreign Office and undermined its traditional role as sole advisor on foreign affairs.[17] The feeling that the Foreign Office was being usurped was compounded by the creation, at the same time, of the Cabinet Secretariat.[18] While the Cabinet Secretariat's role was essentially administrative, it also included the organisation of international conferences, and the handling of relations with the League of Nations.[19] In the eyes of many contemporaries both the Cabinet Secretariat and the Garden Suburb were part of Lloyd George's 'system', and represented his prime ministerial style of government, often seen as domineering and dictatorial.[20]

The Foreign Office had always believed that it was the only body with expertise to present foreign policy issues clearly and objectively.[21] In the post-war period, however, it would seem that anyone within the government could express their opinion on foreign affairs, a trend the Foreign Office deeply resented. As Eyre Crowe (assistant under-secretary of state) put it:

> This growing system of enquiring into other people's conduct by unqualified outsiders instead of entrusting the proper administration of an office to its own responsible head is going to introduce more and more anarchy into the whole service...[22]

Clashes between the War Office and Foreign Office over foreign policy were almost as frequent as those with Lloyd George. Charles Hardinge (permanent under-secretary of state from 1916 to 1920) caustically observed: 'All soldiers regard themselves as Heaven born diplomatists and much prefer diplomacy to military strategy...'[23] As shall be seen, even the India Office would not escape Foreign Office censure when it tried to weigh in on foreign affairs. Coping with a distrustful prime minister, as well as facing various forms of rivalry for its remit over foreign relations, it is perhaps no wonder that the demise of Foreign Office powers has been a dominant theme in the literature. It certainly was for contemporaries. The *New Europe* noted in 1920, 'The Foreign Office seems incapable of asserting its rights to control policy, and has irresponsible competitors, not only in the Garden Suburb of Downing Street, but in the War Office, the Admiralty and the India Office'.[24]

On initial viewing, then, it would appear that Kerr, Sir Maurice Hankey (head of the Cabinet Secretariat), Lloyd George and even officials of the War and India Offices were all more influential in creating Britain's foreign policy after 1918 than the Foreign Office itself. And yet there is reason to believe that actually the Foreign Office was just as important in the post-war period as it had always been. Perhaps we have previously been too quick to accept at face value the testimony of certain contemporaries. G. H. Bennett argues that the tone of historical debate on British foreign policy in this period was essentially set by Lord Beaverbrook, whose biography of Lloyd George laid the idea of a dictatorial prime minister who had almost entire control of foreign affairs.[25] In Beaverbrook's work 'Foreign Secretary and Foreign Office recede to the distant horizon'.[26] Writings by contemporaries appeared to support this concept of a presidential-style foreign policy and historians have been happy to take this idea and run with it.

As has been shown more recently, however, the relationship between the Foreign Office and other government departments was quite complex. For example, despite contemporary apprehension, the Cabinet Secretariat was actually of little challenge to the Foreign Office: the Secretariat held no executive or administrative function and had no authority to take the initiative in any matter.[27] And while it has been taken for granted that the Garden Suburb was a threat to the Foreign Office, it is hard to evaluate the influence of Kerr and his colleagues on policy-making, since their contact with Lloyd George was unofficial.[28]

Part of the problem may have been that by nature Curzon was highly alert to even the slightest indication that his authority might be being questioned; therefore, as foreign secretary Curzon found the very existence of the Garden Suburb unsettling. Such sensitivity thus led to an exaggeration of the threat posed by the likes of Hankey and Kerr. Curzon's issues were not reserved for Lloyd George and his 'system' either. In 1921, the foreign secretary exchanged a series of heated notes with the then secretary of state for the colonies, Winston Churchill, on the latter's supposed encroachment on Foreign Office issues.[29] And while some have argued that the end of Lloyd George's term as prime minister 'freed' Curzon, the foreign secretary continued to chafe under Andrew Bonar Law (prime minister 1922–1923) and Stanley Baldwin (prime minister 1923-1924, 1924–1929 and 1935-1937).[30] Furthermore, despite his personal contempt for Curzon's aristocratic background, Lloyd George did appreciate his foreign secretary's capabilities and realised the importance of having him in the coalition.[31] One did not have to like the foreign secretary to respect him.

It was not only Curzon who fought against a demotion of Foreign Office influence in the years after 1918. Charles Hardinge was almost as important a political operator as Curzon. He had many years of experience in service of the foreign and diplomatic corps, and (like Curzon) had been Viceroy of India. While Hardinge's relationship with Curzon was often contentious, both men did agree on the need to maintain Foreign Office hegemony over Britain's foreign affairs.[32] In March 1918, Hardinge created the Political Intelligence Department (PID) under the tutelage of the Foreign Office in an effort to counter the Garden Suburb. Sometimes known as the 'Ministry of All Talents', the PID was an elite group of specialists tasked with providing the essential information needed for Britain to formulate its policy during the peace process.[33] How Lloyd George and his entourage chose to use such information while in Paris is another matter.[34] The important point is that the Foreign Office was not willing to go quietly into the night. And while Foreign Office officials were largely excluded from the high level decision making at Paris, their participation in the various sub-committees and commissions meant they were still able to influence the peace settlement. Eyre Crowe played a particularly strong role in Paris, occupying Britain's seat when the senior statesmen were away, and ensuring the Foreign Office's influence was felt.[35]

All of which is important in answering the question of who was ultimately responsible for the creation of Britain's foreign policy in the post-war years. Together with housing some of the most experienced and capable men in the government, the Foreign Office was still the preeminent department for information on international affairs, whatever contemporaries might have felt about the Garden Suburb and Cabinet Secretariat. Into the Foreign Office came reports from embassies all over the world, while Curzon's promotion of the government's Code and Cipher School ensured he had access to all the latest intelligence from abroad.[36] Even the Passport Control Office – which often proved useful in monitoring movements of certain persons abroad – came under the Foreign Office's remit. Curzon had control of a vast amount of information on Britain's foreign affairs, while his colleagues in government only had what the Foreign Office supplied or what they could somehow glean for themselves through alternative sources.[37] This is worth bearing in mind, for it relates to the broader question of how the Foreign Office (and Curzon) formulated policy towards southern Asia and Russia in the years after 1918. If knowledge is power, then the officials of the Foreign Office should have been well prepared to handle affairs in Persia, Afghanistan and Russia – they certainly could not blame any mistakes made on ignorance. In the end, while the Foreign Office may have felt that it had less influence after the First World War than before it, it was still the foremost repository of foreign affairs knowledge within the British government.

So far discussion of foreign policy has been rather broad. But what of southern Asia specifically? Indeed, it could be argued that part of the reason for the debate on

Lloyd George-versus-Curzon stems from a focus on European affairs. If attention is shifted to South Asia, it quickly becomes apparent how significant a figure Curzon really was in the creation of Britain's foreign policy. For, given that this was the foreign secretary's area of apparent expertise, Lloyd George was quite willing to let Curzon run affairs in this region, while in turn Curzon was essentially happy to let the prime minister take the lead when it came to Europe.[38] This is not to say that there was not the occasional clash; when it came to relations with Russia, for example, Lloyd George would insist on the creation of the Anglo-Soviet Trade Agreement in 1921, despite Curzon's avid protests.[39] Yet Curzon's personality, knowledge and position of power would enable him to exercise great authority, particularly when it came to Persia.

Before his elevation to the Foreign Office, Curzon initially flexed his muscles over the Mesopotamia Administration Committee, of which he became chair in March 1917. By 1918, the organisation had developed into the Eastern Committee and included members from the War, India and Foreign Offices.[40] Ostensibly, it was the Eastern Committee that was the co-ordinating body for Britain's overall strategy in places such as Persia and Mesopotamia.[41] If one is looking for where the decisions on foreign policy in this region were being made, this should have been the place. However, rather than being a place to discuss and formulate policy, the committee essentially became a vehicle for Curzon's own ego, his practice being to present to the committee draft resolutions he had already written.[42] Sir Robert Cecil (assistant secretary of state for foreign affairs) put it aptly when he complained to Balfour that the existence of the Eastern Committee seemed 'mainly to be to enable George Curzon and Mark Sykes to explain to each other how very little they know about the subject [of the East]'.[43] As will be discussed further in Chapter Two, attempts in 1918 to address the problems of coordination and organisation of Britain's affairs in this region of the world would fail, in large part because of Curzon's refusal to cooperate. Not until 1920 would a Middle Eastern Department be created, and even then Curzon would be quick to quarrel with its head, Winston Churchill, every time he felt the department to be encroaching on Foreign Office territory.[44] A number of short-lived organisations and committees would be created during this time with general remits to collect information and make policy recommendations on issues in this region which might be of importance to the British Empire.[45] Ultimately, however, when it comes to who effectively had the greatest say over foreign policy towards Persia and Afghanistan, George Nathaniel Curzon was first among equals.

The Foreign Office Mind and Mental Maps

It would seem then, that Curzon and his Foreign Office held ultimate sway over the creation of Britain's foreign policy towards Persia and Afghanistan, with the

India Office, the War Office and the prime minister occasionally contributing to discussion and the Indian government relentlessly trying to have its voice heard, to no avail. The next question, therefore, is what factors affected the thinking of those involved in the formulation of foreign policy at this time? To answer it, we must look more closely inside the Foreign Office. Indeed, this was just the thing that many contemporaries were doing immediately after 1918. For in the aftermath of the First World War public opinion towards the Foreign Office had become highly critical. A common belief developed among strands of the population that it had been the secret machinations of the foreign policy-making elite which had brought Britain into a pointless war. This criticism led to calls for reform of the Foreign Office, both in the way it operated Britain's foreign policy and in the very make-up of its personnel.[46] The notion of the Foreign Office as an exclusively aristocratic, nepotistic, secretive institution, conducting Britain's foreign affairs with almost unlimited latitude also did much to damage the department's image in the post-war years.[47] That in order to support oneself while working for the Diplomatic Service one needed a large independent income compounded the concept of an elitist organisation.[48] *New Europe* produced several articles in 1919 which advocated complete reform of the Foreign Office from the ground up.[49] Indeed, even prior to the war, the MacDonnell Royal Commission had recommended wholesale reform, particularly in the recruitment process of the Foreign Office.[50]

However, many in the Foreign Office resisted these attempts at reform. One observer feared that open competition would allow 'Jews, coloured men and infidels' to enter the foreign service (an example of just the type of bigotry it was hoped the reforms would eliminate).[51] Other more open-minded officials, nevertheless, realised that such changes could improve the Foreign Office by injecting it with new blood.[52] By 1919, then, some of the commission's recommendations were brought in, including abolishing the need for the foreign secretary's nomination for candidates, amalgamating the Diplomatic Service with the Foreign Office, and raising the wages of those officials working abroad. Yet, despite the significant pressure on the Foreign Office from the public, Parliament and from within the government itself, the department changed little.[53] By 1930, the majority of successful candidates for the Foreign Office still had a public school background and graduated from Oxford or Cambridge. Personality, rather than intellectual achievement, was still viewed as the key to a successful career in the foreign service and the selection board continued to look for the same kind of man – and it always was a man – as it had prior to the First World War.[54]

The significance of this failed attempt at reform is that it meant that the Foreign Office remained relatively the same department in the post-war period that it had been prior to 1914. In fact, a large proportion of those who served in the Foreign Office and Diplomatic Service before the First World War continued to do so after the conflict.[55] Many of the key players that will feature in this book had long-standing experience of foreign service: Sir Lancelot Oliphant, Sir Percy Loraine and Sir Percy Cox to name a few. Balfour, Curzon and Hardinge were three of the most influential figures within the British government in the first half of the twentieth century. All three had cut their teeth on foreign affairs years before the outbreak of the First World War. Not only did these men share an educational and class background, but the preparation and training for their work in the Foreign Office resulted in an almost homogeneous view of the nature of Britain's foreign affairs. The seasoned diplomat and author, Harold Nicolson, termed this mode of thought 'the Foreign Office mind', while another contemporary referred to the department as 'the brotherhood'.[56] Importantly, those men who made up 'the brotherhood' in the early years of the twentieth century adhered to a certain way of thinking about Britain's foreign relations which has earned them the label the 'Edwardians'.[57] As opposed to the 'Victorians', who eschewed alliances with other powers, the Edwardians championed the concept of a 'balance of power'.[58] Eyre Crowe's 1907 memorandum on Britain's relations with France and Germany has come to be seen as the classic exposition of this doctrine.[59] The fact that the paper was still being read in the 1920s by Foreign Office officials is a prime example of how pre-1914 concepts of foreign affairs were carried into the post-1918 period.[60] That Crowe himself remained a prominent figure within the department after the First World War personified this continuity in the Edwardians' way of thinking.

There has long been a belief/understanding that continuity is important in international affairs and therefore that foreign policy should be above party politics. It is this continuity which allows foreign policy makers to take decisions based on the long-term issues rather than the short-term repercussions. What is more, in Britain, the wealth of knowledge and experience which Foreign Office officials and diplomats carry with them is useful when it comes to tackling the big issues of foreign policy. However, the risk of such uniformity in personnel is that it can leave the Foreign Office vulnerable to 'group think', preventing innovation and dynamism of thought. This was one of the accusations leveled at the British Foreign Office post-1918. The inherent discomfort many in the Foreign Office appeared to have in regard to amending their policies and processes could also prove a hindrance when it came to trying to adapt to the rapidly changing nature of the international scene. Being aware of these internal issues of the Foreign Office goes some way to explaining how foreign policy was formulated within the department.

Understanding the Foreign Office mind is further advocated by the likes of James Joll and Zara Steiner. Joll's concept of 'unspoken assumptions' plays a crucial part in his study of the years leading up to the outbreak of the First World War:

When political leaders are faced with the necessity of taking decisions the outcome for which they cannot foresee, in crises which they do not wholly understand, they fall back on their own instinctive reactions, traditions and modes of behaviour. Each of them has certain beliefs, rules or objectives which are taken for granted.[61]

As Steiner explains further: 'Historical example is used to buttress predetermined conclusions. Experience is assimilated into an existing framework of inherited ideas' – a process termed 'mental maps'.[62] To put it another way, Curzon, Hardinge, Crowe and others would invariably use their knowledge, experience and opinions gained prior to the First World War to help formulate their ideas in the post-war years. The fact that each official within the Foreign Office was of the same cultural, ethnic and class background, and tended to view the world in the same way (the Foreign Office mind), meant that these mental maps were rarely challenged – at least not from within the department. The point is an important one. That men such as Hardinge would rather support Curzon, even though he was often wrong in his assertions, than heed the Indian government, must say something about how the Foreign Office mind functioned.

While recognising that the existence of the Foreign Office mind is important in ensuring proper analysis of how British foreign policy was formulated, this is not to say that all the officials of that department held a single view on all issues. They were, after all, individuals capable of forming their own opinions and debating important matters. The Foreign Office mind simply meant that these individuals shared certain values and that such debates, when they occurred, usually centred on nuances of policy, rather than the larger issues of British foreign affairs.[63] Likewise, it is also important to note that while little distinction has been made thus far between the Foreign Office and the foreign secretary, this does not mean that the two were one and the same. In fact, in the following chapters, Curzon's is the name which appears more than any other, including that of Hardinge or Crowe. The reason for this, as Chapter One will explain further, is simply that Curzon was pre-eminent when it came to British relations with South Asia in the post-war period. The various clerks and under-secretaries of the Foreign Office could offer intelligent and valuable advice to the head of their department, but they could not make him accept it.[64] And, as will come to be seen, Curzon was one who only paid heed to what he wanted to hear, often rejecting anything which did not fit with his predetermined plan of action. If Curzon dominates this book, it is a reflection of how he dominated Britain's relations with South Asia between 1918 and 1924.

Prestige

Having discussed the *processes* of Foreign Office thinking, it is important to look at what exactly officials were thinking *about* when it came to Britain's foreign relations.

And the answer to that is simple – empire. The British Empire in the years after the First World War has been of interest to many scholars, largely because of the debate on the issue of decline which has dominated the historiography.[65] It has often been argued that the First World War set in motion the destruction of the empire by depleting Britain's financial resources to the point where it went from being the world's creditor to being a nation deeply in debt. This economic stress forced Britain to rapidly reduce its military expenditure and placed restrictions on the ability of government officials to use financial leverage in their diplomatic negotiations. Such a loss of economic power is often taken to indicate a corresponding decline both in Britain's imperial status and in the very will of the political elite to hold on to the empire.[66] According to some, in the face of depleted coffers and extensive nationalist uprisings throughout the empire, and without the military resources to assert its authority, London lost all enthusiasm for the imperial mission. The enactment in 1919 of the Montagu-Chelmsford reforms in India, for example, have been seen as an indication by some that Britain knew its imperial days were numbered.[67]

However, the arguments advocating imperial decline after 1918 suffer from certain flaws, not least of which is the emphasis on economics. Peter J. Cain and Antony G. Hopkins, for example, have challenged this traditional concept of Britain's economic decline, arguing that, while Britain's manufacturing output might indeed have fallen after 1918, industrial capability is not the only measure of a country's economic strength. In the opinion of Cain and Hopkins, financial services (such as banking and insurance) were a crucial part of Britain's economy after the First World War, a fact which others have tended to overlook. Indeed, it was this form of 'gentlemanly capitalism' with which the political elite in London had the greatest affiliation, rather than the declining industrial centres of the north. Many in Whitehall were also largely insulated from the day-to-day consequences of financial constraint that the general population may have faced. All of which meant that domestic economic problems did not necessarily affect government figures as much as some have argued.[68]

This is not to say that the British government was entirely unaware of the country's financial problems – budget cuts certainly affected many departments after the war. Rather, it is to question the assertion that these economic issues precipitated a crisis of confidence among the ruling elite of Britain. For one thing, the British Empire was not defined entirely by economics. As Cain and Hopkins explain, 'Power, considered as a measure of the ability to influence others, is relative as well as absolute, and potential as well as real.' Too often economic performance and political strength are assumed to be connected, with little explanation as to how.[69] John Ferris concurs: 'Historians of British power have paid too much attention to economic history and too little to imperial history.'[70] One caveat, however, is the issue of military expenditure, although even here

xviiiThe Decline of Empires

the picture is complex.[71] The correlation between the international standing of
a country and the numerical strength of its military is difficult to define and not
always obvious. For example, in Persia the withdrawal of British troops in the
years after the First World War was seen by some as a sign of Britain's weakness.
Yet there had always been a level of resentment among the Persian population at
the stationing of foreign troops in their country – thus, removal of these soldiers
could be said to have improved Britain's standing in the eyes of some. When it
came to India's military capabilities after 1918, while it was important that Delhi
could command a strong enough force to defeat Afghanistan in the 1919 conflict,
the size of the army was of little relevance to the Indian government's ability
to deal effectively with Gandhi. Indeed, after the First World War overt shows
of military strength within India often harmed Britain's position more than it
helped, as the Amritsar Massacre demonstrated.[72] When it comes to the notion
of 'power' (or 'the ability to influence others') economic capability is thus but
one part of its composition. Perception plays a large role. Britain may have been
economically and militarily weakened by the First World War, but as long as
other nations believed it to be strong, that was the main thing.

That prestige was a crucial asset to the empire was acknowledged by practically
all those involved in Britain's foreign affairs: as Harold Nicolson put it: 'What
credit is to a large firm of bankers, prestige is to the administration of Empire.'[73]
The intangible forces of authority and reputation were believed by British
contemporaries to be particularly important to its position within Asia and the
Middle and Far East. Lord Minto, Viceroy of India from 1905 to 1910, articulated
what many within the government thought when he said that 'We must remember
the huge influence of British prestige... it has solid value in the East'.[74] Despite
what some writers have said, nobody in the British government – either in
London or Delhi or elsewhere – displayed any disillusionment with the empire.
In the post-war years, rather than seeing a beleaguered second-rate world power,
many believed just the opposite: the proven 'greatness' of the British Empire.[75]
Even some foreign observers believed that the empire was still a force to be
reckoned with, as one German noted in 1920:

> [Britain] has strengthened her power and her trade, has gained valuable
> new regions... and her world empire has increased in land-size by around
> 27 percent and in population by almost the same. This has resulted in a
> global power and position as never before; England is the only winner
> from this war, England together with North America: one can see an
> Anglo-Saxon world mastery rising on the horizon...[76]

As for India, if there had ever been doubt prior to 1914, the First World War
had proved beyond measure the value of the Raj to the empire. India's armies

had been instrumental in the prosecution of the war and the country had earned a reputation as 'the battering ram of British power'.[77] Indeed, Edwin Montagu (secretary of state for India, 1917 - 1922) made his position quite clear in 1922 in a telegram to the viceroy: 'Reports are constantly being received in England that we look upon our mission in India as drawing to a close, and that we are preparing for a retreat. Should such an idea exist, it is a complete fallacy.'[78] This determination to hold on to the empire was clear not only when it came to Britain's policies in India but also in its attempts to retain hegemony in Asia and the Middle East at large. As one historian has elegantly put it, 'if the lion had ceased to roar, it was not yet ready to lie down with the lambs.'[79]

Instead, the problem for the British government lay not in *whether* it should hold on to the empire, but *how*. And this was ultimately rooted in the concept of power. For, although officials knew the empire needed to be perceived as strong, how prestige was to be defined and measured – and therefore how it was to be maintained – was another matter. And it is here where opinion divided. Broadly speaking, for Curzon and others in the Home government, Britain's imperial position after 1918 in the likes of Persia, Afghanistan and India was best maintained by an unyielding and unwavering show of authority – diplomatic, economic and military pressure was all to be used to make foreign rulers compliant to Britain's wishes, while any groups or individuals who questioned Britain's authority were to be dealt with swiftly lest the empire appear weak. For the Indian government, however, such an approach to foreign relations in southern Asia would actually prove counterproductive, by aggravating the local populations. Instead, the Indian government advocated making concessions to some of the nationalist and pan-Islamist movements, to demonstrate the empire did not stand in the way of progressive liberal reform in this region of the world. The following chapters will show who was right.

Russia

Together with knowing who was responsible for creating British foreign policy in the post-war period, and in understanding what influenced their thinking, another question to be answered is what role Russia played in these thought processes. The picture is unclear and often times confusing, as British officials contradicted themselves over how much of a threat they viewed Bolshevik Russia to be. Certainly the Bolshevik revolution ushered into Russia a political regime which was anathema to the majority of British officials. Thus, a large section of the literature on Anglo-Russian relations after 1917 focuses on the idea that Britain's policies towards its erstwhile imperial competitor were now conditioned by abhorrence of the Bolshevik ideology.

The problem with this argument, however, is that it oversimplifies a complex topic. Examples of British anti-Bolshevism are often extrapolated to explain the entirety of Britain's Russia policy in this period. For example, while it is more than likely that anti-Bolshevism influenced Britain's participation in the Allied intervention in the Russian civil war, this is not the whole story. As soon as one shifts focus from the north intervention to the south of Russia, one sees that the Malleson mission to Meshed and the Dunsterforce initiative in Baku, for example, were not conceived as part of an 'anti-Bolshevik crusade'.[80] Instead, Malleson and Dunsterville were First World War manifestations of a decades long British obsession with the security of India's borders.

This is not to say that anti-Bolshevism did not influence the thinking of officials in Whitehall. The anarchy and violence which the October revolution ushered in, the decline of Russia into civil war, the betrayal of the Allied cause, the execution of Tsar Nicholas II and his family, all created a feeling of horror among most British officials. Memorandum and reports were constantly being produced by various government bodies detailing the apparent decrepitude of the Bolshevik regime.[81] The problem, however, is when anti-Bolshevism is discussed to the exclusion of all other explanations. By assuming too quickly that ideology was the sole motivator behind Britain's actions towards Russia after 1917, other facets of the topic – such as imperial concerns and the legacy of the past – are sidelined, leaving only a partial picture of affairs.

One of the reasons for this focus on anti-Bolshevism is that for those whose remit is the post-revolution period, the focus has been almost entirely on the idea of change rather than continuity. The Allied intervention, [82] the impact of Bolshevism on British Labour,[83] the Trade Agreement negotiations[84] – all of these topics have monopolised scholarly interest and come to define Anglo–Russian relations in this period. Because a significant proportion of the literature has focused on issues which had no parallel in the nineteenth or early twentieth centuries, this has left the impression that the October revolution constituted almost a complete break with the past. Anglo–Soviet relations are viewed as fundamentally different to Anglo–Russian relations, and because the transformation was due to Bolshevism, the relationship between Britain and Russia after 1917 is in turn defined by ideology. The trouble with this line of thought is that it presupposes that both countries were affected in the same measure by the events of October 1917. Yet, while the Bolshevik revolution may have been of monumental consequence to Russia, the same could not necessarily be said for Britain. This is particularly true in the early years of the revolution, when not only was there limited information on the Bolshevik regime, but there was also little expectation that Lenin and his comrades would survive as a viable government anyway.[85] For most observers among the British political elite, October 1917 was just one further upheaval in Russia's already turbulent domestic history.[86]

Any information the British government did have on the Bolshevik regime mainly focused on their domestic policies. The British representative, Robert

Bruce-Lockhart, and British military personnel involved in the intervention could provide information on affairs such as the Red Terror and the civil war, yet could comment little on Bolshevik foreign policy.[87] Even some of the trips to Russia made by British representatives later on in the 1920s still focused their attention on domestic affairs.[88] The proclamations made by Lenin and his men upon seizing power and during the Brest-Litovsk negotiations were about the only official statements on Soviet foreign policy which British officials could study.[89] From these limited resources, Whitehall certainly realised the anti-imperialist nature of the Bolshevik government. The events of Brest-Litovsk also taught them not to trust the new regime in Moscow. However, little was understood of the practicalities of Soviet foreign policy or about specific Bolshevik intentions towards Asia.[90] With such little knowledge on which to judge Bolshevik foreign policy (particularly in the early years after 1917), many British officials would simply fall back on what they knew – the Great Game. As long as the Great Game mentality existed in the minds of key British officials then the Great Game continued on. To some, while Russian domestic politics were continually turbulent, the one constant had always been that country's ambition in Asia. Thus, in the early years after the October revolution, there were many in London who simply used the same framework they had always used – their mental maps – and formulated policy based on Russia's potential to threaten the stability of southern Asia.

Adding further complexity to the issue of British opinion on Russia after 1917 is the distinction between the Home government in London and the Indian government in Delhi. For as will be seen, Delhi appeared far less concerned with Russia and with Bolshevism than London, and far more interested in the issues of Asian nationalism and pan-Islamism. This appears in part due to the intelligence reports which the Indian government was receiving from its agencies about the progress (or lack thereof) of Russian intrigue within Asia and India itself.[91]

The debates between Delhi and London will be a central feature of the following chapters. What is important to emphasise here is that not enough scholars have taken the time to try to comprehensively explain these issues surrounding the thought processes of those involved in British foreign affairs after the First World War. As can be seen, trying to understand what influenced British government officials and what motivated their advocacy of certain foreign policies is like piecing together a puzzle. The 'Foreign Office mind' and 'mental maps'; the importance of studying individuals rather than only 'issues and impulses'; the notion of prestige and the complexity of how a nation's power is measured; how Russia, Bolshevism and the Great Game influenced thinking – each is a piece of the picture.

*   *   *

By looking briefly at the legacy of the Great Game, and then focusing in detail on the years 1918 to 1923, this work will demonstrate the continuity of thought which existed between the pre-war and post-war period. Utilising primary documents from the National Archives of the Foreign Office, the War Office and the Cabinet, together with India Office papers held at the British Library, discussion will focus on the debates which raged between London and Delhi on all aspects of British policy towards southern Asia and Russia after the end of the First World War. The annotations of Curzon on various memoranda, telegrams and reports – often scathing, sometimes witty, always entertaining – are a particular insight into the mind of the foreign secretary. The numerous letters and telegrams sent between the secretary of state for India, Edwin Montagu, and two successive viceroys, Lord Chelmsford and Lord Reading, also provide particular illumination on the relationship between the Home and the Indian governments. Personal collections of key figures such as the Chief of General Staff, Sir Henry Wilson, and the British ambassador to Tehran, Sir Percy Loraine, also help to provide background.

To be more specific, the following chapters will show that there were those within the British government – and particularly within the Foreign Office – who displayed an attitude towards Soviet Russia and southern Asia that emanated from the decades prior to the First World War. This continuity of thought was rooted in the Great Game, and it is this 'Great Game mentality' that informed the decision-making process of certain government officials in the post-war period. The concept of a Great Game mind-set will be explained in further detail later, but fundamentally it consisted of believing Russia – irrespective of who ruled it – to be a permanent rival for influence within southern Asia, and a threat to Britain's position in India. Indeed, this Great Game thinking tended to over-emphasise the danger of Russia to Britain's imperial interests and, after 1917, often judged Bolshevik foreign policy by that pursued by the tsarist government, thereby failing to formulate policies which would counter the potential for Bolshevism to take hold in South Asia. As pointed out above, southern Asia was where Britain and Russia had traditionally played out their rivalry and Anglo-Soviet relations were still largely defined by interaction in this region of the world. For Britain, the Bolshevik revolution had not constituted a great watershed, and for those of a Great Game mentality, policy towards South Asia and policy towards Russia were largely intertwined.

The legacy of the Great Game also meant that countries such as Persia and Afghanistan were seen by many in Britain only as pawns in the contest with Soviet Russia. The value of these two countries lay almost exclusively in their relation to Anglo-Russian rivalry and the security of India's borders, while their internal politics were generally ignored by Great Game thinkers. This focus on Russia as a threat and this view of Persia and Afghanistan as mere pawns resulted in a failure of some in the British government to recognise the rising strength of the pan-Islamic and nationalist movements taking hold of Asia in the post-war period.

Those who did realise the seriousness of these movements would be largely ignored by the Great Game thinkers. Thus, while the Indian government would try to turn the attention of the Home government from Bolshevik Russia to nationalist Asia, London did not want to listen. Between 1918 and 1923, events would occur that would demonstrate the fallacy of this Great Game mentality, and force those who adhered to it to adjust their policies accordingly. Nonetheless, there is reason to believe that this fear of Russia was never really discarded by many British officials and that the modification of British policy that took place from 1921 was, in fact, simply a pragmatic change of tactics rather than a change of heart.

It is also often just as helpful to know what will not be included in a work as what it will include. This book does not purport to be a balanced exploration of Anglo-Russian rivalry in Asia in this period, but focuses instead on British policy only. Where discussion of Soviet foreign policy towards Asia does occur it is based on work already done by other researchers and is used with the aim of contrasting what British government officials *perceived* Bolshevik aims in Asia to be, not in understanding what such aims actually were. For the purposes of this work, 'South Asia' will largely refer to Persia, Afghanistan and India, with only brief mention of events in Egypt, Mesopotamia, Turkey, the Transcaucasus, Transcaspia and Turkestan as they pertain to Britain's general international situation. In the same vein, this work does not discuss British imperial policy at large and affairs in Ireland, for example, are not mentioned. Aside from the issue of brevity, the reason for this decision of focus lies in the issues discussed above – namely the influence of the Great Game on the thinking of some British officials regarding Russia, Persia, Afghanistan and India. Persia and Afghanistan are singled out here as they were the two countries in which the Great Game most heavily featured in the nineteenth century, and in which Anglo-Russian conflict continued to occur in the post-war period.

Persia and Afghanistan lay directly between British India and Russia, a highly vulnerable buffer zone in British eyes. In effect, all the issues that Britain faced in its imperial policy at large were compounded in Persia, Afghanistan and India by the threat of Russia looming on the border. Furthermore, this work will argue that British officials themselves viewed this region of the world differently to other areas of imperial interest. For the Indian government, Persia and Afghanistan represented a barrier which was in essence the last line of India's defence; for Great Game thinkers, these two countries were prizes up for grabs in the relentless competition for hegemony in Asia. And if further reason is needed for the choice of Persia, Afghanistan and India for the focus of this work, events in these countries in the early twentieth century make them not only interesting but important nations to study. The Persian revolution of 1905 to 1911, the Third Anglo-Afghan War of 1919, the Caliphate agitation and the non-co-operation policy of Gandhi and his followers throughout the 1920s, are just some examples of movements and events which signified the rise of nationalism and pan-Islamism in this region of the world and which directly impacted Britain's imperial interests.

Since it is a contention herein that the Bolshevik revolution was not as seismic an event for Britain as for Russia, the focus of research will begin not at 1917, but at what was the most important marker of this period for British foreign policy – the conclusion of the First World War in November 1918. Chapter Two will thus begin here and end in 1919, exploring how the Great Game mentality of some within the British government influenced policy towards Persia and Afghanistan in these early post-war months. It will contrast this thinking – which was centred largely at the Foreign Office – with the opinions of the Indian government and its preoccupation with pan-Islamism and nationalism. Chapter Three will look at the year 1920 and how events in Persia and Afghanistan came to challenge the optimism and ambition which had characterised the immediate aftermath of the First World War. It will compare the apparent ascendancy of Bolshevism in Central and South Asia to the relative downfall of British prestige in this region and explore the progress of Muslim extremism. If Chapter Two demonstrates the continuity of thought from the Great Game period into the post-war period, and Chapter Three shows how such individuals were forced to face the changed nature of international relations, then Chapter Four will explore how the foreign policy-making elite came to reconcile this disparity between continuity and change in 1921. Chapter Five in many respects will be the culmination of the journey from 1918. It will chart how the optimism and ambition that had characterised British policies pursued in Persia and Afghanistan in 1918 and 1919, were to be replaced with a more realistic and practical state of affairs by 1923. By 1924, a change of government in Britain would see the removal of many key figures from power, and so the story will end there. However, in the meantime, Chapter One will set the scene, by looking at the Great Game and the legacy it left on British foreign policy towards South Asia in the post-war period.

Chapter One

Curzon, Russia and the Great Game

I n the mid-nineteenth century, a young British officer serving in Afghanistan came to believe that it was his 'mission to frustrate Russian schemes of conquest in Central Asia and convince its independent Muslim rulers to band together and seek British protection'. What Arthur Conolly wanted most, he wrote to a friend in 1841, was to play a leading role in this 'great game' in Central Asia. Rudyard Kipling's *Kim* might have helped the term to enter British lexicon, but it was a real life Great Game player who had first coined the phrase.[1] Indeed, within a year of writing to his friend, the unfortunate Conolly would have met an end seemingly taken from the pages of fiction. Having travelled to Bokhara on a mission to rescue a fellow British officer, Colonel Charles Stoddart, from the hold of the capricious emir, Conolly found himself also taken captive. After spending a tortuous few months in a bug infested pit, Conolly and Stoddart were finally executed in 1842 – a death perhaps befitting the ultimate Great Gamer.[2]

If only Conolly could have known the place he would come to occupy in the history books. For the expression he used would become so ubiquitous in the twentieth century that it would end up being used by politicians, journalists and writers to refer to almost any conflict in Asia or the Middle East that involved outside powers. Indeed, for some, the collapse of the USSR and the subsequent opening up of Central Asia has precipitated a second wave of international interest in the region that has come to be known as the 'new Great Game' – a phrase even used to describe the recent war in Afghanistan. And what was once a game played only between Britain and Russia, has now found a third player in the form of the USA.

Yet, the 'Great Game' is not merely a general catchphrase to be applied to any and every issue arising in Asia. Instead, it is an important concept in history, and understanding how the Great Game should be defined is essential. That is not to say that the definition need be rigid. In fact, the concept of the Great Game is much more fluid than historians have hitherto realised. While debate on this subject has nearly always centred on dates and events as defining the Game, it will be asserted that these were manifestations of a certain state of mind, and that it is this state of mind that should be focused on if one wishes to truly understand the Great Game.[3]

Before looking at the Great Game as a mental process, however, it would be useful to understand something of the traditional definitions of the subject. Although, typically, the Great Game refers to the rivalry between Britain and Russia for dominance in Asia between the nineteenth and early twentieth centuries, since the term has grown organically there is little agreement on the specific parameters of the Game. For some, the ambitions of Peter the Great towards Asia in the early eighteenth century was the start of the Great Game, for Russia at least. Yet, for Britain, it was the potential alliance between Napoleon and Tsar Paul I in 1801, which was to really initiate the fear of Russian expansion – a crucial component of the Great Game.[4] Others have started in the early 1800s with the adventures of William Moorcroft, the British veterinary surgeon and horse-trader turned explorer and Great Game advocate.[5] Still others have much narrower definitions, believing that the Great Game effectively began *and ended* with the First Anglo–Afghan War (1839–42).[6] Certainly, this conflict was one of the key events of the Great Game and had a large impact on the British psyche. It also epitomised the nature of British reaction to Russian activity in Asia, the entire affair being precipitated by Russia's attempts to extend its influence within Afghanistan.

Largely in response to Afghanistan's perceived favouritism towards Russia, in 1839 Britain decided to invade that country and replace the current emir, Dost Mohammed, with a much more compliant Afghan ruler. While this initial aim was met, and shah Shujah successfully placed on the Afghan throne, in 1841 an uprising by the Afghan people took place in response to the continued presence of British military personnel in Afghanistan. The British explorer, Alexander Burnes, who had become famous for his travels into Bokhara a few years earlier and who was now a political agent in Kabul, was among the first British victims of the Afghan mob. Within a matter of weeks, the situation had deteriorated so rapidly that the entire British contingent of nearly 17,000 men, women and children were forced rapidly to evacuate the capital. During their retreat towards India through the treacherous gorges and snowbound passes, almost the entire party died of either starvation, cold or at the hands of local tribesmen. The event was a military and diplomatic disaster for Britain, and one that would long remain in the conscience of the public, immortalised as it was in Lady Butler's painting, *The Remnants of the Army*, which depicts Dr William Brydon, said to be the sole survivor of the Kabul cohort.[7] It was this shocking turn of events in Afghanistan that, some have argued, caused the British to realise that the Great Game could, in fact, never be won by them. Instead, they would simply spend the rest of the nineteenth century trying not to lose.[8]

However, this argument suffers from certain flaws, not least of which pertains to the Second Anglo–Afghan War (1878–80), which arguably successfully achieved what Britain had failed to do the first time around. In July 1878, under pressure from Russia, the then emir, Sher Ali, had reluctantly agreed to allow a Russian mission to reside in Kabul, a move which angered Britain even further when their own mission was denied entry into the country. The viceroy of India, Lord Lytton, 'determined to teach the Emir a lesson he would not easily forget, and at the same time make it perfectly clear to St. Petersburg that Britain would tolerate no rivals in Afghanistan'.[9] By May 1879, with large parts of his country under British occupation, the emir's son and successor, Yakub Khan (Sher Ali having died a few months previously), signed the Treaty of Gandamak. By its terms, the new emir agreed not only to cede certain territories close to the Indian frontier to Britain, but, more importantly, relinquished control of Afghanistan's foreign relations to British India.[10] The parallels with the first Afghan conflict are striking – yet again it had been precipitated by British fear of Russian machinations in Afghanistan and a zealous British governor general in India. Unfortunately, Britain had apparently failed to learn the lessons of the 1840s, however, and yet again the British resident sent to Kabul, Major Cavagnari, would soon be massacred by an angry Afghan mob.[11] From 1880 until 1920, no British mission would be kept on Afghan soil. Nevertheless, for the next forty years Britain would retain control of Afghanistan's foreign relations. By the Anglo–Russian Convention of 1907, Russia would also finally officially agree to respect British suzerainty over Afghanistan.[12] One could argue, then, that by the late nineteenth century, Britain had won a decisive victory in the Great Game when it realised hegemony over Afghanistan at the expense of Russian influence there.

The Anglo-Russian Convention

By focusing on events such as war, historians run into difficulties in defining the Great Game. Using diplomatic agreements to set the parameters of the Game is also problematic, as can be seen with the Anglo–Russian Convention of 1907. The culmination of two years of negotiations, the convention was signed between Britain and Russia in August 1907, arguably bringing to an end at least the more overt competition between these two powers that had characterised the Great Game during the nineteenth century. As noted previously, the agreement solidified Britain's position in Afghanistan and also laid out certain terms of interaction in Persia, the other crucial stage of Great Game rivalry. It was the first time that Britain and Russia had managed to negotiate such a truce and, as such, the convention claims great importance in the history of Anglo-Russian relations. Indeed, the nature of the rivalry which had existed between these two nations prior to 1907 makes the creation of the convention all the more significant. As the Russian foreign minister, Serge Sazonov, observed, Britain and Russia's history up until then had been characterised by an 'endless series of political misunderstandings... mutual suspicions and secret and open hostility'.[13] Only a few years prior to the convention, in 1904, these two countries had nearly come to blows over the Dogger

Bank incident, while Britain's alliance with Japan during the Russo-Japanese War had further exacerbated Anglo-Russian animosity.[14]

Given what will be discussed later regarding the 1921 Anglo-Soviet Trade Agreement, it is worth understanding what the 1907 convention represented for relations between Britain and Russia. The parallels between these two diplomatic accords is striking, particularly because while both purported to herald a new era in Anglo-Russian relations, in fact neither document was effective in changing the fundamental dynamic between these two countries. Prior to 1907, tentative attempts had been made to improve the state of affairs between Britain and Russia, but to no avail.[15] By the time of the agreement, however, many factors had come together to create a suitable ground for compromise, not least of which was a growing fear in both Britain and Russia regarding German ambition in the Middle East and Asia. For Britain, Germany had come to be regarded as a potential naval competitor,[16] while the proposed Baghdad Railway – with its starting point in Berlin – was a potential threat to Britain's position in the Persian Gulf.[17] There was also a considerable fear in Britain by the early twentieth century that, should Russia end up allying itself with Germany, France might well be forced to follow suit and Britain could find itself diplomatically and militarily isolated in Europe. It was well known that Kaiser Wilhelm and Tsar Nicholas II corresponded regularly (they were, after all, uncle and nephew).[18] In order not to become isolated and to preserve a balance of power in Europe (that Edwardian obsession), Britain therefore needed to improve relations with Russia. Since it was the scene of the Great Game, Asia, which had always brought Anglo-Russian relations to the boil, in 1907 it was in Asia that a rapport was now sought.

For Russia too, the time was apt for seeking a resolution to the military and diplomatic tension of the nineteenth century. By 1905 not only had it suffered a humiliating defeat at the hands of the Japanese, it had been internally rocked by revolution and mass popular discontent. Domestically in turmoil, Russia needed to find stability in its foreign affairs in order to concentrate on its internal problems. Militarily weakened, there was also a fear that the other major powers would be able to take advantage of Russia.[19] Much like Britain, Russia also hoped that the convention would help to protect it from growing German aggression. Suspicion had begun to develop among many in Russia that, while Germany professed friendship toward them, Berlin was actually more interested in domination than mutual alliance.[20] Wilhelm had greatly encouraged Nicholas II in declaring war on Japan in 1904, and Izvolskii believed that by turning Russia's attention eastward, Germany was trying to secure its own ascendancy over Europe.[21] Hence, it was a common European enemy that ultimately helped to cool down Anglo-Russian rivalry in Asia. And, to some extent, the convention certainly encouraged better relations between the two signatories. Germany's belligerency only increased after 1907, and its actions during the Bosnian Crisis of 1908–1909,[22] served to push

Russia closer toward Britain.[23] Indeed, the agreement paved the way for a meeting between Edward VII and Nicholas II at Reval in 1908,[24] followed in 1909 with a visit to London by officials of the Duma (a courtesy reciprocated in 1912 by Bernard Pares and other prominent Englishmen).[25] Thus, German ambition, which had been the main impetus behind the creation of the convention, also served to keep it alive.[26] By 1914, Britain and Russia would be at war with Germany and, as Sazonov noted, there was little doubt 'that the agreement of 1907 removed many of the obstacles which might have prevented England from joining Russia in the struggle against Germany'.[27]

Yet therein lay the problem with the convention: it was a 'marriage of convenience', designed to draw Britain and Russia closer together in the face of German ambition.[28] It was not actually concluded in order to resolve the outstanding issues of the Great Game, thus, conflict between the two powers continued well after the signing of that document.[29] Indeed, that Britain and Russia were able to move from a state of such tension in the early 1900s to formal allies in a world conflict by 1914 has tended to obscure the fact that the underlying hostility and suspicion between them never fully abated. This is particularly apparent when one looks at Anglo-Russian interaction in Persia during this period. By the terms of the convention, that country was divided into spheres of influence, with Russia in the north, Britain in the south, and a neutral zone in between – an official recognition of what was already the actual state of affairs in Persia by 1907.[30] Yet, the agreement failed to put to bed the rivalry between the two imperial powers - a rivalry which, as we will see, would revive in the years after the First World War.

The convention was unpopular in both Britain and Russia. Izvolskii was accused by some of being too timid in the negotiations and of renouncing Russia's ambitions in Persia.[31] Meanwhile the British foreign secretary, Sir Edward Grey, came under heavy criticism from all different sectors of British society. Since the Russian sphere contained much of the commercial wealth of Persia, many believed that Britain had received the short end of the straw.[32] The most vocal critic of the convention was Lord Curzon, who characterised it as 'deplorable': 'It gives up all that we have been fighting for [for] years, and it gives it up with a wholesale abandon that is truly cynical in its recklessness...The efforts of a century sacrificed and nothing or next to nothing in return.'[33] On 6 February 1908 Curzon even spoke for over an hour in the House of Lords against the convention, attacking it as 'one-sided, unequal and inequitable'.[34] Unfortunately for him, Curzon would have to wait over ten years before he would get the chance to rectify Grey's alleged mistake.

For others in Britain, it was the fact that their government had collaborated with autocratic Russia that proved most odious. As Lord Minto (viceroy of India, 1905–1910), declared: 'we have acted hand in glove with the most abominable autocracy of modern times'.[35] This was also one of those rare moments in politics when both Conservatives and Liberals were drawn together in condemnation of government policy. For, while the former lamented the perceived sacrifice of British rights in Persia, the latter were equally critical of the apparent callous disregard for the interests of Persia itself which the convention entailed. So strong was the reaction against the convention that a 'Grey Must Go' campaign was even conducted in the newspapers *Nation* and *Daily News* between 1911 and 1912.[36] In October 1908, a Persia Society was formed by one of the leading scholars of Persia of the time, E.G. Browne, which voiced vehement criticism of the convention.[37] Browne had the particular advantage of possessing a great amount of information on Persia to which the Foreign Office did not have access – the personal contacts of Browne virtually amounted to an independent intelligence service within Persia.[38] Having been a contemporary of Curzon's at Eton, Browne found the ex-viceroy a useful ally in his fight against the 1907 convention. Indeed, as Browne's co-chair of the Persia Society, H.F.B. Lynch, noted in 1911, 'a nod from Curzon will have more effect upon the Government than the frowns of our collective wisdom'.[39] Yet, despite such confidence in Curzon's apparent influence over the government, the convention remained. Soon, the First World War would prove a distraction and the Persia Society's activities would cease. Grey would also manage to hang on to office, always convinced that the 1907 agreement served as a restraining influence on Russian behaviour in Persia.[40] The idea of controlling Russia via treaty would be used by others later when trying to justify the creation of the 1921 trade agreement.

Such criticisms of the convention are indicative of many of the unresolved problems which lay between Britain and Russia in the early twentieth century. Attitudes and opinions do not alter as easily as treaties are written, and the 1907 agreement did not put to rest Anglo-Russian rivalry. British suspicion of Russian intentions in Asia certainly continued long after 1907. Minto epitomised official scepticism when he argued that Britain would 'gain nothing [from the convention] except a mere phantom of friendship with a Power who will not cease secretly to advance her own interests, regardless of any pledges she may give'.[41] The idea that Russia could not be trusted in its promises was a long-standing feature of Russophobia, which the agreement did little to change. As Lord Hardinge explained when he replaced Minto in 1910: 'In India prejudices die hard, and nowhere so hard as amongst old soldiers who for two generations have been taught to regard Russia as a dangerous enemy.'[42] This distrust was amply demonstrated, for example, during the negotiations over the Trans-Persian Railway. In order to counter Germany's Baghdad railway, and to secure its commercial relations, Russia proposed building a railway through Persia, ultimately connecting with the India network. For Britain, however, the project posed a myriad of problems. While it did not want to alienate Russia by an outright refusal to take part in the scheme, it was highly wary of India's security, and building a railway that would allow the quick transportation of Russian troops through Britain's 'buffer state' was not a scheme it wanted to encourage. This is one example of how, despite the Anglo-Russian Convention, Britain still distrusted Russia. The Russians too, found it difficult to move on from old patterns of behaviour and many veteran Russian diplomats continued to cause problems in Persia after 1907.[43] The Russian minister in Tehran, N.G. Hartwig, for example, 'was one of those who considered at the time of the signature of the Convention, that his country was being deprived of the ripe fruit which was ready to fall into her lap'.[44]

While the convention did not fundamentally alter Anglo-Russian relations, however, it did have important consequences for Britain's relationship with South Asia. For one thing, it served to inadvertently encourage Afghan nationalism. That the emir had not even been consulted about the agreement hurt Afghan pride. (Minto had warned as much, but when he suggested making the negotiations for the convention known to the emir, he had been overruled by London).[45] Nationalists also feared the threat to Afghanistan's independence – until now Anglo-Russian rivalry had prevented the country being absorbed entirely by either power. By laying to rest this competition, the road lay open to greater encroachment upon Afghan freedom.[46] In Persia too, the effects of the convention would be very negative for Britain. Prior to 1907, British officials were generally held in high regard by the Persian people, particularly in the early years of the Persian revolution, when they sided with the reformers against the shah.[47] Indeed, the Persian constitutionalists looked to Britain for inspiration on how to form a democratic system of government while retaining a monarchy.

For Russia, its relationship with the shah was crucial in helping to retain its influence in the north of Persia.[48] This, together with its own domestic political issues, meant that Russia took a natural aversion to the reformers, and made efforts to ensure the shah remained on his throne.[49] That Russia was willing to use force in order to achieve its ends compounded the hostility that the Persian public felt towards its northern neighbour. The Cossack Division,[50] for example, would often be deployed during the revolution in order to quell popular unrest, such as in June 1908 when it occupied Tehran following violent protests by the public against the shah.[51]

From Russia's point of view, it appeared that Persia was gradually sinking into an unacceptable state of disarray – something unwanted so close to its own borders.[52] As one Russian contemporary observed, 'it always happens that the more civilized State is forced, in the interest of security of its frontier and its commercial relations, to exercise a certain ascendancy over those whom their turbulent and unsettled character makes most undesirable neighbours'.[53] Yet, Russian heavy-handedness in trying to secure northern Persia from descending into anarchy ensured the enduring hostility of the Persian people. Britain, meanwhile, although claiming to be non-interventionist, inclined towards a form of constitutional monarchy for Persia. Naturally sympathising with the cause of the reformers, the

British also depended for their commercial prosperity in the south of Persia on the anti-shah tribes.[54] In July 1905, when some 12,000 political refugees sought *bast* (sanctuary) within the British legation in Tehran, not only did the British consul general happily accommodate them, but he even recognised 'many friends and acquaintances' among the Persians, whom he invited for a cup of tea and a smoke in the drawing room.[55] (Three years later, during their occupation of the Persian capital, the Cossack Division would surround the British legation to prevent a repeat of this).[56]

By the 1907 convention, however, Britain's esteemed position among the Persian people was quickly lost. Despite the best efforts of the British minister, Sir Cecil Spring-Rice, popular opinion believed that Britain had betrayed the Persian revolutionary cause by allying with Russia.[57] Indeed, Persian protest at the convention was almost exclusively aimed at Britain, with Russia seldom mentioned. In the words of one historian, after 1907 'Britain fell from grace; but Russia for many years had been accorded no grace'.[58] That the Persian public had no idea of the existence of the 1907 convention until its announcement was particularly insulting, and only helped fuel the rumours and misinformation that tarred the agreement further (yet another lesson that Curzon would fail to learn twelve years later).[59] The idea that Britain had betrayed Persia in order to share the spoils with Russia was hard to counter, particularly when events such as the Shuster Crisis only appeared to corroborate it. In 1911, the American financial adviser retained by the Persian government, W.M. Shuster, was forced out of office on Russia's protest. Grey had been unwilling to risk a breach in Anglo-Russian relations by defending Shuster and his reforms of Persia's finance.[60] The duplicitous nature of Britain, apparently revealed by the 1907 agreement, would have important repercussions in the years to come. The distrust engendered during this period would permeate Persian society, so that by 1919, when Curzon would try to initiate his own agreement with Tehran, he would receive a very frosty reception.

The Great Game Mentality

Despite appearances then, the Anglo-Russian Convention of 1907 did not mark the end of the Great Game. For, while the agreement might have restrained some of the more overt rivalry once displayed between the two countries, ultimately it could not significantly change the feelings and opinions of many Russians and Britons. In effect, it did not alter the official mind set. It has already been noted in the Introduction how important 'mental maps' are to understanding the creation of British foreign policy. Taking this idea further, it starts to become apparent that perhaps part of the reason there has always been such debate around the Great Game is that the parameters of the definition have been wrong. Hitherto writers have been too busy discussing what British and Russian officials were *doing*, not what they were *thinking*. Treaties and events were simply the manifestations of a certain mentality that was determined to view the other imperial power as a hostile rival. And, if the Great Game only really existed as a particular way of thinking (a 'Great Game mentality'), then it could not end simply with the signing of an agreement.[61] Only if the 1907 convention had represented a true change of heart between the ruling elite of each country, could it have been said to mark the end of the Great Game era. But as an artificial construct, created by expediency, it is unsurprising that the agreement only had a limited effect on Anglo-Russian relations after 1907.

Perhaps one way of thinking about the Great Game mentality is by looking at the Cold War. One cannot define this era of American–Soviet competition by simply studying the Cuban Missile Crisis, for example. Instead, only by comprehending the intangible forces of fear, hostility, distrust and paranoia that characterised US and Soviet interaction after 1945 can the Cold War be fully understood. In fact, one could even argue that the Great Game was the precursor to the Cold War. For, if the argument is accepted that the Great Game existed essentially as a certain way of thinking, and that wars and treaties do not serve to define its boundaries, then it becomes clear how the Game could have reverberations throughout the twentieth century.[62] If the analogy with the Cold War is extended, one can even see how the 1907 convention was arguably the equivalent of Détente – a short respite from the otherwise largely relentless endeavours of each power to gain hegemony in South Asia at the expense of the other.

The presumption has always been that in 1917 with a change of government in Moscow came the end of the Great Game. Yet, it is already apparent that if British officials had been used to following a Great Game way of thinking for decades prior to 1917, the advent of the Bolshevik regime was not going to be enough to simply erase that mental process. Men such as Curzon resolutely believed that the British Empire was involved in a battle for supremacy in Asia with a real and committed opponent, a view which the Russian Revolution did little to change. Indeed, so convinced was Britain of the hostile intentions of Russia towards its empire that the term 'Russophobia' was even coined to describe such a fear.

The phenomenon of Russophobia has not received as much attention as it warrants, given its importance within the milieu of Anglo-Russian relations. Yet the term was one recognised by contemporaries and certainly had a role to play within both official and unofficial discourse on Russia. Russophobia was a hostility by certain people in Britain towards Russia, sometimes manifesting itself as an almost obsessive hysteria. In particular, Russophobes tended to view that country with a level of distrust that could not be countered by any Russian official.[63] In effect, no matter what Russia said or did, a Russophobe always attributed the worst of intentions to that country. Literature was one particular area which thrived on Russophobia, with writers such as William Le Queux both epitomising Russophobia and also serving to exacerbate the phenomenon, casting Russia as the principal enemy in adventure and spy fiction. Invariably in such novels, the Russian was 'the picture of savagery' – brutal, uncivilised and criminal. Russian invasion of India, Constantinople, and even England itself, was a further common theme, as was the despotic nature of the tsarist government.[64] While it is notoriously difficult to define 'public opinion', and even harder to track the effect of such popular expression on official policy, the views of the British population towards Russia 'exerted a definite, if subtle and hard-to-quantify influence on the general relations between the two countries'.[65] Russophobia was an important facet of British decision-making towards Russia in the late nineteenth and early twentieth centuries. As will be shown, Curzon provides a prime example of a British official whose Russophobia affected his opinion of Bolshevik Russia.

What is readily apparent from even the limited amount of literature is the continual reiteration, both within official and popular discourse, that Russia was a military threat to Britain and its empire. For all the apparent distaste of liberals regarding the tsarist regime, it was the ability of Russia to mobilise thousands of its men in opposition to Britain which ultimately fuelled Russophobia. In particular, the fear regarding the security and stability of India dominated British policy towards Russia and South Asia throughout this period. This obsession with India governed Britain's preoccupation with naval supremacy, its perceived need to prevent Russia from gaining control of the Straits and the preservation of its own dominance of the Persian Gulf. India was at once Britain's greatest asset and biggest weakness. It was what drove the likes of Conolly and others to implement British hegemony throughout southern Asia, it dictated the creation of Afghanistan, Persia and Tibet as buffer states, and even later of seeking to extend British influence in Mesopotamia, Turkey and the Caucasus. While the many other nations of Asia might have been the stages for Great Game rivalry, India was always the prize.

The problem for Britain, however, was that the very existence of the Raj depended almost entirely on the perceived strength of the British rulers. 'India' was a country made up of hundreds of individual states, some of which were directly possessed by Britain ('British India'), others of which were governed by native Indian rulers under British suzerainty (the 'Princely States'). British rule in India had always relied on the collaboration of native rulers and on the general acquiescence of the Indian population.[66] Any belief that Britain was weak, even temporarily, risked breaking this acquiescence and seeing the Indian population rise up against British hegemony. This was the case both internally in the way the British ruled India, but also externally in the way it defended it from foreign aggression. Should Britain allow Russia to gain any kind of foothold in India, it risked losing any legitimacy it may have had to rule.

Throughout the nineteenth and early twentieth centuries, numerous observers would posit their views on Russia's intentions towards India. In 1829, for example,

Colonel George de Lacy Evans wrote *On the Practicability of an Invasion of British India*, in which he set out to demonstrate the feasibility of a Russian advance towards the sub-continent. De Lacy Evans opened his work with a supposed quote from the Russian envoy to Khiva:

> If we possessed Khiva, of which conquest would not be difficult... then would all the treasures of Asia enrich our country, and we should see realised the brilliant project of Peter the Great... In a word, Khiva is at this moment an advanced post, which ... would become the point of re-union for all the commerce of Asia, and *would shake to the centre of India, the enormous commercial superiority of the dominators of the sea.*[67]

This was the very stuff from which Russophobia was made, and it is not hard to see why de Lacy Evans' work was to have a profound influence on policy-makers in London. Importantly, de Lacy Evans believed that Russia would not actually attempt to conquer India in its entirety, but would instead seek to destabilise British rule there.

This view would be shared by a young Curzon, travelling through Central Asia almost sixty years later to survey the recently constructed Transcaspian railway (Krasnovodsk–Ashkhabad–Merv–Bukhara). Recording his thoughts in *Russia in Central Asia and the Anglo-Russian Question* (first published in 1889) Curzon believed that the full significance of the railway had been overlooked in London. He pointed out how the railway line had made this previously difficult terrain now relatively easy to traverse, enabling Russia to move its troops quicker than ever through Central Asia and up to India's borders. Yet even then, Curzon still believed that no Russian was foolish enough to attempt to invade India completely. Instead, it was probable Russia would try an attack on the Raj in order to distract Britain: 'To keep England quiet in Europe by keeping her employed in Asia, that, briefly put, is the sum and substance of Russian policy.'[68]

Opinion on the relative likelihood of a Russian invasion of India appeared to ebb and flow at various points throughout the nineteenth and twentieth centuries, and of course varied from person to person.[69] For example, in 1884 Sir Charles MacGregor calculated just how many Russian troops could be mustered against the Raj, an exercise designed to highlight the inadequate numbers of Britain's troops in India should its northerly neighbour chose to attack.[70] Even by 1905, Russia's intentions were still being discussed, with Lord Kitchener, commander-in-chief of the Indian army, claiming that the main danger facing India was 'the menacing advance of Russia towards our frontiers'. For Kitchener, the likelihood of invasion was real enough to warrant extensive expansion of the Indian army.[71]

This apparent obsession with the safety of India was not without justification. In 1801 for example, Tsar Paul I looked to take advantage of Britain's troubles with

France by proposing to Napoleon a joint endeavour against India.[72] While Paul I's plans failed to come to fruition, the temptation to try to unbalance British rule in India always remained.[73] And despite later repeated assurances from St Petersburg that it had no hostile intentions towards India, the pace of Russia's expansion into Asia in the nineteenth century was dramatic enough to be of concern to Britain. For four centuries the Russian empire had expanded at a rate of some fifty-five square miles a day, something of which British officials were only too aware. In 1836, Sir John McNeill, the newly appointed British minister to Persia, published a book detailing Russia's territorial gains in Europe and Asia from the time of Peter the Great.[74] Containing a folding map illustrating Russia's expansion over the last century, McNeill's book vividly warned of Russia's apparent inexorable march through the continent.[75] By the late 1800s, the Caucasus, the Trans-Caspian region and the khanates of Khokand, Bokhara and Khiva had all come under Russian hegemony.[76] Moreover, between 1880 and 1904 Russia was busily carrying out a programme of railway construction in Central Asia. At the beginning of the nineteenth century more than 2,000 miles separated Britain and Russia in Asia; by the start of the twentieth century this had shrunk to a few hundred miles.

To many contemporary observers, it must have seemed that the legend of Peter the Great's will was true: that from his death bed, the great Tsar had commanded his successors to pursue what he believed to be Russia's destiny – domination of the world through ascendancy over India and Constantinople.[77] Whatever the reality behind the legend, Curzon for one believed that 'Russia was as much compelled to go forward as the earth is to go around the sun'.[78] As for Russia's true intentions towards India, Curzon and de Lacy Evans were not wrong when they believed that their imperial rivals were too smart to contemplate a full-scale invasion of that country.

Nevertheless, the more astute Russian leaders realised that threatening the jewel in Britain's imperial crown was always a convenient way of gaining leverage in negotiations. Thus, Russia was just as much a player in the Great Game as Britain. It too looked to extend its influence into those countries on its frontiers in order to secure its territories; it too looked to its imperial rival with fear lest that rival gained influence at its expense in Asia; and it too sent numerous agents, spies and adventurers into the arena of the Great Game in order to counter British moves. Indeed, it was the Russian foreign minister, Count Nesselrode, who coined the alternative term for the Great Game, the 'Tournament of Shadows'.[79] Whether Russia was as committed to, or as obsessed with, the Great Game as Britain is perhaps an issue up for debate. However, what is certain is that Britain was not simply playing with its own shadow, nor was Russia simply a passive participant in the process. That Russia was a very real nemesis to Britain in the period prior to the First World War is also important when it comes to understanding the mental maps which might have influenced decision–makers in the post–war years.

Curzon

One figure who epitomised the typical British Great Game player and Russophobe was George Nathaniel Curzon. A notoriously divisive figure, contemporary opinion of Curzon was mixed. To some, such as Lord Beaverbrook, Curzon was 'inconsistent, unreliable, untruthful and treacherous'.[80] A.J.P. Taylor once described him as 'one of nature's rats',[81] while Lloyd George famously revelled in mocking his Cabinet colleague for his aristocratic background. Montagu's feelings on Curzon were complex:

> [He] amuses me, interests me, irritates me. Extraordinarily easy to deal with in the upshot, but, oh! what a process! Do you know that one of my daily duties is to write a letter to Curzon? Every day he wants some information about some Indian matter; every day he is critical about something or other; and he seems to find time to read the million and one papers which a War Cabinet Minister has to read, to write in his own handwriting any number of letters to his colleagues, and it will amuse you that on a day when I know that he had two meetings of the War Cabinet and a meeting of the Eastern Committee, every paper relevant to all three of which he had read, my wife said that she discovered him at Harrod's Stores registering for tea! ... What a man![82]

This mixture of irritation and grudging admiration for Curzon was not uncommon. Curzon's work ethic could not but be respected, yet his arrogance and unbending character meant that he did not win friends easily among his colleagues. Hence, while Montagu would frequently consult Curzon on matters concerning Afghanistan and India, this did not stop him bitterly remonstrating against him in 1922 during the affair of his resignation. There were, in fact, few people with whom Curzon did not clash. His supreme self-confidence certainly did not help matters. As one fellow student at Balliol put it, Curzon's speaking style was 'more inclined to overpower than to persuade'.[83]

Yet, for all this apparent animosity to Curzon, there were some who saw another side of him. To his subordinates, Curzon could be attentive and convivial. One such individual who served under Curzon for three years, produced something like a rebuttal after his master's death. Clement Jones describes Curzon as having shown him great kindness, and of being interested in his family life and attentive to his needs. More telling is Jones' judgement that Curzon possessed something like two personalities: 'For myself, I always felt that, like an actor, he [Curzon] put on the dress suitable for the part which he was going to play.'[84] When Curzon felt the need to be, he could be pompous and arrogant; to those beneath him he could afford to extend kindness. Such an idea is echoed in the writings of Charles Hardinge – colleague in the Foreign Office and fellow former viceroy to India. As Hardinge explained in his memoir:

> I have always maintained that in him [Curzon] there were embodied two entirely different personalities which showed themselves according to surrounding circumstances. The one was a delightful, amusing, clever and most charming companion, while the other was a hard and relentless man, and the more one saw of this side of him the more one almost hated him.[85]

In his biography of Curzon, Sir Harold Nicolson, appears particularly sympathetic to the man, painting a portrait of something like a troubled genius who lacked 'people skills' – a man whose intellectual abilities were so above the average, that it was hard for him to relate to others not as gifted. Hence, Curzon is described as being: irritable, lonely, intelligent, competitive, humorous, genial, emotional, charming, childish, egotistic, and many other things beside. The Earl of Ronaldshay gave positively glowing praise to Curzon in his biography: 'So much courage, so gallant a bearing in face of so great difficulties, such passionate devotion and such high ideals provide an example and an inspiration which will long survive him'.[86] Ultimately, it would seem that Curzon was one of life's dividing figures, eliciting great affection and admiration from some, and extreme hostility and derision from others. His tendency to change personality according to different people and circumstance made it particularly hard for both contemporaries and historians to fully get the measure of the man.

One thing that is certainly agreed upon is that when it came to Asia and the Middle East, Curzon possessed a confidence that propelled him to centre stage of any debate. For the one thing that Curzon aspired to be from an early age was an expert on Asia, and he would devote most of his life to such a pursuit. Curzon's ambition in this arena was sparked while listening to a lecture by the imperialist writer James Fitzjames Stephen at Eton in 1877: 'Ever since that day the fascination and sacredness of India have grown upon me', Curzon confessed.[87] Between 1882 and 1895, he would make six extensive journeys through Persia, Russian Central Asia, Afghanistan, India, China and Japan, experiences which would do 'much to colour his thinking about Britain's place in the world'.[88] Above all, Curzon would be a staunch believer in the civilising mission of the British Empire, and the sacred trust involved in ruling India.[89]

It was this obsession with India that led to Curzon's life-long animosity towards Russia, and his genesis as a Russophobe.[90] Interestingly enough, such a description is one that Curzon would never have accorded himself, declaring that he did not 'class myself either with the Russophiles or the Russophobes'.[91] Yet, in all respects of the word, Curzon personified Russophobia. For, Curzon did not necessarily hate Russia as much as he feared it. Indeed, in some ways Curzon held a certain amount of respect for Russia. In his study of the Trans-Caspian railway he did not hesitate to applaud the technical achievements of the Russian engineers in having completed the task in such difficult desert terrain.[92] There was also an amount of understanding as to why, given its geographical position, Russia did appear compelled to expand into Central Asia.[93] Indeed, one could argue that it was just this acceptance of Russia's needs and its capabilities that made Curzon ardently fearful of the threat that country posed to Britain; for it would seem that the Russian march through to the borders of India was somehow inevitable. Rather than blaming Russia for what it was in its nature to do, Curzon instead tended to criticise the various British governments for allowing its rival to act this way. If Britain was to be gullible and complacent, 'it had therefore no right to complain of Russia's advance'.[94]

Furthermore, Curzon was only too aware that a full-scale military invasion was not necessary for Russia to still create trouble for the British Empire. That the British in India were but 'a little foam on an unfathomable and dark ocean' was something Curzon understood entirely.[95] Without the appearance that the empire was indestructibly powerful, stable, confident and wealthy, Britain's position would be highly vulnerable. For Curzon, to allow Russia to damage British prestige was akin to allowing the destruction of the empire. Hence, his Great Game call to arms:

> Whatever be Russia's designs upon India, whether they be serious and inimical or imaginary and fantastic, I hold that the first duty of English statesmen is to render any hostile intentions futile, to see that our own position is secure and our frontier impregnable, and so to guard what is without a doubt the noblest trophy of British genius.[96]

Throughout his public career, Curzon would be a vocal opponent of any British government policy that appeared to concede too much to Russia's imperial ambitions. For, always, he had in mind not so much the reality of the concession to be made, but of the consequences to the perception of British power. So, for example, while in practical terms the 1907 convention actually gave little to Russia that it did not already possess, for Curzon the agreement in effect admitted that St Petersburg was just as entitled to influence within Persia as London was.[97]

Together with the practical experience and formative opinion that his travels provided, the other important benefit Curzon derived from these years was the creation of a reputation as an expert on this region of the world. Indeed, Curzon always appeared anxious throughout his career to prove himself more than a mere politician. In 1896, when his work *Pamirs and the Source of the Oxus* won him a gold medal from the Royal Geographical Society, Curzon confessed the honour gave him greater pleasure 'than it did to become a Minister of the Crown'.[98] For the rest of his years Curzon would continually refer to this period of travel and the works produced as evidence of the superiority of his knowledge over those in the British government who were less experienced.

In 1889, Curzon completed *Persia and the Persian Question* following a three month journey on horseback through that country. Ultimately, Curzon intended his study to fill a gap he perceived in the British understanding of Persia, and 'to provide an enduring intellectual legacy', reading 'virtually every work published on Persia in a European language' as preparation for his trip.[99] However, although *Persia* received critical acclaim upon its publication,[100] to a modern eye there is an inherent conflict between Curzon's desire to be considered an impartial Persian scholar, and the political bias he brings to his work. Both *Russia in Central Asia* and *Persia* are predicated on analysis of the strategic importance of this area of the world to Britain's interests in India. In *Russia and Central Asia*, for example, Curzon revealed his early thoughts on Afghanistan, when he noted how it 'has long been the Achilles' heel of Great Britain in the East. Impregnable elsewhere, she has shown herself uniformly vulnerable here'.[101] In the opening pages of *Persia* Curzon gives his opinion on the ultimate worth of Afghanistan, Persia, Turkestan and Transcaspia: 'To me, I confess, they are the pieces on a chessboard upon which is being played out a game for the dominion of the world.'[102] At heart, Curzon was a strategist, and not an academic.

Furthermore, the British politician did not speak any Persian, and had to use interpreters during his travels. This meant that, unlike the other renowned Persian scholar, E.G. Browne, who travelled for a year through the country engaging with people from all walks of life, Curzon remained largely isolated from the local people and their culture, his time being spent talking with merchants and officials.[103] His lack of contact with the masses during his time in Persia perhaps goes some way towards explaining why Curzon would fail to recognise the nationalist feelings and popular hostility towards foreign powers that would become crucial to Anglo-Persian relations after the First World War. In contrast, in 1918 when Browne proposed a 'five point plan' for improving Anglo-Persian relations, he was in much better position to gauge popular feeling in Persia at the time.[104] Nevertheless, whether he was really an 'expert' on this region of the world or not, these early years of travel and writing would provide Curzon with the belief that he always knew best when it came to Britain's Asian affairs, and would become his standard justification for advocating policies in the face of opposition from his colleagues.

Having formulated his ideas regarding Russia, India and their South Asian neighbours in his early years of travel and writing, Curzon would have to wait until he was thirty-nine to be able to put these thoughts into action. After gaining his laurels in government as under-secretary of state for India (1891–1892) and under-secretary of state for Foreign Affairs (1895–1898), Curzon achieved one of the central aims of his career, and was appointed viceroy of India in 1898. The position could not have been more suited for a man who combined dedication to the British imperial mission with a pomposity that positively revelled in the ceremony of the viceroyalty. Often seen as the most regal of viceroys,[105] Curzon's tenure in India was marked by a scale of pageantry not seen before, including, for example, 'the biggest show that India will ever have had' in the form of Edward VII's Coronation Durbar.[106] These distractions were not merely created for Curzon's indulgence, however, but were part of his strongly held belief that the 'Oriental mind' thrived on spectacle.[107] In his earlier travels Curzon had quickly discovered that appearances counted for much when it came to Asian rulers – hence the well-known tale of his wearing medals and decorations he had purchased from a costume shop when he had an audience with the emir of Afghanistan.[108] The reaction of the *Times* to Curzon's appointment as viceroy is telling: 'He goes as knowing something of India...but some might say that he knows too much and that he must have a great deal to unlearn.'[109] However, Curzon was not by nature a man open to having his opinions challenged. Indeed, his time spent as ruler of India appears only to have strengthened his convictions in regards to the importance of the Raj to Britain, and of the inherent threat to it posed by Russia. Curzon's inexhaustible capacity for work, combined with his belief that the best defence was offence when it came to Russia, meant that he never relented in pushing for an activist British policy in Asia.

When it came to Persia, for example, the viceroy was highly vocal in his criticism of the Home government's apparent apathy towards that country. Curzon found the attitude of Lord Salisbury and his adherence to the policy of 'splendid isolation' particularly frustrating.[110] In his desire to see a stronger British hand in Persia, Curzon would also often clash with the British minister to Tehran, Sir Arthur Hardinge.[111] While the viceroy was continually criticising Hardinge for apparently failing to deal firmly enough with the Persian government, the diplomat in turn believed Curzon to be impatient, with no appreciation of the art of diplomacy. The trouble was that, as viceroy, 'Curzon was too accustomed to getting his own way quickly' (a telling remark considering Curzon's actions towards Persia after 1918).[112] As Hardinge pointed out, he, as a mere minister, could not bully the Persian government the way Curzon could bully Nepal or Afghanistan. Yet, both men agreed that the Home government lacked a coherent policy when it came to Persia, and blamed Salisbury for such vacillation.[113] With the entrance of Lord Lansdowne into the Foreign Office in 1900, however, Curzon finally appeared to gain an ally in his endeavours. Spurred on by the viceroy, in December 1901 the new foreign secretary sent a lengthy despatch to the Persian government stipulating in no uncertain terms the limit to Britain's tolerance regarding a Russian presence in that country.[114] This was followed, in May 1903, by a pronouncement to the House of Lords that reiterated Britain's determination to retain its exclusive position in the Persian Gulf. Any establishment of a naval base or fortified post in that region by another power, declared Lansdowne, would be 'a very grave menace to British interests, and... we should certainly resist it with all means at our disposal'.[115] At last it appeared that Britain was prepared to send a clear message to Russia that there would be consequences should that country push its luck too far in southern Asia. Curzon was delighted.[116]

Perhaps the most telling event of Curzon's time as viceroy was his sponsorship of the Younghusband expedition to Tibet in 1903, for it epitomised his Russophobia, his determination to extend Britain's influence in Asia, and his tendency to act as he deemed right despite the misgivings of others. For decades, Tibet had been closed to foreigners, but by 1900 there were growing rumours from various quarters that Russia was steadily increasing its connections with that country.[117] Despite the hesitancy of London, Curzon was determined to act before Russia was able to gain a foothold in a country so close to India. He commissioned Colonel Francis Younghusband to advance into Tibet in order to force open the country to relations with Britain. Although sanctioned by Cabinet, the Younghusband mission step by step exceeded its original maxim, encouraged by an enthusiastic Curzon. The upshot of the event was that Younghusband forced his way into Lhasa and in September 1904 made the Tibetans sign a convention with Britain. Those back in London, however, believed Younghusband to have exceeded his initial commission in concluding this agreement. Despite the extraordinary physical achievement he had managed to carry out, rather than the expected hero's welcome, the colonel was censured on his return, and given only the lowest rank of knighthood, KCIE.[118]

The Tibetan mission was, however, Curzon's war, and as Arthur Balfour, prime minister of the time, complained, 'Curzon behaved as if India were an independent country, and not always a friendly one at that.'[119] Curzon's authoritative rule as viceroy was well known. As Younghusband himself noted, 'I fancy from what I saw and have heard that nobody says much against the Viceroy. He does not so much invite discussion as lay down the law and almost defiantly ask if anyone has any objection. If anyone *has* he is promptly squashed...'[120] So often in his career would Curzon become highly frustrated when things did not appear to be going his own way: 'I have a sort of consciousness that my arguments do not produce the smallest effect. If a Government means to sit down...no amount of kicking, even on the most sensitive spot, will induce it to rise...'[121] Curzon often complained during his time in India that the Home government was simply not listening to him and his council in Calcutta. In 1905, he lamented how London often treated his government as if it were a negligible quantity, pointing out to Balfour that 'the Viceroy of India is not an agent whom you send out merely to execute your orders or to act as the instrument of a policy conceived.'[122] For his part, Balfour 'once wrote that Curzon regarded the Secretary of State [for India] not as the Minister responsible to Parliament for the government of India but as the Viceroy's diplomatic representative at the Court of St. James'.[123] Come 1918, Curzon would find the roles reversed, when he was occupying the Foreign Office and the Indian government disagreed with policy emanating from Whitehall. One would have thought that his experience as viceroy would have provided Curzon with an empathy and an understanding for the frustrations of the Indian government in the post-war period, when it complained of being ignored by London. Ironically enough, however, when it came to it, Curzon was just as willing to ignore the voices of dissent in India as his predecessors had been.

In August 1905, Curzon would end up resigning following a dispute with General Kitchener over the relatively minor matter of the power of the military member of the viceroy's council. As viceroy, Curzon had fought incessantly with the Home government to preserve his prerogative to act on matters which he believed to be in his sole remit and when London supported Kitchener in this affair it was too much for him to bear. Later, as chair of the Eastern Committee he would balk at any attempt to reform the committee that appeared to limit his powers over it. As foreign secretary, he would insist on having his own way over Britain's international relations, jealously guarding his authority within the government. He would cajole and bully any who opposed him, and frequently threaten to resign if his wishes were not granted (although 1905 was, in fact, the only time he carried through the threat). For, wherever he was, whatever position within government he occupied, Curzon always believed that he knew best and should be listened to. His ambition, stubbornness and relentless nature, combined with his experience of Asian affairs meant that Curzon's was nearly always the loudest voice in government when it came to Britain's foreign policy in this region. His continual lauding of his own expertise on Asia and the Middle East even became something of a standing joke among his colleagues in government. An encounter during a Cabinet discussion summarises all: as the discussion moved on to Persia, Curzon cleared his throat and began 'You may not be aware...' only for Balfour to quickly interrupt him: 'It's all right George, we all know you have written a monumental work on Persia.'[124]

Bloody Retribution

With the various positions of authority that he occupied, his years of experience with India, Asia and Russia, and the sheer force of his personality, Curzon was a central figure within the British government in the post-war period. As viceroy,

Curzon left his mark on India. As foreign secretary, he was determined to leave his mark on southern Asia. In fact, it seems that, after his ignominious departure from India in 1905, Curzon became even more resolute in the opinions formulated during this first stage of his career. Following his return to England, Curzon was decidedly out of favour in Whitehall, and it would be another ten years before he would finally get back into a position of power within government. His outburst in 1907 against the Anglo-Russian Convention demonstrates how he had lost none of his zeal when it came to Britain's foreign affairs.[125] Yet between 1905 and 1917 he was to be largely frustrated in his ambitions, complaining to an acquaintance: 'As one who was at the Foreign Office for three years, who served in India for seven, and who knows personally almost every country in Europe and Asia, I ought surely to be of greater use that I am now permitted to be.'[126] This period of political marginalisation would mean that when Curzon finally regained some authority in 1918 he would be sure to make it count. Driven by ambition and a redoubtable confidence in his personal knowledge and analytical abilities, Curzon would brook no opposition to his policies in Persia and elsewhere, even if the advice from others was actually sound.

As well as being of interest for the pivotal role he played in Britain's foreign policy in the period after the First World War, Curzon also personified the concept of a Great Game mentality. He carried the thoughts and opinions which he had formulated in his early years of travel and his time as viceroy with him into the Foreign Office. This meant that this Great Game mentality was able to exert an influence over the direction of Britain's foreign affairs, despite the many indicators that such a mode of thinking was outdated by 1918. The days of the Anglo-Russian Convention were gone. No longer could two imperial powers divide Persia between themselves with little regard of the consequences to Persia itself. That the 1907 agreement between Britain and Russia had been sealed in secret, with no consultation with the Persian government, insulted Persian pride. The backlash against Britain, when combined with the civil unrest of the revolutionary period, shows how nationalist sentiment was increasing in Persia even prior to the First World War. Unfortunately, Curzon failed to heed the warning signs. In 1907, despite protests, Britain was still able to exert its authority on Persia; by 1919, the Persian people would no longer allow this.

The reason why the lessons of 1907 were not learnt is that for Curzon and others, countries such as Persia and Afghanistan were viewed almost exclusively in relation to the security of India.[127] The 'buffer state' policy governed Britain's actions towards the Asian states for most of the nineteenth and twentieth centuries; after 1918 the government still pursued the same aims it had done for decades. The only difference was that while the ends remained the same, there was growing debate about the nature of the means. Before the First World War, the main consideration for Britain had been how best to counter the extension of Russian influence into Central and southern Asia. The internal situation of countries such as Persia was a secondary issue, if it was considered at all. Hence, the fact that the Persian people were unhappy with the convention, and that Britain's standing among the masses fell after 1907 was not as important to the British government as was maintaining friendly relations with Russia. Simply put, the consequences of upsetting the Persians were not deemed as problematic to British imperial interests as the consequences of upsetting the Russians. After 1918, however, the growth in Asian nationalism and pan-Islamism would mean that if it wanted to protect India effectively, the British government would need to change its priorities. How to counter internal discontent in the likes of Persia and Afghanistan would have to become Whitehall's focus. Unfortunately, while the Indian government would prove astute at recognising this, the Home government (Curzon being a key example) would utterly fail to note this change of play.

Likewise, when it came to judgements about Russia, Curzon would fail to apprehend the real consequences of the change of regime in Petrograd in October 1917. Just as southern Asia was viewed through the prism of the Great Game, Curzon's understanding of, and opinion on, the Bolshevik regime was coloured by the Russophobia he had developed over a number of years. When it came down to it, Curzon was a Russophobe. He might have deplored Lenin and his comrades for the many reasons that were unique to the Bolshevik creed; however, such anti-Bolshevism was always compounded by a fundamental *anti-Russianism*. Ultimately, Curzon's Russophobia combined with a Great Game mentality that made it difficult for him to comprehend the true subversive nature of Bolshevism. This, in turn, would lead to a dichotomy whereby the foreign secretary feared Russian/Bolshevik influence in southern Asia, yet pursued policies which would only serve to enhance the likelihood of Bolshevism taking hold. Only by understanding the legacy of the Great Game on the thoughts of men such as Curzon can the actions of the British government after 1918 be explained.

Chapter Two

The Iron Hand and the Velvet Glove, 1918–1919

In November 1918, there appeared to be a lot that Britain could be thankful for. The British Empire emerged from the war against the Central Powers not only as a victor but also as a power presiding over a quarter of the world's population.[1] The British imperial army was of a strength not experienced since the Napoleonic Wars,[2] and to many contemporaries the mobilisation of the empire's resources during the conflict had, in the words of Lloyd George, revealed to the world 'that the British Empire was not an abstraction but a living force to be reckoned with'.[3] While the war had seen the demise of three great empires, Britain's was still standing, and its prime minister was about to sit in Paris, as leader of one of the world's greatest nations, to decide the fate of Europe, Asia and Africa.[4] As Curzon put it to the House of Lords in November 1918, 'The British flag has never flown over a more powerful or more united empire.'[5] It is easy, therefore, to see why some contemporaries saw the aftermath of the First World War as a time of confidence and optimism for Britain.

And yet, every silver-lining has its cloud. The war had tested the empire to its very limit, straining Britain's economy and costing millions of lives. The disillusionment of the people against their governments had already created revolution in one major European state and was about to take hold in others. Nationalist and pan-Islamic fervour were simmering in Asia. And, while the rapid increase in imperial territory might be an indication of Britain's power in the post-war period, it also necessitated a requisite increase in military and administrative expense that the country could ill-afford after the strains of the war.

One thing that was for sure was that, for better or worse, the First World War had certainly changed things, as Sir Mark Sykes (expert in all things Middle Eastern), explained to Sir Arthur Hirtzel of the India Office in January 1918:

> If America had not come into the war, if the Russian Revolution had not taken place, if the idea of no annexations had not taken root, if the world spirit of this time was the world spirit of 1887... [But now] we have to look at the problem through entirely new spectacles.[6]

How many other officials in the British government recognised the differences of the post-war world, however, remains to be seen. In the meantime, the period from 1918 to 1919 was one in which Britain, emerging from the battlefields, had to start adjusting its foreign policy from a war-time to a peace-time footing. It was, therefore, a time when some of the greatest debates took place within government, as officials thrashed out their ideas about the empire's future.

Two Voices

One particular problem with Britain's relationship with southern Asia and the Middle East in this period is that there was serious interdepartmental friction and overlapping function when it came to the creation and administration of policy.[7] And part of the issue lay with the role which India was to play in this region of the world. Throughout the history of the Raj, there had been debate about India's contribution to the maintenance of the empire. In 1920, the issue appeared to have been resolved when both the Indian and Home governments agreed that:

> Apart from such 'special cases' as might arise...India should bear primary
> financial responsibility for those geographical regions in which she had
> a 'direct and substantial interest'. Included among such regions were
> Egypt 'so far as the security of the Suez Canal is affected', Persia, the
> Persian Gulf and Afghanistan.

Since Delhi retained consulates in southern Persia and held ultimate control of Afghanistan's foreign relations, such an arrangement appeared reasonable.[8] And naturally, the First World War was just such a 'special case' that India contributed unreservedly to the British cause. Together with supplying a quarter of a million native troops to serve in Mesopotamia, Persia, the Caucasus and Transcaspia, in 1917 India made an outright gift of £100 million towards the war effort – almost double India's net revenue before the outbreak of the conflict.[9]

The result of such an expansion of Indian involvement in southern Asia during the war was both a greater desire of the Indian government to have a political say befitting its military and financial responsibilities and a general confusion of jurisdiction between the Foreign, War and India Offices. In Persia, for example, General Malleson's mission at Meshed and Sir Percy Sykes' South Persia Rifles (SPR),[10] were both Indian government contingents, yet Dunsterforce, in the north-west of that country, was under the command of the War Office.[11] The tradition of having both Foreign Office and Indian controlled consulates in Persia was also problematic. As Montagu pointed out in July 1918, such a set-up meant that Britain effectively had two voices within Persia.[12] In Mesopotamia, Indian troops were instrumental in preventing the country from falling into Turkish hands. However, by 1917 military operations were transferred to the War Office, even though India continued to supply the men and material for the rest of the war, and the civil administration of that country also remained under Indian control.[13] For the government of India, by the summer of 1918 this confusion of authority was becoming increasingly unacceptable, particularly when it was coupled with a lack of political say on India's part. As Montagu pointed out during a debate of the Eastern Committee on Persia, not allowing India to have political control in that country meant that 'the Indian Government naturally said: "why should we give our men and our money to the prosecution of a policy of which we disapprove"'.[14] The solution to both problems, as Montagu saw it, was to have 'the whole war area from Palestine eastward managed from India by the Indian Government, both militarily and politically'.[15]

Unfortunately for Montagu and the government of India, there was little support in London for the suggestion. The Foreign Office argued that the 'feeling in Persia against India and Indian officials is traditional, and were the whole of the policy in Persia to be conducted from Simla that feeling would undoubtedly become aggravated'.[16] The War Office thought that handing control to India would be viewed by the Persian population as nothing less than a step towards the annexation of their country.[17] Curzon cut to the heart of the matter when he pointed out that while it might be irritating for India to not have greater control in Persia, 'it would be not only disagreeable but dangerous to have a Minister at Teheran [sic] who might be pursuing a policy inspired or dictated from Delhi, that did not fit in with the foreign policy of Downing Street'.[18] The supremacy of the Home government was ultimately indisputable. However, the consequences of refusing to allow India a greater say in Britain's affairs in Persia and elsewhere would mean that, very quickly after the armistice, the Indian government would look to roll back its commitments – both militarily and financially – to their pre-war standing. Although necessitated by economic concerns, perhaps India might have been more willing to delay retrenchment had it felt its efforts in this region were appreciated more by Whitehall.

While there was little support for granting the Indian government complete autonomy in southern Asia and the Middle East, the War Office and the Foreign Office certainly agreed that better coordination of policy was needed.[19] Persia appeared the most acute example of overlapping jurisdiction, but by 1918 there was a general realisation within the British government that its policy towards this region should be treated as a whole – that Egypt, Mesopotamia, Persia, Palestine, Arabia and the Caucasus, while representing varying levels of British involvement, were all inextricably linked by geography, religion and history, and that having one body to define, implement and co-ordinate policy across this area would considerably strengthen Britain's presence there.[20] This concept of unifying control was not necessarily a new one – the idea of a Near Eastern Viceroyalty or India–Middle East Empire had previously been floated by the likes of Kitchener and the British Oriental Secretary at Cairo, Ronald Storrs.[21] As the war drew to a close, however, and Britain faced considerable expansion to its territorial responsibilities, the issue became more pressing.

The problem was what form this Middle Eastern/Asian body should take and who should ultimately control it. In the opinion of Robert Cecil, what was needed was the creation of an independent department within the government with control over all political, administrative and military aspects of the region for Britain. However, for Hardinge and Sir Ronald Graham (assistant under-secretary), the creation of a separate department that would challenge the Foreign Office's supposed monopoly over Britain's foreign affairs was inconceivable. Instead, they argued for the creation of a Middle Eastern section within their department.[22] As chair of the Eastern Committee, Curzon too was opposed to Cecil's plans, as it threatened to make his position within government defunct. The ex-viceroy was already annoyed at the frequency with which his committee was bypassed by other departments: 'I observe that no questions are referred to us. We have not been summoned for some two months and the Foreign Office policy as regards these countries is formulated and published without reference to us at all.'[23] Curzon's alternative to the suggestions of Montagu and Cecil was to expand the Eastern Committee to include a staff, and that the chair (i.e. he) should be made a secretary of state for the Middle East.[24] Thus, it would seem that while everybody agreed that a co-ordinating body was needed in order to take charge of Britain's affairs in this region, everybody also believed that their department should be in control and nobody was willing to have their current authority diminished. Eventually, however, by August 1918, Cecil had finally managed to convince Balfour, to allow him to establish a Middle Eastern Department. To conciliate Hardinge, Cecil accepted that the department could not be completely removed from the Foreign Office,[25] and he also gave up trying to dissolve the Eastern Committee altogether, although he did believe that the committee should be concerned only with matters of high policy, leaving the practical administrative issues to the new department.[26]

For Curzon, this was the worst possible scenario. Not only had he been passed over to head the new Middle Eastern Department, but he was in danger of becoming chairman of a largely moribund committee. On 13 August, after a long speech recounting his many numerous qualifications, Curzon threatened to resign as chair if the committee decided to reduce its remit, as was being suggested.[27] In the end, it was only when Curzon was made acting foreign secretary in January 1919 that Cecil was finally able to dissolve the Eastern Committee to be replaced by the *ad hoc* Interdepartmental Conference on the Middle East (IDCE).[28] In the meantime, on 28 August 1918, Eyre Crowe was appointed head of the new Middle Eastern Department of the Foreign Office, although it was agreed that he would share his authority with Hirtzel at the India Office. The Indian government would retain its political authority in Mesopotamia and Persia, while military issues were still to be referred to the War Office. The end result was that, rather than an all-encompassing body with full control over every aspect of British policy in the Middle East and Asia (as Cecil had originally envisaged), the new department was much the same as the old Eastern Department of the Foreign Office, which had been dismantled before the war.[29] The machinery for making policy in this region would continue to be muddled, leading to a lack of coherence in this period.[30] Indeed, wrangling over who was to have authority over this area of Britain's foreign policy was to continue until 1921, when another Middle Eastern Department would be created, this time under the remit of the Colonial Office.[31] In the meantime, Britain would continue to have 'two voices' (and sometimes three or four) in Persia and elsewhere in southern Asia in the immediate post-war years.

Good Red Herring

This problem of coordination would not only continue to cause friction between the Foreign, War and India Offices, but would also allow Curzon to have a resounding say over Britain's relations towards countries such as Persia in this period. For, as will be seen, with nobody to mount an effective challenge against his apparent authority on Asian affairs, Curzon would find himself able to convince others within the government that his way was ultimately the right way. As already shown, Curzon's determination to change Britain's relations with Persia had had a long gestation, and with his re-entry into the government – first with his position on the Eastern Committee and then as acting foreign secretary – he found himself in 1918–1919 finally able to shape Britain's foreign policy. As his biographer Nicolson put it, the post-war period presented Curzon with the opportunity to enact his 'complete, final, perfected plan': to consolidate, once and for all, Britain's presence in southern Asia and secure India from any future foreign threat.[32] In the words of Curzon himself, in December 1918, now was the opportune time for the Persians to 'realise that the iron hand lay beneath the velvet glove'. Curzon's policy towards Persia in 1918 and 1919 would exemplify his Great Game mentality, although he would find opposition to his endeavours at every turn in the form of the Indian government, which much preferred 'to give the "velvet glove" a chance'.[33]

Joining Curzon in his Persian quest in the post-war period was Sir Percy Cox, newly appointed *chargé d'affaires* in Tehran (the previous British minister, Sir Charles Marling proving too inefficient for London's liking).[34] Cox certainly appeared more pro-active than Marling, and immediately upon his appointment, in November 1918, began to inundate the Foreign Office with his ideas for the direction of British policy in Persia. In the opinion of the new *chargé d'affaires*, the collapse of Russia's presence in Asia presented the perfect opportunity for Britain to extend and solidify its position in Persia. Noting that the 'suspension of Russia's existence gives us a free field for our labours', Cox was soon suggesting that Britain should try to gain a mandate for Persia from America.[35] Such a move would give freer rein in Persia, as it would provide international legitimacy to Britain's position of influence in that country. The focus on Russia as the prime target of Britain's policy in Persia matched Curzon's own beliefs. (That Cox and Curzon thought so alike is unsurprising given that the two had a history: Cox had been appointed by Curzon in 1899 as Consul in Muscat and had travelled up the Persian Gulf with Curzon when he was viceroy).[36] The government of India, however, was alarmed at Cox's suggestion, Chelmsford arguing that the cost and military commitment that such a move would necessitate would be a drain on Indian resources that could not be justified so far as India's interests were concerned.[37] Cox countered that the viceroy did not appreciate how much the situation in Persia had changed with the 'alarming spread of Bolshevism and revolutionary ideas... As it is, the Shah is extremely apprehensive of [the] spread of Bolshevism.'[38]

The India government was sceptical, nevertheless, that Bolshevism was the problem Cox believed it to be. Instead, it emphasised the danger of growing pan-Islamism in the post-war years.[39] Prior to 1918, pan-Islamism had already been simmering steadily beneath the surface of India. Since the late nineteenth century, more and more Muslims had come to the realisation that the expansion of European power was increasingly subjecting Muslims to Christian rule. Indian Muslims started to grow suspicious of Britain, and actions such as the 1911 revocation of the partitioning of Bengal did not help matters.[40] Nevertheless, they had remained loyal to the British crown, and the political reforms sought by the Muslim League had always been consistent with the maintenance of British control.[41] That is, until after the First World War. Although many Muslims fought in the Indian army, there was a growing discomfort among them at the fact that they were in conflict with the Ottoman Empire, the last remaining bastion of Islamic power in the twentieth century.[42] Nationalist feeling also mingled with pan-Islamic sentiment, the one serving to encourage the other.

Kemal Ataturk (president of Turkey, 1923–1938) was particularly adept at utilising the Islamic factor to strengthen nationalism, realising that a national Turkish awakening could be achieved through the use and mobilisation could only be achieved by the use of Islamic symbols.'[43] Only through deft handling of Indian, Persian and Afghan affairs during the war had Britain been able to avoid a mass Muslim uprising in support of Turkey. Muslim agitation had not abated with the armistice, however. Rather, it had gained in strength in the immediate post-war years, in part due to the Allied handling of the Turkish peace process.[44]

While there were some in the Home government who paid little heed to Muslim or nationalist discontent in Asia, the Indian government was absorbed by it in the years after 1918. On 3 December 1918, the India Office drew up a memorandum on 'The Future of Russian Central Asia' in which it noted 'that of [the] 10,000,000 inhabitants of various provinces [of the region], only 500,000 are Russian, the rest are fanatical Muslims'.[45] According to this report then, while Bolshevism might prove some irritation to Britain's interests in the region, the real threat came in the form of Muslim extremism. In the post-war years debate would rage as to whether Britain should fear Bolshevism more than pan-Islamism and nationalism. Great Game thinking dictated that Russia, in whatever form, was the avowed enemy of Britain in South Asia. And yet, as the Indian government would consistently argue, when pan-Islamism combined with Asian nationalism it proved a force more potent than Soviet Russia.[46]

When it came to it, the picture on the potential of Bolshevik Russia to be a threat to Britain in southern Asia was somewhat mixed. On the one hand, there were the reports by Cox and news from Malleson in Meshed that consistently noted the possibility of Bolshevism taking hold in Central Asia.[47] A Tashkent Soviet had seized power in September 1917 and in April 1918 had established the first Soviet republic outside of Russia itself – a potentially worrying occurrence for Britain.[48] And yet an uprising by Orenburg Cossacks had left the Tashkent regime completely cut off from Moscow (and they would remain so until September 1919). To the west an anti-Bolshevik regime in Ashkhabad, supported by Malleson, also separated the Tashkent Soviet from the Caspian route of communication, while in the north-east more hostile Cossacks meant that this revolutionary enclave was completed surrounded.[49]

The presence of British and anti-Bolshevik forces in and around Persia also meant that the new Soviet envoy to Tehran, Karl Bravin, was isolated from his Bolshevik masters. Bravin had been the Russian consul in Khoi in Persian Azerbaijan and arrived in Tehran in January 1918.[50] However, the new Bolshevik representative had no credentials from the Soviet regime and although the Persian government had initially been inclined to recognise him, it was soon persuaded to simply ignore Bravin.[51] As he told his superiors, 'in spite of all our expressions of friendship and our cordial demeanour [the Persian government] are obviously laughing at us'.[52] Without the recognition of the Persian government, Bravin was unable to remove the sitting Russian legation, nor did he have access to any funds. Dejected and unable to do any work of substance, in June 1918 Bravin begged his superiors in Moscow 'either to give me speedy assistance or to release me from such an unprofitable engagement'.[53]

Just why the Bolshevik regime gave Bravin such little help in his endeavours is likely due to a number of reasons. For one thing, until the Red Army was able to make progress in the south of Russia, Persia was effectively cut off, preventing the sending of money or other Bolshevik agents into the country. Nevertheless, more effort could have been made to provide Bravin with credentials. There was, for example, a Persian representative in Moscow at this time, Assad Bahador, who could have pressed upon Tehran a Bolshevik desire to have Bravin recognised.

Instead, Assad noted specifically in his reports home that the Bolsheviks 'have not asked for recognition for this person'.[54] Such neglect of Bravin was therefore probably also due to the lack of importance the Soviet regime placed on affairs in Persia at this time. Not only was the civil war occupying much attention but the Bolsheviks were still confused as to what role official diplomacy was to play in its foreign policy. Trotsky had, after all, upon assuming control of the Foreign Office in 1917 declared that he would 'issue some revolutionary proclamations to the peoples and close up the joint'.[55] Such ambivalence towards the traditional channels of international relations was further compounded by the dilemma the Bolsheviks faced in deciding what groups of Persians they should be working with in the first place: should support be given to nationalist and pan-Islamic revolutionary forces, or should these, essentially bourgeois movements, be discouraged in favour of truly communist organisations?[56] While Bravin may have been busy making connections with various Persian malcontents, not until 1920 would this issue be officially worked out.[57] Not until 1921, either, would the Bolshevik regime invest greater resources in their diplomatic endeavours; in the meantime, Bravin was left to his own devices.[58]

Together with Bravin's impotence, there was also reason to doubt that Communism would find fertile ground in southern Asia. In December 1918, the Persian minister, Samad Khan, stated his belief that Bolshevism would never take root in Persia, as the people were not of that militant attitude. Nevertheless the Persian government was suspicious of Bolshevism and, as Cox himself had admitted, the shah was said to be very anti-Bolshevik.[59] In any case, even if Bolshevism was the threat to Persia which Cox argued it was, Lancelot Oliphant of the Foreign Office noted that 'it is open to doubt whether the present sense of feeling here [Britain] or elsewhere would sanction our saving Persia from Bolshevism by military measures'.[60]

Indeed, in a meeting of the Eastern Committee on 19 December 1918 there seemed little enthusiasm for Britain extending its involvement in Persia. Curzon opened the discussion with an explanation of the state of affairs there:

> We are face to face, in the first place, with a country, the Government of which is weak and incompetent, the ruling classes corrupt and extortionate, the monarch worthless and the lower classes in a deplorable condition intellectually, physically and materially. Persia would be bankrupt if it were not for our money, and she would at this moment be in a state of revolution if it were not for our troops.[61]

If Curzon was trying to gain some sympathy for the Persian cause, his plan backfired. Instead, it led Montagu to question the very basis of Britain's involvement there, wondering aloud if the country had ever actually been left to its own devices, free of foreign support. Curzon's response – that such a move would be impossible, since there was no one within Persia capable of running that country properly without foreign aid – led Cecil to ask simply what would be the consequences should Persia be allowed to sink into chaos. Cecil then declared himself in favour of giving up entirely on Persia, including stopping all subsidies and supplies of arms. Sir Hamilton Grant (Foreign Secretary of the Indian government) argued that a certain level of anarchy in Persia would not be disastrous for India. As long as no other foreign power was able to gain a dominant position there, the Indian government cared little for the internal issues of Persia. For his part, Montagu believed that there was something to be said for letting Persia fall so far that it would come to realise, of its own accord, its need for Britain's assistance.

Clearly, Curzon's attempt to galvanise his colleagues into action over Persia was not working. Curzon's scaremongering was also countered by the presence at the meeting of Marling, the recalled minister for Tehran. Marling flatly denied that Bolshevism was the threat to Persia that Cox and Curzon so adamantly claimed it to be. Cecil also expressed his doubt that Persia was under threat from a Bolshevik invasion, arguing that Lenin's regime was as yet unable to organise an operation on such a large scale as would be necessary to successfully attack Persia. As Curzon's irritation appeared at breaking point, Cecil aptly summed up Britain's policy in Persia as being 'neither fish, flesh, fowl, nor good red herring'.[62]

The meeting of 19 December had shown a preference among the majority of committee members to remain distanced from Persian affairs. Curzon, nonetheless, had not been deterred from pursuing a more forward policy and two days after the meeting he received support for his endeavours from Sir Louis Mallet, ex-ambassador to Constantinople and current head of the Middle East section of the Political Intelligence Department (PID) at the Foreign Office.[63] In a memorandum written on 21 December, Mallet argued that to abandon Persia, as Montagu, Cecil and Grant had suggested, would have grave consequences for British interests in Mesopotamia, Afghanistan and India. It would also leave Persia entirely open to Russian advances, be it Bolshevik or White Russian. Mallet's proposal was for Britain, in effect, to go on the offensive and extend its influence into the northern regions. He argued that were Britain not to press forward into 'so fertile a field, just at the moment when our principle [*sic*] rival has disappeared from the scene... a good opportunity would be missed'. Mallet emphasised, in particular, the urgency of exploiting Russia's current weakness before it was able to re-organise and re-assert its authority in Persia. Echoing Cox, Mallet advised gaining a mandate for Persia, in order to allow Britain to 'fortify ourselves against any possible future difficulties with Russia'.[64]

It just so happened that Mallet's thinking was perfectly inline with that of Curzon and of Cox and his memorandum gave added impetus to their cause. At the heart of their argument lay the idea that Britain needed to extend and consolidate its position in Persia as quickly as possible, before the traditional enemy, Russia (be it Bolshevik or otherwise), could regain its influence there. Not only was the possibility of a revived imperial Russia seriously discussed in 1918, but it was actually used by the likes of Cox and Mallet to emphasise the need for haste in this direction. Furthermore, the presence of vestigial elements of imperial Russia in Persia after the 1917 revolution could hardly go unnoticed, given that Britain was financially supporting most of them. Even the post-war concept of seeking a mandate to legitimise Britain's position in Persia still reflected a preoccupation with Russia and the supposition that it would at some point in the future try to challenge Britain's hegemony in southern Asia.

All of this not only reflected Great Game thinking, but was in contrast to the opinion of the Indian government. On 20 December 1918, Hamilton Grant had also written a memorandum further emphasising the points made in the committee meeting the previous day: that the most desirable course, from the Indian government's point of view, was to assist Persia only on a limited scale. Rather than trying to extend its political influence in Persia, the British government should be attempting to ingratiate itself better with the Persian people, who since the 1907 convention had viewed Britain as an imperial exploiter.[65] The violation of Persia's neutrality during the First World War by both British and Russian troops had angered the Persians even further so that by 1918, Britain's standing in the country was at an all time low.[66] As Chelmsford noted, 'until we have regained [the] confidence of [the] Persian people, no Persian Cabinet, however friendly, can work effectively in our interests'.[67] This idea of trying to return to a pre-1907 relationship with Persia had support from others: it had been advocated by Marling in 1917, while in January 1918 the Persian expert, E.G. Browne, had put forth his idea of an Anglo-Persian treaty based on five points, including abolishing zones of influence and allowing the Persian government to recruit advisers of whichever nationality they liked. Browne also advocated filling the Legation in Tehran with those 'who are known to be friendly and sympathetic to the Persian people'.[68]

Curzon, however, refused to acknowledge the changes which had overcome Persia in the last decade and had little time for this 'softly-softly' approach. By 30 December 1918, in another meeting of the Eastern Committee, he appeared to have entirely lost patience with the situation. The acting foreign secretary condemned the idea espoused in the previous committee meeting of leaving Persia to its own devices as 'immoral, feeble and disastrous', adding that 'if anybody imagines that this would really quit us of Persian responsibility he really must be blind'. Continuing his acerbic attack, Curzon mocked the Indian government for believing:

...that we should go on with our present policy, but do it in a more ingratiating way; use rather nicer phrases and try to humour the Persian

National Government more than the Government of India thinks that we have so far done, and that our better manners should take the form of repeating the statements we have already made in a pleasanter way...

Curzon then dismissed this argument by disparaging Indian expertise: 'it is to be noted that all the authorities who speak with actual knowledge of Persia itself are against it'. What Curzon advocated, in contrast, was a set of reforms and economic concessions which were to be pressed upon the Persian government. Should it refuse to accept such an arrangement, Persia would find itself cut off from any future British loans and would face an immediate call on all its current debts.[69] The British government, he argued, 'have never had the pluck to say to them [the Persians]. "You are in our hands absolutely to do as we please.' In his opinion, now was the time to tell the Persian government just that.[70]

The reality, however, was that Persia was *not* entirely in British hands. Despite Bolshevik proclamations renouncing all Russia's foreign interests and an official recall of all Russian staff from foreign soil, in 1918 there remained in Persia an imperial Russian presence in the form of the Russian Legation in Tehran and the Cossack Division. Officially, this Russian presence in Persia remained allied to Britain, and London had been financially supporting both organisations since 1917.[71] As Cox observed, however, there was a great difficulty in having in Persia so many Russian officials 'of [the] old regime who cannot exist without our support, but who not unnaturally resent our predominance...'[72] Both the leader of the Russian Legation, Vladimir Minorskii, and the commander of the Cossack Division, Colonel Staroselskii, regarded themselves as the last bulwark of Russia's presence in Persia. Both also felt responsible for maintaining a semblance of Russian influence in Tehran for as long as was necessary for a new Russian government to form and reclaim its privileges there.[73] For this Russian element, forced to watch Britain's international standing reach its pinnacle with the conclusion of the First World War while their country collapsed into anarchy and civil war, it was hard not to view their old Great Game rivals with jealousy. In November 1918, for example, Cox informed the Foreign Office that Minorskii had been causing a nuisance to the British during his tour of northern Persia.[74] British military personnel, in turn, viewed the Russians with barely disguised contempt.[75] By December, CIGS was forced to instruct Malleson to warn his officers in Persia to refrain from openly showing hostility towards the Russian Legation.[76]

For, despite Russia's weakness in 1918, Britain could not afford to aggravate Minorskii and Staroselskii. For one thing, having been appointed by the Russian Provisional Government, Minorskii was able to disassociate himself from the days of imperial Russian rule in Persia, and represent himself as a progressive liberal, making his standing among the Persian public relatively high.[77] Another problem lay in the fact that 'the mere consideration that they depend on us for their up-keep counts for nothing when Russian interests or those of the Division lie in a direction contrary to those of His Majesty's Government'.[78] This meant that, should they feel the urge to do so, the Russian leaders in Persia could quite simply turn on their benefactors and, while Britain could probably easily put down such a rebellion, it had no wish to incite such a situation. For one thing, the Cossack Division remained a useful resource in the face of any civil unrest or to be employed against any possible Bolshevik incursion into Persia. The division's influence over the shah was also formidable. As Curzon noted, 'the Russian commander of the brigade, Starosselski [sic] was, owing to the size of his force and his easy access to the Shah, dictator of the situation, and, until the circumstances were more favourable to ourselves, it would be impolitic to arouse his enmity.'[79] Nine months earlier, in April 1918, when trying to convince the British government to continue financially supporting the Russian Legation, Marling had warned that without the money, the legation and consulates would be forced to close, and that 'if [the Russian] Minister himself left I am convinced Persian Government would eventually recognise such people as Bravine [sic]'.[80]

In December 1918, Marling continued to argue that, were Russian influence to be eliminated completely from northern Persia, it would create a vacuum and if Britain was unable to fill this vacuum itself, it would 'prove very tempting to some other Power'. While Germany or Turkey perhaps no longer represented a threat, there still remained the possibility of Bolshevism filling that void.[81] Cox also justified his continued political support for the established Russian diplomats by pointing out that should such support be withdrawn, these Russians would soon be ousted by Bolshevik emissaries.[82] While Cox would have liked to have seen the tsarist element in Persia replaced by a British presence, he certainly did not want it exchanged for Bolshevik officials. In Mallet's eyes, however, the solution was simply for Britain to make sure it filled the vacuum itself, arguing that 'there is little to be gained by maintaining Russian interest in N. Persia against Persian wishes'.[83] For Montagu, keeping Russian diplomatic figures afloat was advisable, but he questioned the wisdom of aiding Russia to hold on to its economic interests in Persia.[84] Others in the India Office simply believed that 'this appears to be a quite impossible line of policy'.[85] Oliphant agreed that 'there seems no need to bolster up Russian political interests'.[86] Yet, in January 1918 Oliphant had admitted that in Persia, 'anything is better than Bolshevism',[87] and so for now, maintaining the Russian Legation and the Cossack Division appeared to carry less risk than the potential consequences of breaking with them.

It would seem, then, that the policy that Curzon and his allies were pursuing in Persia in 1918–1919 consisted of supporting one group of Russians against the possible threat of another group, while all the while working to at least undermine, if not remove, Russian influence altogether in that country, to be replaced by a British presence forced upon the Persian government through economic coercion.

This was a policy that the Indian government vocally opposed. By April 1919, Chelmsford was arguing that the 'existence of anti-British feeling among Moslems in Egypt and India... coupled with unsettled condition of Afghanistan, renders the present a highly dangerous moment for initiation of so hazardous an experiment'.[88] In February 1919, the emir of Afghanistan, Habibullah, had been assassinated, sparking a succession crisis,[89] while in India Chelmsford was facing rising popular unrest following the enactment of the Rowlatt Bill and the infamous Amritsar Massacre on 13 April.[90] While they were struggling to keep a check on events within India itself, the viceroy and his government were cautious of giving Muslims in South Asia any further excuse for agitation.

Yet such protests seemed to be having little impact on Curzon, and Chelmsford complained continually to Montagu that the government of India was being treated 'as if we were a *quantité négligeable*'.[91] In December 1918, Montagu himself had threatened to completely withdraw India's share of Persian expenditure if the Foreign Office did not stop sending instructions to Tehran without prior approval from the India Office.[92] In response, Crowe argued that 'the attitude of the India Office is unreasonable. The fact is that the India Office do everything to substitute their authority for that of this dept., not only in Mesopotamia and kindred questions but also in regard to Persia, where, I gather, Mr Montagu is bent upon leading us into a policy of scuttle and complete abandonment of our position.'[93] This struggle over control of Persian policy was compounded by the Foreign Office's apparent disregard of the Indian government's opinion and its claim to expertise in Asian affairs. Despite the viceroy's assertion that the Indian government held 'a greater knowledge of the facts than they [the Home government] could possess',[94] the Foreign Office believed 'that knowledge and experience gained in Persia is to be found far more easily in London than it is in Simla or Delhi'.[95] This attitude Chelmsford attributed to the report of the Mesopotamia Commission 'which had blackened our faces in the eyes of the world and discredited us as a Government'.[96]

Curzon, for his part, was growing increasingly impatient with Chelmsford's opposition. At an interdepartmental conference in May 1919 the acting foreign secretary blasted the government of India for refusing to underwrite a large loan to Persia needed to push through his planned reform package. The issue of finance was, indeed, the one ace up the viceroy's sleeve, for without India's resources the Home government would struggle to maintain its interests in Persia, let alone extend them (as Curzon was trying to do). Threatening to withhold such finance, as Montagu had done in December, was the one way of getting the Home government to listen to India. It had certainly caught the attention of Curzon, who fumed at the Indian government's attitude, arguing that the whole plan he was trying to enact in Persia was being carried out for the benefit of India in the first place, by creating a stable buffer state.[97] Curzon apparently failed to understand why the Indian government objected to being forced to pay for a policy that it opposed while all the while being scolded that it was for India's own good. The problem for Chelmsford came when Montagu was finally persuaded to support Curzon's plan. In the structure of authority, the viceroy was subservient to the secretary of state for India and, thus, while Chelmsford could continue to rail against the Home government's plans in Persia, Montagu ultimately had the final say. Once the secretary of state had been brought around to the opinion that it was worth running the risks that Curzon's Persian policy held for the potential beneficial results, Chelmsford had to acquiesce.[98]

Once Montagu had capitulated and Cecil had been brought around, there was little opposition left to Curzon's proposed plans. (It is worth noting that the reason for Cecil's change of heart was not that he became fearful of a Bolshevik threat to Persia but, rather, that he had grown apprehensive over the position of power in which Staroselskii and the Cossack Division would be left should Britain withdraw from Persia.)[99] By August 1919, the Anglo–Persian Agreement was finally concluded. Curzon considered this an important personal achievement, although lamented the fact that others did not recognise this. As he wrote to his wife:

> The papers give a very good reception to my Persian Treaty, which I have been negotiating for the past year, and which is a great triumph, as I have done it all alone. But not a single paper so much as mentions my name or has the dimmest perception that, had I not been at the Foreign Office, it would never have been at all.[100]

The agreement allowed for the supply of British advisers for Persia's administrative departments, for the encouragement of Anglo–Persian enterprise for the extension of Persia's railways and roads and for a military commission to assess Persia's military situation (with a view to creating a uniform force, officered by the British and which would ultimately absorb the South Persian Rifles and the Cossack Division). Together with a substantial loan of two million pounds sterling, to be levied on certain concessions, the agreement also stipulated the creation of a joint commission to investigate a revision of the Persian customs tariff.[101] When the finalised text of the Persian agreement was circulated through the War Cabinet for approval, Curzon justified the agreement by arguing that 'if Persia were to be left alone, there is every reason to fear that she would soon be overrun by Bolshevik influences from the north'.[102]

The idea of an imminent threat of a Bolshevik takeover of Persia was also reflected in many British newspapers that reported on the agreement. The *Times* believed that the Bolshevik regime was at that very moment 'preparing a war of conquest in Persian territory',[103] while *The Daily Telegraph* argued that there was every reason to believe that if Britain refused to help Persia, 'that in a very short time the whole country would be overrun by Bolshevik agents'.[104] The *Manchester Guardian* ominously noted that, for Persia, 'there are always the Bolsheviks looming on the horizon, and it is impossible to say...what engines of war of the most "modern type" may not be needed in order to counteract the inflow, if not of Bolshevik arms, yet of the more deadly Bolshevik doctrine'.[105] How far Curzon was really fearful of a Bolshevik incursion into Persia, and how far it was a convenient way to justify his expansionist ambitions is questionable.[106]

Whatever Curzon's real motivations, for all this anti-Bolshevik rhetoric, it was to be the White Russian element that was to be the most immediate threat to Britain's interests in Persia in late 1919. The Bolsheviks of course immediately denounced the agreement as 'a scrap of paper', refusing to recognise its legitimacy, but offered no real help to the Persians. Those Russians who ran the legation and Cossack Division, however, were able to cause much more trouble for the British. For the officials of the former tsarist regime, the agreement not only represented the strengthening of Britain's presence in Persia, but an extension of that influence into ostensibly 'Russian' territory. For the Cossack Division, the concept of a uniform force, with British rather than Russian officers in command, obviously constituted a great threat to its position in Persia. On 29 August 1919, Cox was asked outright by the Russian minister whether the agreement marked a change in Britain's policy towards Russian interests in north Persia. While Cox replied in the negative, this did little to reassure Russian officials.[107] On 1 September, it was reported by Cox that Minorskii, together with Staroselskii, had been in close communication with M. Bonin of the French Legation since the announcement of the agreement (both France and America had denounced the terms of the accord and the secrecy in which it had been negotiated).[108] As Cox explained to the Foreign Office, the 'attitude of Russian Legation is that [the] agreement [is] obviously most injurious to Russia, and that [the] Russian Legation, being in too weak a position to offer any effective opposition to it, look to [the] French to do their best to support Russia in connection "*dans les interets des deux pays*"'.[109]

More worrying than the Russian Legation's overtures to the French, however, was the possibility that Russian officials in Persia, particularly the officers of the Cossack Division, might actively try to impede the treaty. Since March 1919, the British together with the Cossack Division had been sporadically fighting an uprising in north-east Persia by the Jangali group led by Mirza Kuchuk Khan.[110] By October, Lord Derby in Paris was relaying warnings from the Persian minister for foreign affairs that the Russian constituents of this campaign were stirring up intrigue against the Persian government, particularly in the northern provinces: 'They even go so far as to wish to create relations between Persian elements of disorder and Bolsheviks.'[111] The Persian prime minister himself was fearful of the Russian reaction to the agreement and asked Cox to implore the British government 'to recognise that it is in our joint interests that steps should be taken without delay to make position safe both as regards Bolshevist menace in northern provinces and in regard to Cossack Division, whose loyalty can now no longer be relied upon'.[112] British officials were quickly finding that their policy of supporting the Russian presence in Persia was coming back to haunt them.

Although it was the only force capable of repressing any disturbances in northern Persia, the Cossack Division had now become worse than redundant, constituting a threat in itself. Talk from Staroselskii of removing his force to Persian Azerbaijan and Gilan in order to put down the Jangali uprising, was met with suspicion by the British government. By taking his division from the capital, the Cossack commander would not only prevent his men from being absorbed into the proposed new uniform force, but he could potentially re-enforce his troops with men from the Caucasus and even liaise with General A.I. Denikin, the White commander in south Russia, to intrigue against Britain in Persia.[113] As Cox himself noted, it 'seems quixotic that we should be giving so much help to Denikin, and should have maintained [the] division itself for so long, and now allow them to remain a serious menace to successful progress of our policy'.[114] For whatever reason, Curzon had apparently failed to appreciate the risk that lay in providing financial support to an armed Russian contingent in Persia while simultaneously trying to undermine the basis of that force. He had failed to predict just how far the agreement would antagonise the Russian Whites and had arguably made Britain's position in Persia less secure by it. In effect, the Great Game thinking that had informed his actions in this period re-awakened many of the Great Game tensions that had lain dormant for the past five years.

The Wasps' Nest

While the Indian government struggled to have its authority taken seriously in London in relation to Persia, when it came to Afghanistan things should have been more clear cut. Not only was Afghanistan inextricably linked to India via proximity, religion and its connections with the tribes on India's North-West Frontier, since 1880, with the conclusion of the Second Afghan War, the Government of India had had control of Afghanistan's external relations.[115] Nevertheless, this did not prevent the Home government from interfering when it could. In June 1918, for example, in a meeting of the Eastern Committee, Chief of Imperial General Staff (CIGS) Sir Henry Wilson questioned the Indian government's judgement over Afghanistan. Wilson advocated persuading emir Habibullah to join the conflict, arguing that, with the collapse of Russia, Afghanistan had become extremely vulnerable to penetration by the Central Powers.[116] He accused the Indian government of being 'diffident about formulating any definite course of action' in regard to Afghanistan, and pushed for the War Cabinet to take control of policy towards that country.[117] Curzon too was keen to make Afghanistan a formal ally, believing that together with Persia it could form 'a Moslem nexus of states' which would stop a German and Turkish advance into Asia. Yet again, Curzon also tried to exert his authority over India, pointing out during the meeting that 'the Viceroy of India and his Government were in these matters advisers to the Home Government, and that in the last resort it rested with the latter to decide'.

Balfour, however, quickly poured cold water on Curzon's implications that London should proceed without listening to Delhi.[118] For Chelmsford believed that open revolution would ensue there should the emir ally himself with Britain against Turkey. Habibullah was already facing intense pressure from his subjects to provide support to Muslim Turkey, and was only just managing to maintain his country's neutrality by arguing that Afghanistan would be ruined by entering the war.[119] Trying to get Afghanistan to support the British cause was therefore simply unfeasible. Luckily, on this point Chelmsford had Montagu's support, who argued in the next Eastern Committee meeting that, 'as the Indian Government had hitherto been successful throughout the war in their dealings with the Amir, he thought the Committee should trust their judgement in the present case'.[120]

As already noted, one particularly important reason the Indian government was so reluctant to become overly involved in Persia was the problems it was facing in Afghanistan. The murder of the emir Habibullah had proved a great blow to Britain, not least because of the unrest it created in Afghanistan. Habibullah's willingness to stay loyal to Britain despite strong pressure from his people to support Turkey, was invaluable to Britain, although it may have actually cost the emir his life.[121] Whatever the cause of it, Habibullah's death set off a chain of events that would culminate in the Third Anglo–Afghan War. While Habibullah's brother, Nasrullah Khan, immediately announced himself the new emir, this was contested by Amanullah, Habibullah's third son. By 4 March, Nasrullah had given up his claim and Amanullah had been proclaimed emir.[122]

Unfortunately for Britain, Amanullah was well known for his nationalistic, anti–British tendencies, and from the outset of his reign the new emir seemed determined to be antagonistic towards his imperial neighbour.[123] Traditionally Britain's relationship with the ruler of Afghanistan was one of 'gentle bondage' – the emir was expected to be a complaisant liege and in exchange he received a generous subsidy.[124] While many of Amanullah's predecessors had grumbled about this arrangement, he was the first emir to reject it entirely.[125] Pronouncements declaring the independence of Afghanistan externally as well as internally were followed with the appointment of a Commissary of Foreign Affairs, under Muhammad Tarzi.[126] As well as being Amanullah's father-in-law, Tarzi was the founder and owner of Afghanistan's only newspaper of the time, the *Siraj-al-Akhbar* ('Spotlight on the News'), a paper that specialised in vitriolic attacks against Britain and which had spent the entire First World War espousing the

Turkish cause.[127] Such actions boded ill for the Indian government, which by April 1919 was facing its own problems with extensive internal unrest. The announcement of the Rowlatt Bill, followed by the tragedy of the Amritsar Massacre, was used by the new emir to denounce Britain's rule in India.[128] Finally, following minor skirmishes along the borders, Afghan troops violated Indian territory on 5 May 1919. Indian forces were mobilised to counter the attack, and by 11 May Amanullah had announced a *jihad* against Britain. The conflict was short-lived, as Afghan troops and civilians became quickly demoralised by the Indian government's campaign of aerial bombardment, and by 28 May Amanullah had despatched a request for a ceasefire.[129]

With such events in Afghanistan and India dominating his attention, it is unsurprising that Chelmsford was reluctant to become more deeply involved in Persian affairs. Signs of a link between the Bolshevik regime and the problems in Afghanistan were also highly worrying. Throughout May, Malleson had been reporting on the increase in pro-Bolshevik, pro-Islamic and anti-British propaganda being distributed in Meshed, Turkestan and Afghanistan.[130] On 30 May, Malleson had told CIGS that the Bolshevik government had officially recognised emir Amanullah and the independence of Afghanistan,[131] while, for his part, one of the first acts of the new emir was to congratulate the Soviet regime on their successes in Russia.[132] On 6 May, the Director of the Eastern Section of the People's Commissariat for Foreign Affairs in Soviet Russia had described Afghanistan in the paper *Izvestiia* as being 'of first class importance for the propaganda cause in Asia...Afghanistan is historically and geographically a passing stage from India to Central Asia...it exercises an enormous influence over the 70 million mussulman population of India'.[133]

This description of Afghanistan as 'a passing stage' would not have escaped the notice of the Indian government. The Bolshevik regime's relationship with exiled Indian dissidents, some of whom had at one stage or another resided in Kabul, only compounded India's fears. The Muslim agitator Maulana Barakatullah, for example, had been part of the German–Turkish mission to Afghanistan in 1915, and in 1919 arrived in Moscow claiming to have been specially sent by the new Afghan emir to establish relations with the Soviet government.[134] The Indian revolutionary also tried to assert that 'the ideas of communism have thoroughly penetrated into Afghanistan and even into neighbouring India', although both these claims were simply wishful thinking on Barakatullah's part.[135] The year 1919 also saw the arrival in Moscow of Mahendra Pratap, the head of the 'Indian Provisional Government' – an organisation set up in Berlin during the First World War by exiled Indian revolutionaries. After discussions with Lenin, Pratap travelled to Kabul later in the year, where he was joined by Karl Bravin who, being unsuccessful in Persia, was now trying his luck in Afghanistan.[136] The new emir was more than welcoming to these Bolshevik and Indian malcontents, allowing them unlimited freedom of movement and association.[137] Thus, in 1919 it appeared that Afghanistan had the potential to be a hotbed of anti-British intrigue.

Nonetheless, for all the apparent affinity between Afghanistan and Bolshevik Russia, there remained doubt among many in the Indian government that Bolshevism alone was the threat to Britain's interests some claimed it to be. Just as with Persia, there was scepticism that Bolshevik ideology could take hold in Afghanistan, with its religious and monarchical political structure. H.R.C. Dobbs, chief commissioner of Baluchistan, noted that it was 'inconceivable that present-day Bolshevism should make any impression on the social structure of Afghanistan'.[138] Hamilton Grant, in his talks with the Afghan delegation during the peace negotiations following the Third Anglo-Afghan War, even expressed amusement at the concept that 'a State ruled by an autocratic King and supported by an aristocracy' would 'amalgamate and work in sympathy with a violent rabble who hold that Kings must be murdered, that Monarchies must be abolished, [and] that aristocracies must be swept away'.[139] While the *Times* might argue that the civil unrest that had preceded the Amritsar Massacre was a result of a Bolshevik 'conspiracy',[140] the Political Department of the India Office pointed out that 'there is little evidence to support the theory of Bolshevik or enemy instigation' in the outbreak of the Afghan war. Instead, the report contended, it was the weakness of the new emir's position, combined with the news of unrest in India, that encouraged Amanullah to take the opportunity to strike and re-assert Afghanistan's international authority.[141] Hamilton Grant concurred, believing that one of the chief reasons for the outbreak of the conflict had been the mistaken belief in Afghanistan that the tribes along the Indian border, together with the Indian people, would rebel against the British government.[142]

Furthermore, there was evidence to suggest that the Afghan government was using relations with Moscow as a bargaining tool against Britain. As Hamilton Grant reported to the Indian government, the Afghan delegation at Rawalpindi 'was obviously briefed to try and frighten us with the Bolshevik bogey'.[143] Indeed, they openly threatened the Indian government when they asserted during the negotiations that 'if you fight with us we can fight with you, and we will get help from the Bolshevists and fight against you. If the Bolshevists fight against you, we shall help them and welcome them. But if you are our friend, we can prevent them by force.'[144] Aware of the vulnerability of his position, Amanullah was effectively playing the best card he had – inviting into his country Bolshevik and Indian revolutionaries in order to demonstrate his ability to cause trouble for the Indian government.[145] Hamilton Grant's reaction was, in effect, to call the Afghans' bluff, by arguing that Britain had no fear of Bolshevism taking hold in India, since the Indians themselves would not let that happen, and that the government could quite easily close all the northern passes between the two countries if need be.[146]

Nevertheless, while Hamilton Grant could not afford to appear anything less than entirely self-assured in front of the Afghan delegation, this did not mean that the Indian government totally dismissed the potential danger of Bolshevism. For, as Dobbs explained, the Bolshevik regime 'might ally itself with Afghanistan and help it with men and arms against India. Or it might conceivably conquer Afghanistan as an obstacle on the road to plunder India.'[147] This threat was, however, not entirely different to that which had been posed by the tsarist regime and had, indeed, been the very basis of the Great Game. The Indian government well understood how to counter this by making friendship with Britain appear the better option than co-operation with Soviet Russia.

The second layer of Soviet foreign policy, however, was one that few in the Home government appreciated: the spread of ideology and encouragement of popular unrest as a means of undermining rival governments.[148] While there was much talk in London of the threat of invasion by Bolshevik forces in places like Persia, it was the Indian government that appeared to understand that Bolshev*ism* spread quickest and most effectively where there was mass discontent. Thus, in the Indian government's opinion, the more Britain undermined the sovereignty of the rulers of Persia and Afghanistan by imperialistic coercion, the more it inflamed nationalist and pan-Islamist feeling, then the more likely it was that Bolshevik agitators would find a ready following in these countries. If, on the other hand, Britain treated the people of southern Asia with tact, and proved an attractive ally to the shah and emir, it had little to fear from Bolshevism. Fundamental to the Indian government's policy towards Afghanistan then, was an understanding – perhaps not explicitly verbalised but certainly apparent from its handling of the Afghan peace process – of how the Bolshevik regime functioned in its international dealings.

For Delhi, then, it was imperative that the peace negotiations with Afghanistan were handled correctly, with enough firmness to disavow the Afghan delegation of any notion of the Raj's weakness but without risking pushing them into Bolshevik arms. The Home government, however, did not share this view and from the outset Chelmsford and Hamilton Grant faced criticism from London. In June 1919, Montagu complained of having not been consulted before the viceroy had arranged the armistice, particularly as he felt that the emir's letter preceding the ceasefire had not displayed enough deference. Not only had Amanullah not apologised for his actions in causing the conflict, but he had even had the audacity to compare Britain's air raids on Afghanistan to the German bombing of London during the First World War – a reference almost designed to earn the animosity of the British government and people. Montagu was worried that the viceroy had shown himself too keen for peace and that the emir had not been properly castigated for his impudence towards the British Empire.[149] Chelmsford, nevertheless, stood by his decision to accept an armistice. He insisted that the letter from Amanullah needed to be understood in light of 'Afghan psychology'. He explained:

> We can, of course, vanquish Afghanistan, but only at a cost of prolongation of war with its attendant dangers – probable breakdown of stable Government in Afghanistan, thereby opening Afghan doors to Bolshevism, probably necessitating occupation of parts of the country by our troops...Bolshevik propaganda skilfully manipulated from Tashkend [sic] is preaching that we are bent upon an aggressive war on one of the few remaining Moslem powers. Had we resumed hostilities after the Amir had fulfilled our demand [for a ceasefire]...we feel that this would have been [the] interpretation placed on our action by the Moslem world...[150]

The alternative to accepting the armistice, in the opinion of the Indian government, would have meant continued military action and the weakening of Afghanistan. This would subsequently result either in exposing that country to Bolshevism or of having to make it a British protectorate, a prospect nobody relished. As the secretary of the Military Department of the India Office, Lieutenant-General Sir Vaughan Cox, aptly put it, 'I cannot imagine a less profitable country to "protect" than Afghanistan – a veritable wasps' nest.'[151]

   This was, of course, assuming that India would continue to be victorious should the conflict resume. The Third Anglo-Afghan War had, in fact, highlighted the weaknesses in the Indian army following the First World War. Not only were its numbers depleted, but those soldiers who remained were often undisciplined and inexperienced in frontier fighting. The Indian troops faced a hard enemy in the tough and skilled tribesmen who had joined the war with Afghan encouragement,[152] and there was a genuine fear that should the conflict resume, India might not be able to defeat Afghanistan, at least not as quickly and resoundly as should be expected from the larger power.[153] It was also clear that a speedy resolution to the current crisis was in the interest of India's domestic concerns. The scars of the Amritsar Massacre were yet to heal, and Gandhi's nationalist agitation was gaining momentum. While the Indian population had failed to rise up with the outbreak of the Afghan War, this was not to say that it might not do so should the conflict continue. In 1919, the viceroy's entire attention was therefore needed at home. While Montagu was admonishing the Indian government to remember that 'we, and not he [the emir], are the victors',[154] Chelmsford appeared more realistic about India's current weaknesses. His aim in the peace negotiations was to deal firmly and resolutely with the emir in order to bring about a peaceful resolution as quickly as possible and in such a way as to maintain a strong yet friendly Afghanistan and prevent it from becoming a hostile centre of pan-Islamic and Bolshevik propaganda.[155]

Indeed, the Anglo-Afghan peace negotiations and the treaty that would eventually be proposed were designed to achieve a quick resolution to the conflict by creating a temporary basis for a firm peace: in Chelmsford's words, 'first peace, then friendship'.[156] The biggest issue, nevertheless, would prove the hardest for the Indian government to try to postpone, for it soon became clear that the Afghan delegation would refuse to come to any agreement that allowed for Britain's continued control over their country's external relations. Chelmsford tried to convince Montagu of the impracticability of insisting on retaining the right to conduct Afghan foreign affairs:

> During the past year there has been a profound change in political outlook in [the] middle East, including Afghanistan. General unrest awakened national aspirations, President Wilson's pronouncement, Bolshevik catchwords and other influences have been at work. This change of outlook is evidenced in Amanulla's first utterances as Amir, basis of which was the sovereign independence of Afghanistan, and the complete freedom of his external relations.[157]

It is this recognition of the changing times that set Indian government opinion apart from much of the foreign policy-making elite in London. Afghan intellectuals such as Tarzi had done much over the last few years to spread concepts of freedom, modernisation and independence among the Afghans.[158] Habibullah himself had tried to regain control of Afghanistan's foreign affairs at the end of the First World War, to no avail.[159] Indeed, the desire for self-determination was one of the very reasons Amanullah had gone to war with India in the first place. For, as Vartan Gregorian explains, 'In 1919, no ruler could have succeeded in establishing a strong hold over the Afghan nation without pledging himself to the cause of total Afghan independence.'[160] From Delhi's point of view, the British Empire simply could not deal with its Asian neighbours as it had done before 1918. If the Indian delegation forced a provision regarding Afghanistan's foreign relations on Kabul, all that would happen was that the emir would break the terms anyway, leaving Britain in an awkward position, whereby it would be forced either to ignore this treaty violation or to resume hostilities in order to save face.[161]

Realising it could no longer use force to retain its predominance over Afghanistan, the Indian government instead hoped to be able to gain Afghan confidence and friendship to keep that country allied to Britain. As Hamilton Grant tried to explain to Sir George Roos-Keppel, chief commissioner of the North-West Frontier Province:

> It is obviously imperative for us so far as possible to exclude this force [Bolshevism] from Afghanistan. We cannot do so by military measures...

The only alternative appears to be to secure the genuine friendship and trust of Afghanistan, and to convince the Afghans of the danger of the inroad of Bolshevism.[162]

Roos-Keppel, who had led troops into battle during the Anglo–Afghan War, doubted that there had ever been 'any really friendly feeling among the Afghans towards the British Government and I do not think there will ever be. As regards mutual trust the past has shown that we can never trust Afghans.'[163] According to Chelmsford, however, Roos-Keppel 'is confessedly an Afghanphobe. He hates the Afghans and, I think I may say with confidence, he would like to see Afghanistan thoroughly conquered.'[164] The Indian government maintained that Britain had little choice but to give up control of Afghanistan's foreign affairs. Much as it had advocated with regard to Persia, the Indian government believed that a stronger alliance could ultimately be made with Afghanistan through mutual confidence and co-operation than through interference in that nation's affairs: the choice of the 'velvet glove' rather than the 'iron hand'.

By 8 August 1919, Hamilton Grant was able to report the signing of a treaty with Afghanistan.[165] The terms of the peace included an end to the subsidy the Indian government had paid to the previous emir, the removal of the privilege of allowing Afghanistan to import arms and munitions through India and the provision that the Indian government would be prepared to receive another Afghan mission in six months to discuss greater measures of friendship, should Amanullah prove his sincerity towards the British government. In a letter that Hamilton Grant handed to the Afghan delegation alongside the official treaty, the Indian government further stipulated how the new emir could prove this sincerity, naming certain Bolsheviks and Indian revolutionaries who were to be expelled from Afghanistan. Most importantly, however, the letter also noted that the treaty had made no mention of the issue of Afghanistan's foreign relations. Since all previous agreements between the two governments were accepted as void by the creation of this treaty, this by default left the Afghan government independent in both its internal and external affairs.[166] Thus in this roundabout way, the Indian government relinquished its official hold over Afghanistan.

The reaction in London, however, was not good. Certainly, this was not what Curzon had in mind when he was thinking of his 'Moslem nexus of states'. Montagu sent the viceroy a rebuke for presenting the Afghan delegation with the treaty and letter before having gained approval from the Home government. And, for the secretary of state, the more information he received on the peace with Afghanistan, 'the more [,] I am sorry to say [,] I dislike it'. In Montagu's opinion, it seemed Hamilton Grant had given away a considerable amount for little in return.[167] Indeed, it was hard to see what punishment the Afghans faced for having waged war against the British Empire. There was also some evidence that the Afghan government was flaunting the new treaty as a triumph. As Roos-Keppel's secretary noted, 'a General Sarsarus has been saying that Afghanistan got the main things it wanted, independence and certain tracts of land and that others – importation of arms, subsidy and better treatment of Indians – had been postponed until excitement in India had subsided'.[168] Thus, while the Indian government believed that by the treaty it had taught Afghanistan its place, 'the position of a petty state in relation to her powerful neighbour',[169] Montagu had to point out that:

> The fact remains that a great deal of disquiet was felt here by myself and my colleagues, and has been shared, as I must assure you, by that part of the public which takes an informed interest in Afghanistan, as to whether the Afghans, under what may have been a show of bluff, have ever truly realised that they were not the victors.[170]

Ultimately, however, in a role reversal (which was perhaps apt considering the situation in Persia), there was little Montagu (or Curzon) could do once Chelmsford had decided on his course but to impotently complain that his opinion was not valued by the Indian government.

Blown Sky High

By August of 1919, the British government had concluded two new treaties with two of the most important nations bordering its imperial field of interest, each one reflecting the views of the main negotiators on Britain's future in southern Asia. The Anglo–Persian Agreement represented the 'iron hand' of Curzon and his allies, while the Anglo–Afghan treaty was a demonstration of the Indian government's preference for the 'velvet glove'. When it came to Persia, Curzon's thinking was conditioned by his Great Game experience which placed Russia front and centre in his considerations. Yet whether it was the new Bolshevik regime in Moscow or the old tsarist presence in Tehran that Curzon's policy was designed to combat is difficult to tell. Indeed, Curzon's policy towards both White and Red Russia was complex and often contradictory. From what was known and understood of Bolshevism, it was clear to London that the new regime in Moscow was a potential threat to the British Empire.[171] It was just such a danger that was used by both Curzon and Cox as a reason for forwarding Britain's presence in Persia. Furthermore, the possibility of the Bolshevik regime penetrating Persia, either politically or militarily, was one of the main reasons given for the continued maintenance of the Russian Legation and the Cossack Division.

However, as much as Curzon and Cox may have feared a Bolshevik incursion into Persia in the immediate future, it was the possibility of a resurgence of an imperial Russia that was, in their opinion, the greatest long-term threat to Britain's interests in southern Asia. Reflected in Curzon's haste to push forward his Persian policy in 1918–1919 was the belief that Britain should take the opportunity to gain the upper hand while its old imperial rival was weakened. The assumption that Russia would eventually re-constitute itself in something of its old form and try to pursue that which it had temporarily lost with the Bolshevik revolution seemed supported by the attitude of the Russian Legation and the Cossack Division in Persia. Indeed, the Great Game appeared personified in these relics of the old order and in the day-to-day feuds between the likes of Minorskii and Malleson. Yet this inability to detach his thinking from the old pattern of Anglo-Russian rivalry meant that Curzon followed a line in Persia in this period that really did seem 'quixotic', in the words of Cox: the propping-up of the imperial Russian presence in Persia, while simultaneously working to undermine its position within that country. Indeed, it is hard to understand how Curzon and Cox failed to predict the hostility that the Russian Legation and Cossack Division would have against the Anglo-Persian Agreement when it was finally made public.

And although others within the British government who were sceptical of Curzon's proposals for Persia in 1918–1919, the acting foreign secretary was able, through force of will, to push through his plans. As one historian has explained, when it came to Persia, 'Curzon was able to exploit his ministerial seniority and his special expertise in Eastern affairs to overcome or evade criticism or opposition'.[172] Throughout this time, however, the Indian government remained a vocal critic of Curzon's Persian policy. For, when it came to the issue of Bolshevism, Delhi was adamant that the new regime in Russia only constituted a real threat to British interests if the South Asian people and their governments were mishandled so much as to push them towards Moscow.[173] In contrast to Curzon and Cox, Chelmsford and Hamilton Grant were apt to downplay the threat of Bolshevism to Afghanistan. Indeed, the Indian government appeared to recognise that while there may have been a new government in Russia, Afghanistan was using old tactics in trying to play its neighbours off against each other: using fear of Bolshevism to try to gain concession from the Indian government. In these respects, when it came to handling the three-way dynamic between India, Afghanistan and Bolshevik Russia, the Indian government was more astute than its colleagues in London gave credit for.

Delhi also appeared attuned to the changes that had occurred in southern Asia since the First World War, so that imperial dominance was no longer simply an accepted fact and that the threat of force was increasingly coming to lose its potency in the face of potential mass Asian nationalist and pan-Islamist unrest. It understood, for example, that 'a genuine nationalistic spirit was alive in Iran, despite its seeming confusion, and...felt that this force should be recognised and conciliated'.[174] British policy was going to have to change. Indeed, when Montagu argued that the viceroy was going against 40 years of tradition in his handling of the Afghan peace process Chelmsford responded: "'It has been the cardinal policy of His Majesty's Government for the past forty years....'" and the whole world has blown sky high in the last four!'[175] The Indian government also realised that while Britain may have just 'issued triumphantly from a struggle with the greatest military power the world has ever seen', economically and militarily it had been weakened by the experience.[176] A large part of its southern Asian policy in 1918–1919 was, therefore, conditioned not only by its views on the potency of nationalism and pan-Islamism but by the basic premise of incurring the least amount of strain on India's resources, particularly when the country itself was undergoing so much domestic unrest. After all, alliances based on trust and friendship ultimately cost much less than those based on financial and military inducements. In this respect, then, the agreements of 1919 reflect the optimism of Curzon against the realism of Chelmsford. Curzon's imperialistic rhetoric, when it came to 'doing as Britain pleased' with Persia, is an indication of the confidence he appeared to have in Britain's capabilities in the post-war period. It also reflected, perhaps, a concept of the British Empire as a force that needed to continually expand and strengthen lest it flounder. For its part, the Indian government was more conservative in its expectations of the empire after 1918. It was more willing to accept a limited British presence in southern Asia and called for a reduction in Britain's military and financial involvement in that part of the world. In the opinion of the Indian government, it was far worse for the empire to have to face flagrant violation of unenforceable treaties, or even military defeat, than to admit its limitations and tailor its policy accordingly.

For Curzon, the post-war period provided the opportunity to extend and consolidate Britain's imperial influence in southern Asia once and for all (creating his 'Moslem nexus of states'), using all the financial and military coercion the empire could garner to forcibly achieve this position of hegemony. For Chelmsford, this was a time to resuscitate Britain's reputation among the South Asian population, to seek to find an accord with the forces of nationalism and pan-Islamism and to maintain Britain's imperial position through a more subtle form of influence, by appearing as the friend and benefactor of the Muslim world. Eventually, the course of events in the next few years would come to vindicate the Indian government's point of view. In the years 1918 to 1919, however, Delhi was doomed to play Cassandra, unable to make itself heard in London, despite the astuteness and foresight of its opinions.

Chapter Three

A Nice State of Affairs, 1920

In a speech given to the Central Asiatic Society towards the end of 1920, Curzon – now fully foreign secretary[1] – declared that Britain 'must face the fact that the expansion of the British Empire in Central Asia is at an end, and rightly at an end'. The problem, however – as the *Times* newspaper saw it – was that while this fact was accepted readily by the British public, 'we are by no means sure that the Government are doing so, or even that Lord Curzon himself appreciates the full significance of his own words'.[2] The observation was telling, for, as this chapter will show, despite this pronouncement Curzon had spent most of 1920 categorically refusing to abandon his ambitions in South Asia or accepting the limitations that now existed on Britain's foreign relations. If the years 1918–1919 had been a time of optimism for the British government – emerging as it did a victor of the First World War – the events of 1920 would soon bring an end to that feeling. The failure of the Anglo–Persian Agreement, the invasion of the Persian port of Enzeli by the Red Army, nationalist discontent in India, a restless Afghanistan and the possibility of a mass pan-Islamist movement across Asia all threatened to destabilise Britain's position in that part of the world in the post-war period. Quick to realise the potential of this popular discontent, the Soviet regime threatened to add to the explosive mix with the dissemination of anti-British, anti-imperialist propaganda throughout the region.

1920 was the year in which the forces of nationalism, pan-Islamism and Bolshevism would come to the fore of politics in South Asia. That such events coincided with (or marked) the military and political ascendancy of the Bolshevik regime within both Russia and Asia, compounded Britain's problems. Nonetheless, old habits die hard, and despite the arguments of the Indian government and the War Office, there were those in government who could not evolve beyond their Great Game thinking, or the optimism of 1918, to accept the realities of 1920. By their stubbornness, the likes of Curzon and Lloyd George arguably made what was a bad year for the British Empire even worse.

Mutiny and Revolution

Compounding the difficult international scene, Britain was facing its own domestic problems in 1920. Although the country had experienced an economic boom in the months immediately after the armistice, this was short-lived. By 1920, rising inflation and unemployment were causing widespread public discontent within Britain, and the year would experience a surge in labour unrest and industrial action.[3] Particularly worrying, however, was the apparent influence of Bolshevism on Britain's domestic strife at this time. The 'Hands off Russia' movement, for example, organised protests against the government's involvement in the Soviet–Polish conflict of 1920.[4] In January 1919, during violent clashes between police and workers in Glasgow, a red flag was raised on the flag pole of the city chambers. That troops, tanks and machine guns were called in to occupy the city and end 'The Battle of George Square' is indicative of just how much the British government feared a Bolshevik-style uprising in the country.[5]

To make matters worse, in 1918 and 1919 the police force themselves had gone on strike, and could no longer be entirely relied on to keep the peace in the face of other workers' protests.[6] As for the army, in January 1919 troops stationed in Dover and Folkestone had rebelled at the slow demobilisation process.[7] By 1920 there was a likelihood that should a general strike occur – as the Triple Alliance was threatening in the autumn – the authorities might find the police and a large group of ex-soldiers joining the workers.[8] As a report of the Home Office put it, 'in the event of rioting, for the first time in history the rioters will be better trained than the troops'.[9] So seriously did the Chief of the Imperial General Staff (CIGS), Sir Henry Wilson, view the situation that, in January 1920, he set his men to prepare plans for 'mutiny and revolution' in Britain.[10] Such fear regarding Britain's domestic situation goes some way perhaps in explaining the Home government's consistent preoccupation with the threat of Bolshevism.

With Britain in domestic turmoil, drastic measures were needed in order to bring the economic problem under control and thus reduce popular agitation.[11] Given the financial constraints facing the government, an extensive military machine was an obvious target for cost-cutting. By April 1920 the army constituted about 173,000 more men than seven years earlier, and cost approximately twice as much.[12] Unsurprisingly, the secretary of state for war, Winston Churchill, faced intense pressure to reduce the financial burden of the army on the Treasury. However, the cost of the army was clearly a reflection of its size, which in turn was a consequence of the large number of arenas where British forces were stationed. After 1918, British troops were to be found in countries across the northern hemisphere, including, among others, France, Germany, Italy, Greece, Austria-Hungary, Serbia, Bulgaria, the Ottoman Empire, Persia, Mesopotamia, Egypt, Ireland and not forgetting the interventionist forces in Russia.[13] Thus, there was a fundamental disparity between the need to rapidly reduce the army and the level of responsibility that the British Army held in the post-war period.

Something was going to have to give and for Churchill, it was going to have to be the extent of Britain's military presence in Asia. In February 1920, for example, the secretary of state attacked the excessive price of maintaining troops in places such as Mesopotamia.[14] To Wilson, however, Mesopotamia was one of five countries that were essential to the security of the British Empire as a whole.[15] The director of military operations, General Radcliffe, also agreed that a reduction of British forces in Mesopotamia would lead to anarchy, which could have negative consequences for India.[16] Nevertheless, Churchill would not let the matter of Mesopotamia rest. In May, he submitted another memorandum to Cabinet in which he tried 'to draw the attention of my colleagues to the waste of money entailed by our present military and administrative policy in Mesopotamia', and asked them to make the decision for 'a prompt and drastic curtailment of expenditure'.[17] In his cost-cutting endeavours the secretary of state for war even explored using the RAF in Mesopotamia.[18] In the opinion of Wilson, Churchill 'regardless of safety and hoping that any disasters may come after he has left office, is trying to gain credit and make a name by saving money'.[19]

Whatever the strategic benefit of Mesopotamia to Britain, where both Churchill and Wilson agreed was that the security of India did not lie in Persia. The main debate on Persia, prior to May 1920, concerned whether the country was at risk from a Bolshevik attack and to what extent Britain was prepared to help the Persian government should such an event occur. One of the justifications for the Anglo-Persian Agreement used by Curzon had been the need to protect the country from a Bolshevik incursion, which could have repercussions on Britain's position in South Asia at large. By 1920, the consolidation of the Soviet government within Russia and its actions in Central Asia made this threat more credible. In the Russian civil war the White Russian commander, General Denikin had been defeated outside Moscow in October 1919 and subsequently driven south to Novorossiisk before escaping in a boat to Constantinople.[20] By March 1920 the Red Army had consolidated its hold on the North Caucasus and pushed on into Daghestan and Azerbaijan, capturing Baku on 27–28 April and setting up the Azerbaijan Soviet Socialist Republic. In Central Asia, a protracted battle between the Red Army on one side, and General Kolchak and the Orenburg Cossacks on the other, had finally ended in September 1919 when forces of the Tashkent Soviet joined with the Red Army to defeat Kolchak. By early 1920, the Turkestan Army Group had destroyed all remnants of the Orenburg and Ural Cossacks, while the Transcaspian Government of Ashkhabad was gradually forced back towards the Caspian, with Krasnovodsk finally being captured in February 1920.[21] A few months later Russian forces would help overthrow the Khan of Khiva, with Bukhara soon following suit.[22]

Unsurprisingly, this rapid southern progression of the Red Army alarmed some British observers. While for 1918 and most of 1919 Persia (and Afghanistan) had been somewhat cushioned from Bolshevism by the presence of anti-Bolshevik factions throughout southern Russia and Central Asia, by 1920 the borders of these countries were now looking decidedly vulnerable. In a Cabinet meeting that January it was admitted that:

> The Bolsheviks had now a very powerful army, consisting of all their best troops...Every day they were making great strides towards the East, in the direction of Bokhara and Afghanistan. They were carrying out a regular, scientific and comprehensive scheme of propaganda in Central Asia against the British. We ourselves had no military forces wherewith to oppose them; in fact, at the moment, our troops were at their lowest ebb...[23]

Whether the current success of the Red Army meant that the Soviet government would attempt an attack on Persia, however, was unclear. In the opinion of the Indian government, the real danger lay in Bolshevik emissaries and propaganda infiltrating Persia, rather than military action.[24] (In January 1920 the first 'Red Train' left Moscow for Turkestan, laden with propaganda materials.)[25]

The question remained, however, as to whether Persia was actually worth saving from a Bolshevik military attack if it came to it. For the Indian government, the answer was much the same in 1920 as it had always been: that Persia simply was not worth the cost, particularly if it meant using Indian resources. Indeed, Montagu had already let Curzon know that India could no longer be responsible for the cost of retaining Malleson and his force at Meshed. In the opinion of the secretary of state for India, any danger which Bolshevism posed to Persia was 'largely the fault of the Home Government in their anti-Mohemmedan policy'[26] and defending Persia was 'not an Indian matter'.[27] The refusal of the Indian government to provide more men for Persia was particularly important given the small number of British troops stationed in that country at the time. As the CIGS made clear, Britain could not save Persia in the face of a Bolshevik attack even if it wanted to. In which case, 'If His Majesty's Government has no intention of assisting Persia to defend her territory by the use of British troops, the logical course is for the North Persian Brigade to be withdrawn.'[28]

Nevertheless, in the early months of 1920, if the soldiers and diplomats did not always entirely agree on the course to be pursued in Persia, there was at least an understanding that the situation was complex. As the general staff explained:

> ...there can be no question but that the withdrawal of this force from North Persia at the present juncture would exercise a deplorable effect on the political situation generally. It would leave Teheran [sic] a prey to the Bolshevik sources should the Soviet Government decide actually to invade Persia, and in any case it would shake the stability

of the Persian Government and expose them to all the anti–British propaganda that would most certainly be instituted...[29]

Even the Indian government agreed that there was no simple answer, noting that withdrawal of its troops from Persia could affect Britain's reputation both in that country and in other southern Asian states, such as Afghanistan. (Although, it also pointed out that since India was little affected by events in Persia, it really raised no objection to such withdrawal.)[30] Ultimately, at a meeting of the Eastern Committee on 12 January 1920, it was decided that no reinforcements were to be sent to Persia and that none of the troops there were to be withdrawn either.[31]

Churchill took exception, protesting to the Cabinet at the apparent absurdity of retaining within Persia a force that, while being an enormous drain on the military's finances, was insufficient to prevent any serious attack on that country anyway.[32] Despite Churchill's complaints, however, it was agreed in Cabinet on 18 February that the general officer commander in Mesopotamia would be directed to hold his forces at Enzeli and attempt to bluff the Bolsheviks out of making an incursion there. Should this fail, however, and an attack took place, there was no intention of holding on to Enzeli and the troops should retreat.[33] For, as Curzon pointed out to Cox, it was not really 'understood by us why a country with a population of 10 millions, even if it be Persia, should allow itself to be conquered by a few thousand armed robbers from without'. In any event, 'it is most improbable that [the] Bolsheviks will make any attack in force against Persia, and [the] possibility may practically be discounted'.[34]

I Told You So

In the diary of Wilson there is an entry on 19 May 1920 that notes with some bitterness that 'at 6:30pm came a wire from Teheran [sic] to say our garrison at Enzeli on the Caspian had been surrounded by Bolsheviks & made prisoners! A nice state of affairs which will have a *bad* effect in the East.'[35] The improbable had occurred. The retreat of British troops in the face of the Red Army was a humiliation that struck at the very heart of Britain's prestige in South Asia. Officially, the Soviet government denied sanctioning the attack on Enzeli, claiming that it was only informed after the operation was complete[36] – a claim the British government and press found dubious, and rightly so.[37] Trotsky had apparently planned the event the previous month, cabling Lenin and Chicherin to tell them of the operation.[38] On 23 May the Soviet government sent a congratulatory message to the sailors of the Caspian Fleet, thanking them for the 'fatal blow' that had now been dealt to the 'international counter-revolution'.[39] Aside from causing the British government a major embarrassment, the immediate effect of the landings was to open up communication between the Bolsheviks and the various revolutionary agitators in Persia and, in particular, to provide support to the Janglis. Indeed, collaboration between the Bolshevik regime and the Janglis would see the takeover of the provincial capital of Gilan, Recht, and the ultimate creation of the Soviet Republic of Iran.[40]

This Republic, however, was to prove short lived. For although they may have been busy sending the Red Army into Persia, the Bolshevik government had still not resolved the contradictions in their policy towards Asian nationalists, pan-Islamists and Communists. Confusion over who they should be supporting hampered the Bolsheviks in these early years when it came to extending their influence in Persia. Hence, while there were those in Moscow who warned against trying to impose communist practice on the Persian people too soon, others disagreed. Unruly local Ghilan Communists ignored Lenin and his comrades and set about encouraging class terror, creating peasant Soviets and unveiling Muslim women.[41] Such radicalism, however, alienated Kuchik Khan and his Janglis and spelt the downfall of the Soviet Republic in Iran.[42]

Meanwhile, back in London, Churchill was furious. Despite its earlier vacillations, by early May the general staff had actually warned that the situation following the collapse of Denikin had deteriorated to the extent that Norperforce was now extremely vulnerable. As such, on 13 May it recommended moving the troops from Tabriz and Enzeli to Kazvin.[43] However, at a meeting of the Eastern Committee a few days later, to which neither Churchill nor Wilson were invited or even had knowledge of, the decision was taken against evacuating Enzeli. 'In consequence of this, our force has first been rounded up and then allowed to retire in circumstances of great humiliation to the British arms', Churchill fumed at Curzon.[44]

Recrimination was followed by counter-recrimination. Wilson could not resist his own taunt at Curzon, asking the foreign secretary if he might in future 'trust, a little, in the advice of the responsible military advisers'.[45] Curzon, however, was not prepared to take the blame for the situation and acidly replied to Wilson that it was the War Office that had consistently given the wrong information regarding Enzeli:

> Who was it who wrote the telegram of Feb. 13 telling the Enzeli force to hold on?...not the FO but the WO...Who was it who came repeatedly to E[astern Committee] Conferences and told us that the WO view was that the Bolshevik policy in Persia was not military but propaganda? Not I but General Radcliffe. Therefore do not my dear Field Marshal accuse me of being indifferent to military advice. I have trusted it too implicitly![46]

In the days, weeks and months that followed Enzeli, debate over Persia would become intense. Despite the humiliation of what had occurred, there were still those within the British government, such as Curzon and Milner, who believed that complete withdrawal from Persia 'would weaken our whole position in the East'.[47] The War Office, on the other hand, vehemently pressed for the evacuation not only of the force at Enzeli, but all the various troops stationed in north Persia and in Batum, to fall back to Mesopotamia over the next few weeks in order to avoid any further embarrassment.[48] As Churchill pointed out in a letter to Curzon on 20 May, 'If we are not able to resist the Bolsheviks in these areas, it is much better by timely withdrawals to keep out of harm's way and avoid disaster and shameful incidents such as that which has just occurred...I must absolutely decline to continue to share responsibility for a policy of mere bluff.'[49] On 18 June both Wilson and Churchill continued to press their views, warning that should the Cabinet ignore their advice and 'decide to continue the attempt to maintain simultaneously our existing commitments at Constantinople, Palestine, Mesopotamia and Persia, the possibility of disaster occurring in any or all of these theatres must be faced, and the likelihood of this will increase every day'.[50] As Wilson noted in his diary, however, his recommendation to withdraw from Persia 'brought Curzon and Milner to their feet, and it was quite clear they would resign if it was done'.[51] In a letter to Curzon a few days after the Enzeli attack, Churchill vented some of his frustrations: 'It is a great pity that we have not been able to develop any common policy between W.O. and F.O. I have to bear the abuse of F.O. policy and to find the money for it. Yet there is no effective co-operation or mutual support.'[52]

The humiliation of the events of May 1920 was compounded for Britain by the ultimate failure to convert the Anglo–Persian Agreement into a meaningful relationship between the two nations. Indeed, the hostility of the Persian public to the agreement was a demonstration of the low standing that Britain now appeared to have in that country. The prevailing belief that by the agreement Persia had become a British protectorate was one that both Cox and his successor, Herman Norman, found hard to counter, particularly when it was coupled with the accusation that Persian government figures had received bribes from the British government in exchange for supporting the agreement.[53] Public opposition to the agreement came from many sections of Persian society, including religious leaders, constitutionalists, nationalists, journalists, civil servants and even poets.[54] As one contemporary observed: 'The entire Near and Middle East is in the grip of Anglophobia, which unites the Muslims from India to Turkey, from Turkestan to the Persian Gulf.'[55] In trying to force British patronage on the Persian people, Curzon had simply failed to grasp the idea that 'The Orient of 1919 was completely changed from the Orient of 1890'.[56]

The practical effect of this opposition came with the ratification of the agreement. Under the terms of the Persian constitution, any foreign treaty or agreement had to be ratified by the Persian parliament, the Medjliss. With such public and international condemnation of the agreement, the Persian government was understandably reluctant to put its terms into effect. To the annoyance of Curzon, delaying the summoning of the Medjliss became a convenient way for the Persian government to thereby delay acting on the agreement. Matters were made worse when the Persian prime minister, Vosugh ed-Dowleh, was forced to resign in June 1920, the Enzeli attack being the final nail in the coffin of his unpopular tenure.[57] Unfortunately for Britain, Vosugh's successor, Mushir ed-Dowleh, was not a supporter of the Anglo–Persian Agreement and was even more keen to delay its ratification. Such feeling, nonetheless, did not prevent the Persian ruling elite from seeking other concessions from the British government. As Curzon explained to Norman, the Persian prime minister refused to draw on the loan which was provided as part of the agreement, or to make use of the British officers of the military commission sent to Persia in December 1919, or to let Armitage Smith, the British financial adviser, begin his work. Yet the shah was currently pressing for the retention of British troops in Tehran, the Persian government was drawing on a monthly subsidy provided by Britain, and the Persian ambassador in London was pressing for a supply of arms and munitions.[58] As Curzon complained, the 'Persian Government cannot repudiate or ignore the obligations which the Agreement imposes and at the same time claim all the advantages which it confers'.[59]

Unfortunately for him, however, there was little Curzon could do in the face of Persian delaying tactics. After May 1920, the Persian Government began to claim that the Bolshevik invasion had caused distraction from the task of electing the Medjliss.[60] By November, Curzon appears to have lost his patience, complaining to Norman that 'though it is now fifteen months since the agreement was signed, no serious attempt has been made by two successive Persian Governments to submit it to the approval of [the] Persian Parliament'. He simply could not allow this filibustering to continue and demanded the Medjliss to be called within the space of a month.[61] By December, it had become clear that the Anglo–Persian Agreement had died an ignominious death, when the new Persian prime minister, Sepahdar-e Azam, hinted to Norman that the agreement would probably be accepted if certain people were bribed.[62] Ultimately, the Indian government proved to be correct with its warning in 1918 that Britain should seek the friendship of the Persian people before trying to conclude an agreement with the Persian government. In a letter to Montagu in December 1920, Chelmsford could not resist gloating slightly:

> We have carefully abstained from saying 'I told you so', but anyone who takes the trouble to peruse our telegrams from the very beginning of the Persian negotiations will see that we have been strenuous opponents of the Curzon policy and that we wished to confine our interference in Persian matters within much smaller limits.[63]

In ignoring the forces of nationalism within Persian society, Curzon and Cox had made a grave error. They had believed that any opposition would be inconsequential and easily subdued. Curzon appeared to believe that the majority of the Persian public still saw Britain as they had done prior to 1907 – as a friend and protector. Perhaps Cox was at fault for not enlightening his superior about Persian feeling after 1918. However, Cox appears to have seen what he wanted to see when it came to analysing Persian sentiment towards Britain. Both men had failed to appreciate that the days when governments could entirely ignore public opinion on foreign relations had long gone, even within the relatively politically backward nations of Asia.

The ignominy of Britain's position in Persia in 1920 was further demonstrated by its complete impotence when it came to the Cossack Division. A key part of the Anglo-Persian Agreement had been the idea of creating a Persian force that would assimilate the Cossack Division and the South Persian Rifles, thereby relieving the British government of the financial responsibilities for these troops. With the Persian government refusing to enact the agreement, however, this project was being held in limbo, leaving the Cossack Division still active in Persia. Indeed, given the shortage of troops in Persia in 1920, the Division was to prove invaluable following the Bolshevik landings at Enzeli. For Britain, the Division continued to be a mixed blessing. While it undoubtedly relieved some of the pressure off the British military in Persia, the force continued to be a financial drain. Again, one of the benefits of the Anglo-Persian Agreement, as argued by its advocates, was that it would bring an end to British patronage of Persia's armed forces. Indeed, Montagu had made quite clear that his support for the agreement was based solely on the idea that it would relieve the Indian government of much of its financial responsibilities in Persia. From December 1919, the India Office therefore refused to share in payment of the subsidy.[64]

British financial support of the Division was thus supposed to end in March 1920, although with some wrangling Norman and the Foreign Office managed to extend it until June.[65] Nevertheless, come July, Norman was asking for further payments to be made, since the Persian government was not ready to deal with the Russian officers of the Division.[66] Thus, the same problem which faced the British government in 1918 was hampering its actions in Persia in 1920. If the Division was not paid, it would leave a large number of unemployed, disaffected Russian officers within Persia, with nothing better to do than cause trouble for Britain there. As long as the Persian government refused to draw on the loan provided by the Anglo-Persian Agreement, it could not afford to support the Division on its own. Therefore, the burden remained with the British government, and Norman would spend much of his time in 1920 trying to find ways of providing for the Division until its final dissolution in 1921.

Just as in 1918–1919, a further reason for continuing its support for the Cossack Division in 1920 was that the British government could not afford to risk making its leader, Staroselskii, an outright enemy. In June, Norman telegrammed Curzon to report that 'Colonel Starosselski [sic] was again in communication with Bolsheviks and was working actively to spread Bolshevik principles amongst officers and men of [the] Cossack Division'.[67] And yet, still, the British government could not quite make up its mind as to what it feared most – the new Soviet regime or the old tsarist Russia – and the landings at Enzeli simply added to the confusion. The Persian government had little choice but to send the Division to quell the rebellion of Kuchik Khan and his men. For Britain the problem was three-fold: should Staroselskii succeed in his endeavours, his prestige and standing in Persia would rise to such an extent that it would be even harder to have him removed as leader of the Division. Should he fail, however, the Bolsheviks would increase their campaign and it would fall to Britain to prevent Persia disintegrating into anarchy. And should the British government's suspicions turn out to be true and Staroselskii actually defected to the Bolsheviks, it would be almost impossible to prevent the greater part of Persia from coming under Russian control.

Indeed, the success of Staroselskii in July in putting down a rebellion in the province of Mazandaran was contrasted unfavourably with the decision of the British government a few days later to evacuate their troops from Menjil in the face of tribal unrest.[68] By the end of August, the Division leader and his men had recaptured Recht and pressed on towards Enzeli, where they found themselves under heavy fire and were forced to retreat. Throughout September and October the Cossack Division would make several attempts to take Enzeli, but with no British support it was difficult to face the Bolshevik fleet.[69] While in 1920 the Cossack Division, the Red Army and the Persian rebels were busy fighting, the British forces seemed merely to be retreating – an unfortunate metaphor for Britain's position in Persia in general and a policy which made them more unpopular among the Persian people. Some saw the retreat as a sign of Britain's weakness; others thought that it was a calculated move because Britain did not care much about Persia; and some believed that the British were deliberately trying to frighten them by allowing Bolsheviks into the country so that the Persians would then clamour to Britain for help.[70]

As a reward for his efforts against the Bolsheviks, however, Staroselskii soon found himself deposed as the Cossack Division leader. Taking advantage of a temporary absence of the colonel in October, General Ironside – who was now commanding Norperforce – took control of the Division.[71] Simultaneously, Norman pressed upon the shah to dismiss the colonel; charging Staroselskii with incompetence and corruption, Norman threatened to withhold the royalties of the Anglo–Persian Oil Company from the government should the shah refuse. The shah had little choice but to acquiesce.[72] Although there was some criticism in London of the coup that Ironside and Norman had enacted, something had finally been done to end the absurd position which the British government had allowed itself to get into by its patronage of the Cossack Division.[73]

Thus, by the end of 1920, the British government faced a catalogue of humiliations in Persia. The inability of Curzon to have his agreement ratified by the Persian Parliament was just one indicator of the loss of status and prestige which Britain now experienced in that country. The forced retreat of the British army from Enzeli in the face of a Red Army incursion was only made worse by the comparative successes of Staroselskii and his Cossack Division. It is, therefore, unsurprising that in 1920 the Persian government came to the conclusion that it could no longer rely on Britain for financial help and military protection. In December 1920 Edmund Overy in the Foreign Office accused the Persian government of touting to America those concessions which had previously been in Russia's possession. Now that the Persian government had 'practically exhausted the milch cow of the British Government', it was evidently looking to America for financial aid; an act which displeased the British Foreign Office but one which it could do little about.[74] It could also do little to prevent Persia from seeking an alliance with the Soviet government either. In July, Norman reported that Mushir ed-Dowleh was talking of despatching a Persian mission to Moscow in order to discuss the recent events.[75] From the Persian point of view, such a move was essential. The actions of May had marked the ascendancy of the Soviet government on the international stage, and the Persian government could no longer afford to pursue its hitherto policy of ignoring the Bolshevik regime. As Norman explained, the 'weakness of Persia's geographical and military position obliges them to make such an agreement [with the Bolsheviks], more especially since they have more than once [been] told that Great Britain cannot defend her against serious invasion'.[76] For the British government, the attempt – which had characterised its foreign policy in 1918–1919 – to take advantage of Russia's weakness to bring Persia under its sole influence appeared to have failed.

Bolshevist Bogeys

For the Indian government in 1920, the main issue when it came to Bolshevism was not so much the latter's military capabilities but its subversive activities. In India, the threat of Bolshevik propaganda creating unrest among the population was particularly great when combined with nationalist and pan-Islamist agitation. One of the key challenges facing the Indian government in 1920, then, was the prevention of Bolshevik agents and propaganda from infiltrating India through Afghanistan. Immediately upon gaining independence of their foreign relations in 1919, the Afghan government had invited a Bolshevik mission to Kabul, headed by Karl Bravin, the former Soviet envoy to Persia.[77] Indeed, the British agent in Kabul complained how Bravin and his cohort could be seen riding around the city in a particularly nice coach lent by the emir himself, while the British were assigned a much more inferior mode of transportation.[78]

Despite appearances, however, there was reason to believe that the relationship between Soviet Russia and Afghanistan was not as solid as either nation would like India to think. On 24 August 1919, British intelligence intercepted a message from Bravin to Tashkent, informing his government that:

> Afghan policy towards Russia is now absolutely clear. Amir only desired our friendship for security of his northern frontier...He has invited us to his palace merely that we may become hostages. Of course Amir uses us as a bogey to frighten British by threats of alliance with us, and will show us at Kabul as evidence of his power.[79]

For all his flirting with the Soviet government, it seemed that the emir did not entirely trust the new Russian regime. In the autumn of 1919, with the defeat of the hostile Cossack forces at Orenburg, the Soviet regime at Tashkent had finally been able to turn its attention to the Bokharan and Khivan states. By April 1920, Russian forces had facilitated the collapse of the Khanate of Khiva and the establishment of the Khorezm People's Soviet Republic in its place. By the end of the year Bokhara would have followed suit. On both occasions, the Bolsheviks claimed to be helping to 'liberate' the people of Bokhara and Khiva from despotic rulers.[80] The removal of khan Abd Allah and emir Alim (and the Bolshevik justification for their actions) was unsurprisingly a concern to the emir of Afghanistan. Amanullah's own position was somewhat unstable and his control within his country 'loose and undefined'.[81] To align himself too firmly with the Soviet government could place the emir in danger of one day being deposed just like his fellow Muslim rulers. Nevertheless, the emir was also aware of the advantages that were to be had 'by raising Bolshevist...bogeys' against Britain.[82] For the Indian government's part, while it could not allow Afghanistan to use Bolshevism as blackmail to force concessions, it was also aware that having its neighbour, at the very least, as a neutral buffer against Soviet Russia was invaluable.

The Indian government's objective during 1920, therefore, was to prevent Afghanistan from moving closer to Soviet Russia, by emphasising the dangerous potential of friendship with the Bolshevik regime as compared to the benefits of good relations with Britain. While this had always been the policy of Chelmsford and his men, with the Bolshevik successes in Asia in 1920 it became even more imperative to keep Afghanistan on side.[83] Hamilton Grant had noted himself, as

early as November 1919, the opportunity that existed to drive a wedge between
the Bolshevik regime and Afghanistan:

> There is every indication that the Amir's ambitions are for the moment
> turned mainly towards enlarging his borders or influence in Central
> Asia. We hear that his representatives at Merv and Bokhara are
> posing as protectors of Mussalmans against the tyranny of Bolshevist
> [sic] communism; and if this policy is pursued, it seems bound to
> bring Afghanistan into collision with the Bolshevists [sic] and to
> throw them definitely into our arms. But the decision hangs in the
> balance.[84]

The question, as Montagu put it, was whether the Indian government could
'hold out inducements to him [the emir] that will suffice to turn [the] scale
against [the] Bolsheviks and in our favour'.[85]

One way to find this out was with the Mussoorie Conference, which took
place between British and Afghan delegates in the summer of 1920. As may be
recalled, the Anglo–Afghan Treaty of August 1919 had been concluded as a peace
treaty only, with an agreement of friendship to follow. Thus, in December 1919,
Amanullah wrote to Chelmsford suggesting the conclusion of such an accord.[86]
The problem was, however, that the Afghan government had failed to uphold the
conditions which the Indian government had set for such a treaty of friendship,
including the expulsion of Indian and Bolshevik seditionary characters from
Afghan territory. Therefore Chelmsford suggested a meeting between the
two sides 'for the purpose of frankly examining any obstacles which may now
exist to a good understanding and to preparing a firm foundation on which a
treaty of friendship can afterwards be erected'.[87]

Just as with the Rawalpindi negotiations, however, the Home government was
suspicious of the emir's calls for friendship with Britain, and wary of the Indian
government appearing weak to the Afghans.[88] Nevertheless, in the viceroy's
opinion, the Indian government needed to do something to 'dispel this atmosphere
of probably genuine suspicion' that was developing in Afghanistan against
Britain.[89] As H.R.C. Dobbs (Hamilton Grant's successor as foreign secretary)
emphasised, the longer Afghanistan and Britain remained estranged, the more that
suspicion between the two nations would grow and the more success Bravin would
have in misrepresenting British intentions to the emir and his government.[90]

Thus, on 14 April 1920, a conference between British and Afghan delegates
opened in Mussoorie, in the United Provinces of Agra and Oudh. As well as lengthy
discussion on issues such as tribal unrest on India's borders, the conference served
to confirm the Indian government's opinions on the state of Afghan–Bolshevik
relations.[91] On 30 April, the Afghan representatives openly admitted to Dobbs, who

was heading the British delegation, that they would much rather be Britain's friend than Soviet Russia's, since Britain:

> is an ancient, powerful and well-established State, which the Bolsheviks are not, and because she is wealthy. We can easily get rid of our connection with the Bolsheviks and restrain the Indian seditionists if it is made worth our while. But we want to know how much Britain will give.[92]

As Montagu had predicted, Afghanistan was, in effect, trying to precipitate a bidding war between Soviet Russia and India. For his part, Dobbs tried to emphasise the danger to Afghanistan if it chose to trust in the Bolshevik regime. For, if the Afghan government allowed Bolshevik propagandists to travel freely through its territory into India, it was inevitable that some of that propaganda would be spread through Afghanistan itself.[93] By September, the Indian government's handling of the situation appeared to be having some success; the Foreign and Political Department reported that the Afghan government was opening its eyes 'to the dangers which they would invite by permitting Bolshevist agitators to enter Afghanistan ostensibly to promote agitation in India and by having too intimate relations with the Soviet Government'.[94]

Together with trying to prevent Afghanistan from becoming a channel for Bolshevik propagandists, the Indian government was also sensible enough to be taking precautions within India itself. In October 1919, it proposed appointing a special officer attached to the Foreign and Political Department 'whose duty would be the reception, collation, digestion and dissemination of information regarding activities of Bolshevists, indeed specially to study the whole problem', as well as increasing intelligence staff in the provinces and enacting special legislation that would prohibit anyone from possessing the rouble note.[95] This last measure, passed on 6 December 1919, proved so effective (depriving, as it did, Bolshevik agitators of the means of directly financing propaganda within India) that the temporary ordinance was prolonged in June 1920.[96] To a large extent, these measures were pre-emptive, as the secretary to the Indian government explained to the local administrations: 'Though actual proof of Bolshevik activity in India itself is small, the Government of India think that a serious situation may develop unless systematic protective measures are adopted.' The government's defensive policy was thus to include not only the officer attached to the Foreign and Political Department whose focus would be on Bolshevism outside of India, but also one on the staff of the Department of Criminal Intelligence (DCI) who was to seek out Bolshevik activity within the country. The DCI officer was to be in close contact with a colleague of similar function in each province. For the local administrations, the role of their officer was to regularly liaise with officials in the province, explaining to them the various guises Bolshevik propaganda could take. He was to 'make enquiries as to the presence of Bolshevik Agents, collect evidence of Bolshevik activity, endeavour to trace the source of pro-Bolshevik writings in the press, and especially watch for any attempts of Bolshevik agents to create new sources of credit'.[97]

These measures, taken in late 1919, to create an efficient web of communication between the local and central Indian administrations on Bolshevik activities, demonstrate the foresight of the Indian government. For 1920 was to prove the year in which the Bolshevik regime would come to organise itself in Asia, both theoretically and practically. From the outset Lenin and his comrades appeared to recognise the importance of Asian feeling to their success. Within the borders of Russia alone there resided approximately twenty-five million Muslims in 1917,[98] while the possibility of co-opting Islamic discontent for its own revolutionary struggle was not lost on the Bolshevik regime. Together with its appeal to working Muslims, in January 1918 the Soviet government established a Commissariat for Muslim Affairs.[99] From the early days of the revolution it also maintained contact with various Indian revolutionaries and agitators,[100] and in June 1918 produced a blue book which spoke of the role Soviet Russia was to play in a future Indian revolution.[101] Yet, other than these tentative first steps, the Bolshevik regime appeared a little lost in the early days as to how to deal with Asian affairs. The problem was that Marx himself had failed to focus on this area of the world, since it had been assumed that the Communist revolution, when it came, would invariably occur in the advanced nations of Europe. Early Communist thought on this issue was thus limited to some discussion on the nature of Britain's rule in India,[102] and statements which were 'sometimes contradictory, and often... distinctly ambivalent'.[103]

In 1916, Lenin had himself tried to fill in some of the gaps with his work *Imperialism, the Highest Stage of Capitalism*. In it, the Bolshevik leader argued that the 'super-profits' the capitalist countries gained from their colonial holdings – such as India – had thus far stifled proletarian unrest in the West. Lenin concluded that any nationalist movements in the colonies should therefore be supported by Communists, in order to break the capitalist hold and remove their resources.[104] It was not until the 1920s, however, that this theory would be put into practice, as the steady gains of the Red Army in the Russian civil war gradually opened up Asia to Bolshevik influence. A key event in the evolution of Soviet policy towards this region of the world was the Second Congress of the Comintern. Founded in March 1919, the Third Communist International (Comintern) was intended as a replacement for the Second International, which had been denounced by Lenin and his regime during the First World War. Despite arguments by the Soviet government that the Comintern was a global political organisation, over which it had no control, it has been shown that the International's hierarchy was dominated by members of the Russian Bolshevik party.[105] Indeed, one historian has argued that the Chairman of the Comintern (Grigory Zinoviev) was a much more 'weighty political figure' than the Soviet Commissariat for Foreign Affairs (Georgii Chicherin).[106]

It was at the Second Congress of the Comintern, which convened in Moscow on 19 July 1920, that the relationship between Bolshevism and Asia was discussed in detail for the first time. It was here that Lenin developed his ideas from *Imperialism* to answer this fundamental question and effectively lay the foundation for all future Communist practice in Central and southern Asia. Discussion on India particularly dominated the meeting in July, largely because of the debate which ensued between Lenin and M.N. Roy – a well-known Indian Communist – on the question of the progress of Communist revolution in that country. While Lenin argued that, as a backward nation, India needed to experience a bourgeois revolution before it was able to progress to a proletarian one, Roy believed that the Indian workers and peasants were advanced enough for a proletarian uprising – with aid from Soviet Russia – to succeed there.[107] In essence, the debate centred on the larger issue of whether or not the Comintern should encourage Asian nationalism and pan-Islamism – how far it should support movements such as that being orchestrated by Gandhi or Kuchik Khan, for example. While Roy believed Gandhi was a 'reactionary', and should be denounced by the Comintern, Lenin believed that the Indian leader was a 'revolutionary' deserving of all encouragement Communist organisations could give.[108] By supporting the likes of Gandi, the Bolshevik leader argued, more headway would be made in removing British influence from South Asia which was a fundamental step in securing Soviet Russia and in furthering the general revolutionary cause. In effect, the nationalist and pan-Islamist were to be used for their ability to cause general disruption in the region – Communist revolution could then follow.[109] This was the tactic Lenin chose to advocate in Persia, India and Central Asia where alliances where to be made between the Bolsheviks and Muslim modernist and nationalist groups such as the Jadids.[110]

Ultimately, the Bolshevik leader's opinions held sway over Roy's, and the congress agreed that support should be given to the nationalist movements across Asia. From this meeting arose the 'Directives on the Nationality and the Colonial Question', signed by Lenin and from here on out the guiding document for the Comintern on all its Asian affairs.[111] Finally, it appeared that some order was to be brought to Bolshevik policies towards Central and South Asia. Efforts were to be made to pander to nationalist sentiment and Communists were to tread lightly with Muslim revolutionaries in order not to cause an Islamic back-lash against the Bolsheviks. However, while the theory had been worked-out, the practicalities of such policy was another matter, as shall come to be seen.

The debate on Gandhi and the issue of Asian nationalism at the Comintern congress would have been particularly worrying to the Indian government in

1920. A report by the Home Department in February had noted that 'there is no evidence in our possession to show that Bolshevik agents have reached India and started direct propaganda, but certain extremists...have been presenting Bolshevik theories in most favourable light'.[112] As the year was to develop, the growth of nationalist agitation in India threatened to bring Bolshevism into the country despite all of the government's endeavours. In May, old wounds were reopened when the Hunter Commission published its report into the events of April 1919 in India and the actions of General Dyer at Amritsar. While the Hunter report condemned Dyer for using excessive force and for not providing aid to the injured, there were some who lauded the general as 'the saviour of the Punjab'. A collection was set up for the general in which over £26,000 was raised,[113] and Montagu and Chelmsford were even criticised for their treatment of him. The council of the European Association of India, for example, announced that '[the] General body of Europeans in India strongly uphold Dyer and condemn [the] actions of [the] Government of India and Secretary of State'.[114] During a debate in the House of Commons on the Hunter Report, there was a strong reaction among some of the Conservative politicians to Montagu's speech against Dyer[115] (although one observer believed most of those involved were 'less Pro-Dyer than anti-Montagu').[116] The CIGS himself believed that in this time of troubles, the British government should be standing by the actions of its soldiers.[117] Such defence of Dyer, however, was resented by many Indians. As a consequence, at the Indian National Congress of September 1920 it was decided to adopt Gandhi's resolution for a programme of non-co-operation with the Indian government.[118]

For Chelmsford, the best way of dealing with this action was to largely ignore it. He believed that the Indian public would realise the 'folly' of non-co-operation.[119] As one historian has put it, 'Chelmsford's slogan was "caution and watchfulness"'.[120] In a letter to the viceroy, Montagu voiced his support: 'I believe your treatment of Gandhi will be successful...I am quite certain that if you have to move against him, he will hunger-strike and die in prison, and then I don't know where we should be.'[121] Chelmsford, nevertheless, faced criticism by others in London, who 'want to know why you don't lock him [Gandhi] up at once because they disapprove of him'.[122] However, the viceroy and his colleagues were well aware that Bolshevism thrived on popular discontent, and they were not about to provide fodder for Bolshevik propaganda by creating martyrs of Gandhi and his followers.

Potentially more dangerous than the Bolshevik interest in Gandhi and Indian nationalism, however, was Moscow's involvement in the nationalist and pan-Islamic agitation in Central and southern Asia during 1920. When it came to Islam the Bolshevik regime had to tread carefully, as instructions from Moscow pointed out to its party members in February: 'Religious prejudices are much stronger among the Mussulmans than among Russians or other European peasants and workmen...great caution must be exercised in the struggle against religious prejudice.'[123] Lessons also appear to have been learnt about Asian nationalism from the early Bolshevik encounters in Central Asia. In March 1918, the first Bolshevik attempt at deposing the Bokharan emir had failed, largely because Alim had been able to gather widespread support from his subjects in the face of what was a blatant foreign invasion.[124] When Russia tried again in 1920, it was careful to first orchestrate a 'spontaneous' uprising by the Young Bukharans before sending in troops to aid them.[125] This subtle manipulation of nationalist feeling to ultimately achieve revolutionary ends is indicative of how far the Bolsheviks had progressed from their early confusion and heavy-handedness in Asia.

Fortunately for Lenin and his colleagues, 1920 was a year of particular Muslim unrest, largely as a result of the Caliphate affair. If the loss of Enzeli was the biggest military blunder of the British government in 1920, its handling of the Caliphate issue was arguably the greatest diplomatic mistake of the post-war period.[126] The problem centred on the fact that the Sultan of Turkey was also the Caliph, the ostensible head of Islam. Thus, when Allied forces took control of Constantinople in October 1918 following the armistice of Mudros, there was immediate fear throughout the Muslim world that the Caliph would have his power and status significantly curbed. The defeat of Turkey – the last truly independent Islamic power – was difficult enough for Muslims to have to stomach, without seeing their spiritual leader degraded too. In India, as pan-Islamic feeling had grown, so too had sympathy with the Caliph in Istanbul. After the Indian Mutiny and the deposition of the last Moghul emperor, Indian Muslims needed a symbol of Muslim solidarity and the Caliph appeared to be it.[127]

Hence, in the aftermath of the First World War, the Caliphate issue had the potential to create mass discontent among Indian Muslims, a fact that was recognised by the India Office: on 5 January 1920, at a conference of ministers, Montagu argued that harsh treatment of Turkey would have a great and negative effect on India. It was pointed out that nearly all Indian (and Mesopotamian) experts agreed that if the Allies removed the Sultan/Caliph from Constantinople, there would be dangerous consequences. For Curzon, however, the only way to assure Britain's security from Turkish ambitions in the future was to relieve the Sultan of his standing in the Islamic world.[128] As for causing unrest in India, the foreign secretary branded such agitation as 'fictitious' or, at worst, 'short-lived'. It was also pointed out that, when it came to expertise, as ex-viceroys, Curzon and Hardinge had a combined experience of twelve years in India, and both doubted the agitation would amount to anything. Montagu countered that things had changed dramatically since Curzon and Hardinge's days and that India was actually 'in a more dangerous state today than it had been for the last thirty years'.[129] The following day, at a Cabinet meeting, Churchill added his weight to Montagu's argument, bowing 'to the overwhelming evidence, supplied by the secretary of state for India, of the resentment that would be excited in

India and throughout the Mohammedan world by the expulsion of the Turks from Constantinople'. Ultimately the decision of the Cabinet was that the Sultan and his government should be allowed to remain at Constantinople, although without a Turkish force under their control; Curzon dissented from a decision he believed to be a mistake.[130]

To the Caliphate movement that had formed in 1919, this assurance was not enough.[131] For the Caliph to be stripped of his powers and to become a mere figure-head and potential puppet of the West was unacceptable. For, as was explained by an Indian Caliphate Deputation when it visited Lloyd George in March 1920, the temporal and spiritual power of the Caliph could not be separated in the eyes of Islam. The Caliph, the deputation argued, was required to hold extensive temporal power in order to have the strength to act as protector of the Muslim world. According to the deputation, Arabia, Syria, Palestine and Mesopotamia all had to be under Muslim control, as well as the holy places of Mecca, Medina and Jerusalem. What was ultimately demanded by the Caliphate movement, which the deputation represented, was the 'restoration of *status quo ante bellum*'.[132] As Lloyd George pointed out, however, it had been Turkey that had declared war on Britain, and not vice versa. To accuse Britain of being anti-Turk, or even anti-Islam, as some were doing, was simply unfair, not least as both Germany and Austria-Hungary had faced harsh peace terms, even though both were Christian countries. Why should Turkey be allowed to escape justice?[133]

As to the need for the Caliph to hold such temporal power, there were even those among Muslims who disputed this, and did not recognise the Caliph as their leader, including the Arabs.[134] As Dobbs argued when the Afghan delegation at Mussoorie brought up the issue, 'At one time there were three Khilafats in simultaneous and rival existence...This shows how very careful you should be in laying down the law and making all sorts of statements about the Khilafat.'[135] In fact, in the opinion of some in the British government, the Caliph issue was simply an excuse for anti-British propagandists, 'who have in past times betrayed no great interest in the fortunes of the Ottoman Empire'.[136] Indeed, with Gandhi lending his support to the Caliphate movement, Crowe argued that this was 'further evidence that the religious side of the movement is purely fictitious. It is a nationalist and anti-British movement of all extremist parties'.[137]

Whether the Caliphate agitators were genuinely moved by religion or not was somewhat irrelevant to the matter at hand.[138] The Nizam of Hyderabad summarised the issue to Chelmsford:

> The Headship of Islam has been a polemic for years during which it did
> not rise beyond academic interest, but the present situation has given
> it a turn which defies sober reasoning and theological examination.

> Popular psychology is not necessarily logical or answerable to historical
> verities, and in practical politics what counts is fact and not theories.[139]

In effect, the Caliphate issue was a convenient rallying point for all the discontent
that was accumulating in India and South Asia at large in the post-war period.[140]
Muslims who had once shown complete loyalty to the Raj now felt 'thoroughly
ashamed of themselves' for having fought in the British Indian army against
their co-religionists; 'They had joined the Christian powers to fight against
Muslims and had not received any reward for that, neither any degree of self-
government for India nor any particular advancement in the status of the Muslim
community.'[141] Kemal Ataturk was astute in exploiting such feelings of Muslim
solidarity and the Caliphate issue was one which captured the imagination of
the public.[142] As one historian has explained, 'Turkey became a symbol of the
past greatness of Islam and its predicament in a hostile world in the twentieth
century'.[143] And with Gandhi encouraging Hindus to support the Muslim cause,
the movement gained true mass appeal in India, much to the discomfort of the
government.[144]

In January, Chelmsford tried to diffuse the situation by reassuring a Caliphate
deputation that the views of Indian Muslims were being strenuously pressed at the
peace conference in Paris, and that within the British Empire the religion, lives
and property of Muslims had and always would be protected.[145] Unfortunately
the viceroy's statements did not convince the deputation, which put out a
statement that 'should the peace terms result unfavourably to Muslim religion
and sentiments, they would place undue strain upon Muslim loyalty'.[146]At a
Caliphate conference held in Bengal on 28 February 1920 a resolution was passed
stating that:

> if the settlement of peace with Turkey is in any way against the religious
> injunctions and demands of Islam, that is, if the dominions of the
> Khilafate are not kept intact as they were before the war, then Muslims
> in obedience to the laws of Islam will be compelled to cease all relations
> of loyalty with Great Britain and shall be duty bound to assist their
> Khalif against all his enemies by all possible means.[147]

Despite the viceroy's attempts to prevent it, the sentiment was growing in the
Muslim world that the British Empire, once the friend of Islam, was increasingly
its enemy.

Unable to counter the Caliphate movement with reason and theory, and finding
that its calls for Muslim loyalty were also being rebuffed, the Indian government
chose to handle the situation by remaining as uninvolved as possible. Chelmsford
explained to Montagu in March, that 'at the present moment the extremists are

somewhat in a quandary. They would like to attack the Government of India, but there is nothing on which they can take hold because the Government of India have [sic] been uniformly in sympathy with their desires.'[148] Just as with the Gandhi issue, however, the Indian government came under criticism from the Home government for its reticence in being heavy-handed with the Caliphate movement. The Foreign Office believed the Indian government was simply looking on and watching the opposition grow,[149] while Curzon argued that the movement was being 'rendered formidable by [the] shocking weakness of the Gov. of India'.[150]

The first test for the Indian government's policy came on 15 May when the proposed Turkish peace treaty was made public. Among the terms was the removal of Smyrna and Thrace from Turkish authority to be placed in Greek hands.[151] This move was actually opposed by a number of figures in the British establishment, particularly among military members and the Indian government, who believed not only would it incite Muslim unrest but that Britain lacked the military capability to enforce it. However, as Wilson noted in his diary in June 1920, Lloyd George 'is as much convinced as ever that the Greeks are splendid soldiers and the Turks perfectly useless. It is a most dangerous obsession.'[152] Indeed, if Curzon was the champion of Britain's Persian policy in 1920, then the prime minister was the key orchestrator of the Turkish peace. It was due, in large measure, to the anti-Turkish-pro-Greek 'personal policy' of Lloyd George that the British Empire was to become even further estranged from the Muslim world in 1920.[153] As Admiral de Robeck warned, 'the proposal to dismember the Ottoman provinces of Turkey in the interests of Greece will drive the remaining Turks into the arms of the Bolsheviks, will set the Near East and Central Asia aflame, and will intensify the menace of Bolshevism to the British Moslem world'.[154]

In an effort to temper any potential trouble, Chelmsford published a message to all Indian Muslims acknowledging that the proposed treaty terms must be painful to them and asking them to accept the agreement 'with resignation, courage and fortitude and to keep your loyalty towards the Crown bright and untarnished...'[155] Despite such worries, however, the immediate reaction to news of the proposed treaty was actually relatively muted. The disturbances which the Indian government had been bracing themselves for did not materialise.[156] Instead, it seemed that the extremists of the Caliphate movement had succeeded through their violent speeches in frightening away more moderate supporters to their cause.[157] The policy of the Indian government, which had been to largely ignore the extremists and allow them to talk themselves out seemed to have been successful. The Indian government remained cautious, though, for, as Chelmsford noted, it was still early days and there was no way yet of knowing whether the anti-government agitators were simply lying low for now, making underground preparations.[158]

The greater test for the policy of the Indian government came with the involvement of Afghanistan in the Caliphate issue. On 3 March 1920 Chelmsford had relayed to Montagu the emir's wish to send a deputation from Afghanistan to Britain in order to make his sentiments known there on the Turkish peace. As the viceroy noted, such a move was probably designed to enhance Amanullah's reputation in Asia by making himself appear as the champion of Islam. While Chelmsford wanted to encourage such ambitions in order to bring Afghanistan and Soviet Russia to clash over Asia,[159] Montagu vetoed the idea, fearing that allowing the emir a say over the Turkish peace would only enhance his ability to influence Muslim hostility against Britain.[160] It was with the signing of the Treaty of Sèvres by Turkey in August that the real trouble began, however. It was a 'great disappointment' for Indian Muslims.[161] Amanullah had made known through a proclamation that he would welcome into Afghanistan any Muslims who wanted to escape from their ruler for religious reasons. With this encouragement, some 20,000–30,000 Muslims decided to perform *Hijrat* (religious migration) during the month of August, as a protest against the treatment of Turkey by the Allies.[162] A Central Hijrat Office with branches all over India was opened, and a propaganda campaign launched.[163] With such a large movement of people, the Indian government was unsurprisingly anxious, particularly Hamilton Grant, who was now chief commissioner of the North-West Frontier Province, from where the majority of the *Muhajirun* (those performing *Hijrat*) originated. Nevertheless, despite such worries, Grant also realised that the least interference that his administration made in the movement, the better.[164] In this policy of allowing things to take their course Grant was supported by Chelmsford. For one thing, as was observed, 'the people are extraordinarily orderly' and there was little need for action in order to keep the peace.[165] Indeed, Grant believed that his policy of non-interference was one of the very reasons for the relatively calm proceedings of the *Hijrat*.[166]

For another thing, as the viceroy explained to Montagu, although led perhaps by political extremists, 'the poor misguided folk who have left their homes have left them because they genuinely thought that they were bound to do so on religious grounds. It was all important therefore that we should give no ground for the suggestion that we were interfering with a religious movement.'[167] Once again, the Indian government was vindicated in its policy of non-interference. By late August, the *Muhajirun* were flocking back to India after a less than warm welcome from the Afghan government. Amanullah had been expecting more prosperous and educated Muslims to migrate to his country; when he learned that the vast majority of the *Muhajirun* were the poorest elements of Indian society, he quickly lost enthusiasm.[168] With no help from the Afghan government, and no resources of their own, the *Muhajirun* were forced to return home.[169] Reports soon spread through India of the hardship endured by the *Muhajirun*, many of whom died on the return journey from exhaustion and disease – the road from the Frontier to Kabul was said to be dotted with *Muhajirun* graves.[170] All together, the episode constituted a major setback for the Caliphate movement. As Grant observed, '[the] Khilafat Committee realise that they have aroused forces they cannot control and are paralysed with fear of [the] public who are bitterly resentful at having thus been duped'.[171] The affair was also a disaster for Amanullah, resulting as it did in a blow to his prestige across Central and southern Asia.[172]

While the policy of the Indian government had helped avert an even bigger crisis for the British Empire, the Caliphate movement and the general Muslim unrest that was felt in South Asia in 1920 was ultimately a gift to the Bolsheviks. Not only did it create a group of captive discontents, it also allowed the Bolshevik regime to paint the British government in the light of imperialist oppressors, while posing itself as the friend and ally of the Muslim world – which was just the aim of the First Congress of the Peoples of the East, held in Baku in September 1920.[173] According to Bolshevik figures, 1,891 delegates attended representing a number of Asian countries and various extremist movements.[174] (This was certainly much better attendance than its pre-cursor, the first All-Russian Congress of Muslim Communist Organisations, had garnered in November 1918).[175] An account given by H.G. Wells describes the Congress's Chair, Zinoviev, and his colleagues holding an event at Baku 'at which they gathered together a quite wonderful accumulation of white, black, brown and yellow people, Asiatic costumes and astonishing weapons. They had a great assembly in which they swore undying hatred of capitalism and British imperialism'.[176] Zinoviev claimed that the event showed 'the living strength of our revolution', and even went so far as to call for a *jihad* against British imperialism.[177]

The practical effects of the Baku Congress, in bringing about an understanding between Bolshevism and pan-Islamism were, however, limited. Instead the Congress revealed that all Zinoviev had to offer 'was empty rhetoric', rather than a well-conceived plan.[178] One report to reach British Intelligence stated that while many violent speeches were made, the general effect was spoiled by large numbers of the Muslim representatives going outside to say their prayers and that 'not the faintest notice was taken of most of the numerous speeches made, the delegates being far more interested in each other's swords and revolvers'.[179] Far from being a vehicle for open debate and discussion, the Congress consisted of a list of speakers that had 'been made beforehand and consisted only of Russian Communists', with few being allowed to speak freely: 'Several of the Mussulman orators made an attempt to speak but were not allowed to continue.'[180] One delegate described the Congress as 'a badly-acted comedy...a mere farce, having no significance for Eastern peoples, especially for Moslems'.[181] Wells himself admitted the event was 'an excursion, a pageant, a Beano. As a meeting of Asiatic proletarians it was preposterous'.[182] British Intelligence even reported that one of their agents had seen a telegram from Zinoviev to Lenin admitting that the Congress was a failure.[183] The chairman's rant against Muslim clergy, labelling them parasites and oppressors, did not go down particularly well with his audience.[184]

However, while Zinoviev and his colleagues may have been clumsy in their handling of the delegates to the Congress, as a work of propaganda the event was a huge success. As the report by British Intelligence concluded, if the delegates to the Congress were really elected by the people they claimed to represent, the Bolsheviks had done themselves great harm in the East by the bad impression they had given. However, 'If it was merely a plan to collect together a heterogeneous mass of Asiatic undesirables with a view to enlisting them as agents and agitators, then the Bolsheviks appear to have been most successful.'[185] The gathering together of a large number of anti-British malcontents was a worry in itself for Britain. As one Tiflis newspaper pointed out, at the Congress the representatives of the revolutionary and nationalists movements 'will have facilities for meeting and discussing mutual measures and co-operation. If they do this, then the Conference will serve as the first step towards a union of the forces of the Eastern peoples...'[186] The last thing the British government needed was for the revolutionary movements in Central and southern Asia to combine and organise themselves. Indeed, one of the few practical results of the Congress was the creation of a Council of Propaganda and Action in the East.[187] Two months after Baku, a school would also be set up in Tashkent under the direction of M.N. Roy with the specific aim of training Indian and Asian malcontents in Communist revolutionary theory (its first students were a handful of *Muhajirun* who had not returned to India with the others).[188]

The crucial result of the Baku Congress then, was that it served to disturb the British government (and would contribute to the seeking of an accord with the Bolshevik regime in 1921). Furthermore, the Congress was an apt summary of the relationship between Bolshevism and the pan-Islamist and nationalist movements in Asia in the post-war period. In true Great Game style, it was an event of all show and little substance, just as the relationship between these groups did not go much deeper than a mutual anti-British fervour (not only was this the First Congress of the Peoples of the East, it was also the last). For the British government, however, any level of collaboration between these movements was enough to make it uncomfortable. Montagu summarised the situation when he wrote to Chelmsford in September 1920:

> What does alarm me is that up till now it has always seemed to me that extremism in India has really been either anti-British or national. It seems to me that it is going to be international. The Bolsheviks, in their animosity to all settled government, are using the grievances of the Mahomedans, and what frightens me is the way in which Pan-Islamism

which, as I think foolishly, we have made hostile to the British Empire, is taking charge of the extremist movement.[189]

That the actions of the British government had helped foster Muslim opposition to the empire in the post-war period was certainly true. While the Indian government tried its best to mitigate the problem, ultimately it could not overcome the attitude of some in the Home government towards Turkey or make them fully appreciate what bad policy was contained in the Treaty of Sèvres.

An Act of Dementia

The year 1920 was one of extraordinary strain for the British Empire. It seemed that, on all fronts, it was facing popular unrest and waning international influence. In India, the government struggled to deal with mass popular discontent that was becoming ever more vocal and organised under the leadership of Gandhi and of the Caliphate movement, while all the while trying to pacify a fickle neighbour in the form of Afghanistan. Throughout Asia an over-stretched and under-resourced army was being called upon to maintain Britain's imperial influence against a surge of a pan-Islamist and nationalist feeling that was gradually engulfing this area of the world. At home, the British government faced economic decline, rapid unemployment and mass industrial unrest; while in Persia, its inability to enforce the terms of the Anglo-Persian Agreement, or to prevent Staroselskii reaching dominance over the military operations of that country, was matched only by its impotence in the face of the Red Army landings at Enzeli. Indeed, compounding all of these troubles facing Britain in 1920 was the ever-present shadow of Soviet Russia, its propaganda efforts threatening the very core stability of the empire, its growth in strength and confidence in Asia high-lighting even further Britain's own relative decline. Any one of these issues would have been enough to place pressure on the resources of the British Empire, and test the abilities of the country's leaders; combined as they were in a synergy of opposition and hostility toward Britain and it created at this time the possibility of a very real crisis. It was how the British government addressed these issues in 1920 which determined just how big of a crisis would develop.

Unfortunately, the British government was inclined to make things worse for itself and in this Curzon and his Foreign Office held great responsibility for the policy that was ultimately pursued. Curzon's authority on foreign affairs in South Asia had been given further impetus by his gaining sole control of the Foreign Office towards the end of 1919. By 1920, the belief that Curzon was a driving force behind Britain's affairs in South Asia was so prevalent among contemporaries, that the foreign secretary was forced to defend himself in the House of Lords:

Incidentally I have noticed in some quarters that our policy in that part of the world is described as an act of dementia on my own part, dragging after me a body of reluctant colleagues...It is unfair to assume at any moment that an important branch of policy, even of foreign policy, is the work of any individual Minister.[190]

While it is true that government foreign policy cannot be solely blamed on one person (Curzon was supported in Persia by Milner for example, and had Cox telling him what he wanted to hear), there is no doubt that Curzon proved a stubborn obstacle in the way of a more prudent military policy in South Asia at this time. It was due to him 'more than to anyone else' that British forces were maintained in their position in Persia.[191] For while Churchill, Wilson and the Indian government were preaching military retrenchment, Curzon would do nothing to risk jeopardising an Anglo–Persian Agreement which was already clearly defunct. In allowing his ambition to override military caution Curzon must take the bulk of the blame for Britain's humiliation in Persia. The reluctance of the foreign secretary to accept a more limited role for Britain in Persia and elsewhere in Asia, was eventually, however, to have repercussions for him. For as Chelmsford pointed out to Montagu in December 1920, 'When one considers the failure of his [Curzon's] policy in Persia and Mesopotamia, one is at a loss to understand how he can retain the position of an authority on Eastern affairs.'[192] Wilson summed up his regard for the Foreign Office when he noted in his diary how the newly appointed ambassador to Constantinople, Sir Horace Rumbold, had come to see him; in their half hour talk, Rumbold had learnt more 'than in all the Foreign Office palavars and papers. That Foreign Office and Curzon are hopeless. They have not even got maps.'[193]

The lacking of maps aside, the most crucial mistake that Curzon made in 1920, however, was to inadvertently encourage a greater affinity between Bolshevik Russia and the Muslim world. In December 1919 the First Lord of the Admiralty, Walter Long had tried to warn of the progress Bolshevism was making in Asia:

The recent Bolshevik successes are likely to give an impetus to what is, it is submitted, one of the most important of Bolshevik aims, namely, to turn the Moslem world against the British Empire... Skilfully making use of every circumstance lending itself to mis-interpretation or distortion, the Bolsheviks have succeeded to make large numbers of Moslems in various parts of the Near and Middle East honestly believe that Great Britain is the enemy of Islam...Very skilfully, too, the Bolsheviks are contriving to turn the somewhat vague and unformed aims of the Pan-Islamic movement, such as it is, into anti-British channels.[194]

Indeed, the ability of the Bolshevik regime to subvert the more extreme points of its doctrine in order to try to appeal to Asian and Muslim malcontents is testament to the pragmatism and opportunism of Lenin and his colleagues. Long's warning that the danger of a Bolshevik–pan-Islamic combination was not fully realised by some in the British government would indeed appear to be true, given the policy which both Curzon and Lloyd George insisted on pursuing with Turkey. For Curzon in particular, such blindness was at odds with the almost obsessive warnings he had made in 1918–1919 over the Bolshevik threat to Persia. It would seem that when it suited his ambition to see a weakened and dismembered Turkey, Curzon found it convenient to downplay the Bolshevik regime's ability to exploit pan-Islamic agitation.

In comparison to the Home government, the Indian government was to prove its shrewdness when it came to dealing not only with the Bolshevik danger to India, but also with the pan-Islamic and nationalist movements that threatened to undermine Britain's position in that country. By refusing to engage with Gandhi, by allowing the *Muhajirun* to proceed freely, and by letting the Caliphate extremists talk themselves out of mass support, the Indian government was in effect allowing the popular unrest in India to run out of steam. By its determination not to provoke further unrest or make martyrs of the cause, the Indian government also robbed the extremists of what would have been an even greater anti-British rallying point – government-sponsored oppression.

In its dealings with Afghanistan, the Indian government further demonstrated the realism and practicality of its approach to foreign affairs. While the Home government may have worried about a loss of prestige for India, by appearing too keen for Afghan friendship, Chelmsford and his colleagues realised that the greater loss would be to India's security should a hostile Afghanistan develop on its borders. Again, it is to the Indian government's credit that it realised the crucial component in combating Bolshevism in India was information. The web of communication that was set up between the central and the peripheral administrations ensured that the government was able to maintain a clear picture of the level of Bolshevik agitation occurring in India and, therefore, to take appropriate action, such as the extension of the rouble ordinance. That, in 1920, relatively little Bolshevik agitation occurred in India must be, at least in part, attributed to the government's measures. Despite the criticism it often faced from some in the Home government, the choices made by the Indian government in dealing with its problems in 1920 proved to be correct. Indeed, there is some irony in the fact that the Foreign Office was so quick to disparage Delhi's policies – with Gandhi, for example – when the latter proved far more successful in its endeavours in 1920 than the former.

The year 1920 was one in which the British government had been forced to face its limitations. For some, the struggle between ambition and pragmatism continued for longer than it did for others. The following year, 1921, would be one in which the government would have to come to terms with these changes. For, while 1920 had proved the military and seditious capabilities of the Bolshevik regime, 1921 would demonstrate how far their diplomatic abilities could take them. The Soviet agreements with Britain, as well as those with Turkey, Persia and Afghanistan in 1921 would signal a marked evolution in the progression of Bolshevik Russia from its status as an international pariah in 1918.

Chapter Four

Making Friends, 1921

T he events of 1920 had shown that Curzon had been wrong in the
policies he had tried to pursue in Persia. The 1919 agreement had been
categorically rejected by the Persian people, and the Enzeli debacle had
exposed the impotence of Britain's military for all to see. What is more, given the
state of its economy, Britain no longer had the physical resources to support the
forward policy which the foreign secretary favoured. Unfortunately for Curzon,
Britain's position as unrivalled authority in South Asia was not to be. A change
was now needed in Britain's foreign policy. But how far did the foreign secretary
recognise this? And what was the change to be?

1920 had been a rude awakening for those in London who had been overly
optimistic about the empire's capabilities in the post-war period. By 1921 it
appeared that realism needed to be the order of the day – the guiding principle
which the Indian government had been following itself since 1918. However, while
Delhi was confident that Britain could still play a central role in South Asia even
from a position of retrenchment, the Home government was not so convinced.
Prestige was always a key factor in the international standing of the empire, but
by 1921, without any economic or military clout, prestige appeared to be of
even greater importance to many in London. How the empire was to pull back
from its current position without appearing weak was a particular worry to the
Home government, and one which would bring it into conflict with the Indian
government yet again.

The changes which 1921 wrought on British foreign policy have been noted
by other authors, albeit for quite different reasons. The Anglo–Soviet Trade
Agreement was signed by Britain and Russia in 1921, and for some, this event
has been seen as a watershed moment in the relationship between these two
countries, marking, as it did, a level of recognition of the Soviet government
by Britain that it had never previously admitted.[1] Some have argued that the
accord represented a turning point, not only in Britain's policy towards Russia,
but in its perspective on its foreign relations in general – a move from the
militaristic frame of mind that had dominated Britain's immediate post-war
foreign policy, to a peacetime mentality.[2] The continued attempts in those years
to curb military expenditure certainly support this argument. However, others
have argued that the trade agreement in no way represented a change in the

actual attitude of the British government. Instead, the diplomatic manoeuvres involved in the trade negotiations 'in political terms represented a continuation of the military intervention of the immediate post-revolutionary period'.[3]

However, what is interesting is not only this debate as to what the agreement meant for Anglo-Russian relations in general, but also what the agreement tells us about Britain's imperial outlook in this period, for as has been demonstrated throughout this work, the problem of Bolshevism was inextricably linked with the issues of pan-Islamism and Asian nationalism when it came to Britain's imperial interests. The connection between Britain's relations with Soviet Russia and with that of Persia and Afghanistan is clear, even from the terms of the trade agreement. While the document was supposed to be concerned with trade relations, the preamble required both parties to refrain from any hostile undertakings against the other (including, importantly, conducting propaganda). Accompanying the agreement, moreover, was a letter from the British government to the Soviet government, detailing the current areas in which Bolshevik subversive activity was being conducted and demanding this be stopped.[4] In September 1921, when a note was sent to the Soviet government protesting against alleged violations of the trade agreement, the examples cited were that of Bolshevik sedition towards India and within Persia and Afghanistan.[5] Hence, when it came to Russia, Persia and Afghanistan (or Bolshevism, Islamism and nationalism), the three were hard for Britain to separate in the post-war period.

In fact, the trade agreement was not the only accord to be signed that year. Indeed, 1921 could be termed the year of the treaty. For, Moscow would sign agreements with the governments of Afghanistan, Persia, Turkey and, of course, Britain, while the latter would conclude its own treaty with Afghanistan.[6] How these treaties all affected one another is a question, however, which has yet to be fully explored. So, while others may have asked what the Anglo-Soviet Trade Agreement meant for Anglo-Russian relations, the following pages will focus instead on how affairs with Russia affected Britain's policies towards Persia and Afghanistan in 1921. Furthermore, this chapter will try to understand to what extent the British government underwent an actual change in attitude regarding not only its policy towards Soviet Russia, but, more specifically, towards Persia and Afghanistan; it will try to see how far any such change was real or simply superficial. Finally, given the setbacks he had experienced, had the Great Game mentality of Curzon actually died a death by 1921 or was it struggling on?

Shadow for Substance

In a speech to the House of Lords in July 1921, Curzon described the situation in Persia as one which left him with 'a feeling of disappointment, almost of despair'. All his previous efforts in Persia he believed to have been in vain, and he was 'unaware of any encouragement at the present moment to persevere in this task'.[7] This was an apt summary of Curzon's feelings in 1921, as well as a telling indication of the change that the foreign secretary had undergone in relation to Persia in the last year or so. As noted, Persia was Curzon's apparent area of expertise, and the policies pursued by the British government towards this country in the post-war period were created and driven almost entirely by him. It is therefore hardly surprising that the foreign secretary should feel such despondency when surveying what the last two years of his handiwork had done to Britain's position in Persia. Rather than attaining a position of unrivalled hegemony over a secure and stable buffer state, Britain's standing in that country – and its reputation in Asia at large – appeared to have sunk to an all time low.

And yet, rather than realising the error of his ways, and admitting that he may have failed to appreciate the nature of the post-war world, Curzon was to react as if he had been personally insulted by the Persians. Even at this point it would have been possible to negotiate an agreement more in line with the suggestions of the Indian government and E.G. Browne's five point plan, and potentially save Anglo-Persian relations from sinking any further. Instead, after 1920 the foreign secretary commenced on what can only be described as a monumental sulk towards Persia. In January 1921, the Persian government was still obfuscating when it came to ratifying the agreement with Britain. When Norman enquired as to the possibility of modifying the agreement to make it more palatable to the Persian public, George Churchill of the Foreign Office noted quite plainly that such action seemed pointless.[8] Curzon made clear his position a few days later when he explained to Norman that he was now 'wholly indifferent as to whether [the] Medjliss is summoned or not'. The time for submitting the agreement had passed six weeks ago and now Britain's only interest was that a decent government be formed for Persia's own sake.[9] When Norman further suggested annulling the current agreement and creating another to replace it Curzon responded:

> I have no desire to negotiate a new agreement...Personally I will never propose another agreement with the Persians. Not unless they came on their knees would I even consider any application from them...In future we will look after our own interests in Persia not hers.[10]

The bitterness in Curzon's reply is palpable. Having invested so much of his time, energy and reputation in the Persian agreement, the failure of the Tehran government to ratify the document had apparently resulted in the foreign secretary washing his hands of the entire matter.

Although it was not interested in negotiating an amended or entirely new agreement with the Persian government, neither did the British government have the 'slightest intention of denouncing the agreement themselves and of accepting thereby the responsibility for a proceeding the blame of which must rest exclusively upon Persian shoulders'.[11] For Curzon, it no doubt seemed that denouncing the agreement amounted to admitting that it had been wrong to create it in the first place. In Norman's opinion, such sensitivity was a mistake: by officially declaring the agreement to be defunct, the British government could start to repair the damage done to its reputation.[12] However, by leaving it neither enacted nor annulled, the agreement hung like an albatross around the neck of Anglo-Persian relations – a focus for anti-British feeling within Persia and for Britain a reminder of its failure to bring Persia under its control.

Norman was not alone in believing that his government should distance itself from the accord. Unsurprisingly, Chelmsford supported this view:

> it seems to us essential that we should seize every possible opportunity of working back to our old role of champions of Islam against the Russian ogre. At present the roles are reversed and our position not only in Persia but throughout [the] Middle East is one of greatest difficulty in consequence. Scrapping of Anglo-Persian Agreement would go far to right the matter.

Curzon's minuted response was typical of the ill feeling he constantly displayed towards the viceroy:

> Considering that the Gov. of India decline to take the slightest interest in Persia, have steadily opposed the Anglo-Persian Agreement from the start, cut off their expenditure there without even a reference to us, and wash their hands of all responsibility – I regard the above with which they so liberally regale us as an impertinence and would not pay it the compliment of a reply.[13]

But despite Curzon's dismissal of Chelmsford's opinion, the idea that the agreement was now worse than useless was growing within the British government. Even Sir Percy Cox, the chief architect of the agreement (and now high commissioner of Mesopotamia), had come to concur with Norman and the Indian government. In his opinion, the agreement 'has become such a red herring to the Bolshevik[s] and such a pretext for extremist propaganda, that I agree with the Government of India that we must drop it in its present form as a basis of policy'.[14] Curzon's minute that Cox was closer to the mark than anybody else when it came to Persia shows that the Indian government's ideas were always more palatable to the foreign secretary when they were proposed by anyone other than the viceroy![15]

Unfortunately for Norman, Curzon appeared just as willing to ignore him as the viceroy. Cox had been Curzon's man and his recommendations on British Persian policy had been exactly what the foreign secretary had wanted to hear. Norman, however, had a different perspective to his predecessor. While he had served in Egypt and Turkey, he had also held positions in the US, Latin America and Europe. Before his appointment to Persia he had been part of the British Delegation to the Paris Peace Conference. Norman had therefore 'seen a wider changing world and witnessed the rising tide of nationalism', whereas Cox had spent much of his career 'dealing with hereditary sheikhs and tribal leaders'.[16] Norman also had no personal attachment to the 1919 agreement and was therefore perhaps more objective. Unfortunately, although he was a man of 'intelligence and vision', Norman's views of the Persian situation were not what Curzon wanted to hear. Try as he might, the diplomat was unable to make the foreign secretary listen to him. Indeed, the relationship between the two became so bad that when Norman finally left Tehran in October 1921, Curzon refused to see him when he arrived in London (as was the general courtesy when a diplomat returned from abroad).[17]

Despite the pleas of Norman to abrogate the agreement, nevertheless, Curzon remained unmoved. As one historian puts it: 'This stubborn clinging to an obviously imperialistic treaty could only make the worst impression on nationalistically minded Iranians.'[18] The situation became even more farcical when the new Persian prime minister, Seyyed Zia'eddin, took it upon himself to denounce the agreement.[19] On 26 February 1921 in a declaration to the Persian public, Zia'eddin explained:

> The occasion of the conclusion of this agreement was a different world situation, and the causes which obliged us to profit by it are no longer existent...I announce the denunciation of the Anglo-Persian Agreement that it may not have a bad influence on our conduct of affairs...[20]

The wording of the declaration demonstrates Zia'eddin's efforts not to offend the British government by his actions. Indeed, he even suggested that Curzon send a note to the affect that the British government had concluded the agreement because it believed it to be in the best interests of the Persian people, but in no way insisted on its acceptance by the Persian government. Publication of such an announcement would 'at once add very greatly to our popularity and prestige here', as Norman put it.[21] Curzon responded that he had no time 'for a Gov. that simultaneously denounces and fawns'.[22]

The foreign secretary's reply to Norman not only illustrates the bitterness now apparent in his attitude towards Persia, but also hints at a cynicism in regards to that country's government. The rulers of Persia were in a difficult situation in this period: they did not want to alienate the British government, but needed to distance themselves from an agreement so derided by the Persian public that it had contributed to the downfall of the men who had aided its creation. As Zia'eddin tried to explain to Norman, 'if Great Britain wished to save her position here she must sacrifice shadow for substance, remain in the background and help Persia effectively but ostentatiously'.[23] For Curzon and others in the Foreign Office, however, such caution by the Persian government was taken as proof of its insincerity towards Britain. The attempts made by Zia'eddin in April of 1921 to enlist American advisors to help with some of Persia's administrative issues – including bringing back W.M. Shuster to head a Persian national bank – appeared to confirm such suspicions.[24] While Norman tried to explain that the Persian prime minister was simply hoping to create a strong and reformed Persia by seeking any help he could,[25] to Curzon such courting of Washington amounted to a betrayal of Britain.[26] The foreign secretary was apt to believe that the Persian political system was much as it was prior to the war – based on personalities – and that the way to achieve anything was to work with sympathetic individuals.[27] Much of Norman's communication with London was spent trying to explain that the old system was in decline. As he told the Foreign Office in April 1921, the forces of nationalism within Persia were now so strong that any prime minister that hoped to survive had to harness this force and, hence, had to be seen to be internationalising and reforming the country.[28]

Just how precarious a position any Persian government was in is apparent simply from looking at how short their terms of office were. Seyyed Zia'eddin had come to power following a *coup d'état* by the commander of the Cossack Division, Reza Khan (Staroselskii's successor), who had claimed that he was 'tired of seeing one inefficient Government succeed another at Tehran'.[29] Yet, within a few months, Zia'eddin had been ousted – ostensibly because of his 'pro-British attitude' – and replaced with Qavam os-Saltaneh.[30] Such political turbulence did not make for better relations between Britain and Persia. Probably aware of his precarious position, the new Persian prime minister, os-Saltaneh, immediately sent to London a communication of friendship. He hoped, of course, that the British government realised that he had to remain 'impartial', in Persia's foreign relations, but that this would not prevent Britain from giving its support to himself and his new Cabinet. Nevertheless, Lancelot Oliphant epitomised the British Foreign Office's view when he noted that it appeared that 'the new [Persian] Cabinet wished to keep their cake and yet eat it': it wanted to place all nations with an interest in its country on a par, and yet gain all the advantages which Britain had bestowed on previous Persian governments 'which had actively worked with us'.[31] Curzon, meanwhile, was apparently entirely sick of a succession of Persian ministers 'all taking anti-British action but sneaking round to protest British sympathies'. As for the constant interchange of personnel in the Persian government, this elicited in the British foreign secretary 'no more concern than the rapid and inevitable fall of (British) wickets in an International test match'.[32]

What made the Persian government's position even harder in 1921 was the decision by the British Cabinet to recall its troops from north Persia by the spring of that year. This resolution sent panic through the officials in Tehran, and prompted the shah to ask Norman 'whether withdrawal of British troops indicated that His Majesty's Government had ceased to take any interest in Persia'.[33] While the British minister tried to reassure that this was not the case, such worry was understandable.[34] The presence of its troops on Persian soil had been a crucial component of Britain's policy since their arrival there during the First World War. Curzon himself had argued throughout 1919 and 1920 that Norperforce was instrumental in preventing a Bolshevik penetration of Persia.[35] Thus, by removing its troops, Britain was potentially opening the door for Soviet Russia to gain an ascendancy in Persia. Norman for one firmly believed that the removal of Norperforce 'will be immediately followed by a Bolshevik occupation, or, at least, by arrival of numerous Bolshevik agents' into the country.[36]

Nor was the British minister alone in his fears. The head of the Persian Imperial Bank believed that for Britain 'to desert before we are compelled by force...will be simply doing what [the] Moscow Government are anxious we might do'.[37] The India Office too, was anxious about what the recall of Britain's troops would mean for the growth of Bolshevik influence in Persia. As Montagu explained to Chelmsford, any Bolshevik advance into that country:

> would not necessarily take [the] form of military invasion. More probably
> it would follow customary line of political propaganda among disaffected
> elements of [the] population...We must therefore be prepared, if we
> withdraw from Persia...to see [the] whole country fall under direct
> Bolshevik influences, which will then extend right up to [the] frontiers of
> India and Mesopotamia.[38]

In Hardinge's opinion, Britain was 'simply throwing away the fruit of a hundred years of effort in Persia for the sake of the withdrawal of three or four thousand men.'[39]

The viceroy, however, was one of the few who did not share these concerns. Since 1918, Chelmsford had been advocating a reduced role for Britain in Persia anyway, arguing that the current policy towards that country was contributing to anti-British feeling in the Muslim world that was making the Indian government's job that much harder. Hence, his reply to Montagu:

> Unpleasant though Bolshevism up to our border would be, it is to us
> questionable whether it would be more dangerous than the present
> position when...British attitude in Persia is regarded in Moslem Asia,
> especially in Afghanistan and largely in Moslem India, as another example
> of Britain's crushing of Islam.[40]

As ever, pan-Islamism and Asian nationalism were of more concern to the Indian government than Bolshevism. Thus, the withdrawal of British troops from Persia was practically welcomed by the viceroy.

Together with the abrogation of the Anglo-Persian Agreement, Chelmsford no doubt hoped the removal of troops represented a change in Britain's Persian policy. Indeed, in January 1921 the Indian government made clear its intention to end its share of the maintenance of the South Persia Rifles (SPRs), effective at the end of March.[41] As the Indian government had been threatening since 1918 to bring its financial contributions to Persia to a close, this announcement regarding the SPRs should not have been a surprise to the Foreign Office. Nevertheless, it helps explain, in part, the animus displayed by Curzon towards the Indian government as expressed above. The foreign secretary was not the only one unhappy with this decision regarding the SPRs, however. In February 1921, the British financial adviser in Tehran, Sydney Armitage-Smith, composed a memorandum outlining his opinion on the Persian situation and arguing that the SPRs would now play a crucial role in that country following the withdrawal of Norperforce:

> I am still not without hope that when the Government of India fully understands the hideous results of a complete abandonment of Persia and the disruption of the only disciplined force which can maintain law and order, they may yet consent to make a further contribution to the upkeep of the South Persia Rifles after 31 March.[42]

Like many in the Home government, Armitage-Smith failed to understand the Indian government's perspective on Britain's Persian relations. As long as the Persian government and people were not overtly anti-British to the point of becoming a threat, and as long as the southern and south eastern borders were relatively stable, Chelmsford and his colleagues were unconcerned with the internal state of that country, particularly if such a concern required expenditure of Indian resources – financial or military. This had been made clear in the original Eastern Committee debates in late 1918, and was perhaps the most consistently held view within the British government in this period.

As is hinted at in Armitage-Smith's statement, the arguments over the maintenance of the SPRs represented a wider issue for Britain's position in Persia at this time. One of the main reasons others had acquiesced to Curzon's plans for Persia in 1919 is that many were willing to defer to the foreign secretary's apparent knowledge of that country. Now that it had become apparent what maintaining a significant presence in Persia was really costing the British government – both financially and in terms of reputation – withdrawal was advocated.

Some British officials now began to believe that if they did not have the military and economic means to hold onto a position in the north of that country, then they might as well cut their losses and concentrate their limited resources in the south. Churchill gave a good summary of this view in February 1921:

> The withdrawal [of Norperforce] from Persia leading to the loss of the Northern part of Persia may be attended by the moving of the capital from Teheran [sic] to Ispahan. This is surely very much in our interest, but it is impossible unless the South Persian Rifles are maintained...It might indeed have been impossible for us to hold North Persia as long as an unfriendly and uncivilised Russian Government is in existence, but South Persia ought certainly not to be thrown away without an effort.[43]

Although it begs the question as to when was there ever a Russian government that would have been happy to see a British hold on north Persia, Churchill's statement appears logical. After all, it was in the south of Persia that British interests had traditionally been centred prior to the First World War. Protection of, and access to, the oilfields in the south was of vital importance to the British Navy, as the Admiralty had reminded the Foreign Office in December 1920.[44] W.A. Smart, the Oriental Secretary of the British Legation in Tehran, also advocated a shift in focus towards the south. Writing in June 1921, Smart argued that by that point the north of Persia had become so infested with Bolshevik agents that the British Legation simply did not have the resources to counter them. Smart believed the British government should be realistic regarding the Persian situation, and retreat south to make its stand against the Bolsheviks.[45] In Armitage-Smith's words: 'Let the North have its taste of Bolshevik rule; let the experiment of reconstruction be tried in the...South.'[46]

Curzon, however, was opposed to the 'southern policy'. In a telegram to Norman the foreign secretary asked (rhetorically) whether 'damage to our prestige, of which you complain, only be enhanced by a precipitate retreat and abandonment of whole of Northern Persia to an enemy, whose advance is by no means certain, and a revolution which can probably still be avoided [?]'.[47] Perhaps surprisingly, the Indian government agreed with the foreign secretary in regards to the southern policy, albeit for different reasons. Although Delhi's interests in Persia certainly lay in the south, in Chelmsford's opinion, having 'a Soviet Government in the north, and a Shah Government, supported or dominated by Britain, in the south', would have an equally bad, if not worse effect on India as Britain's current Persian policy.[48] The Indian government welcomed the removal of British troops because it saw it as a step back from Persian internal affairs; what it did not want was for Britain to simply turn its attention from the north to the south of that country. It had been just such an attempt to carve up Persia into spheres of influence that had gained the British the animosity of the Persian people in the first place. Indeed, the plan as advocated by Churchill of bringing the Persian capital south under British auspices seemed likely to cause even more resentment towards Britain than the 1907 Anglo–Russian Convention had done. Instead, Delhi would rather leave Persia to its own devices, interfering only as far as was necessary to secure the southern borders and protect its interests in the south should they be threatened – which was far from the case in 1921.[49]

It is perhaps no wonder, then, that the Persian government was feeling decidedly nervous in 1921. The Red Army landings at Enzeli the previous May had shown that it could not rely on British military support to protect it from Bolshevik aggression. Now, the withdrawal of Norperforce, the disinterestedness in the Anglo–Persian Agreement, and the seeming willingness of the British government to abandon north Persia to the Bolsheviks as it scuttled south, all left the Persian government feeling somewhat abandoned by Britain. It is, therefore, hardly surprising that Zia'eddin or his successors sought the financial and administrative help of America, or wanted closer relations with France, or even that they tried to enlist Swedish officers to help organise a national army.[50] Curzon may have seen this as a betrayal towards Britain, but one wonders what other choice Persia really had in 1921.

It was just this lack of options that would lead to what one would have thought was the greatest blow to Curzon's Persian policy of the entire period – the signing of a 'treaty of friendship' between Persia and Soviet Russia on 26 February 1921.[51] In Norman's opinion, at least, it was Britain's lack of commitment to Persia that had directly contributed to the creation of this treaty. In January the minister had warned that the withdrawal 'of our troops and discontinuance of financial assistance must sooner or later involve loss of our influence over [the] Persian Government, who, having nothing to hope for from us, must turn elsewhere for help'.[52] In May, he expanded further:

> When once we had abandoned the Transcaspian railway, evacuated the Caucasus and surrendered control of the Caspian Sea itself, and, still more, when our troops had retired before Russian aggression in Ghilan... it was obvious that a helpless Persia had no alternative but to negotiate with an enemy firmly established on Persian soil.[53]

Moshaver ul Mamalek, the Persian envoy who had been dispatched to Moscow following the Enzeli affair, certainly believed that, should Persia refuse to sign a treaty with the Bolsheviks, it would 'be attacked from all sides, Gilan, Azerbaijan and Khorassan. The English will not make any resistance...'[54] By signing the treaty, the Persian government hoped to convince the Russians to remove their troops from northern Persia.[55]

Indeed, it would seem that many in the Persian government remained suspicious of the Bolshevik regime. The Persian consul general in Georgia believed that 'All their promises are false, and they are only trying to deceive us',[56] while Norman noted that Zia'eddin 'fears Russia, and his nervousness regarding her policy appears to increase as Soviet Minister draws nearer to Tehran'.[57] Hussein Ala, the Persian minister in Washington told the US State Department that the signing of the treaty 'does not mean that our country wishes to come under Moscow's influence or accept Bolshevik doctrines. We were obliged to reach a modus vivendi with a powerful neighbour because of territorial closeness.'[58]

Whatever the reasons that motivated the Persian government the reaction of the British government to the Soviet-Persian Treaty, particularly the Foreign Office, was somewhat surprising. In contrast to the virulent anti-Bolshevik rhetoric that Curzon had used in 1918–1919 to justify his Anglo-Persian Agreement, the Foreign Office response to this turn of affairs was muted. When the treaty was published in the *Manchester Guardian* in March 1921, Oliphant simply described the document as 'absurd'. As he pointed out (somewhat amusedly), if Article I of the agreement (which renounced all prior treaties between Russia and Persia) was to be taken literally, it would mean the surrender to Persia of practically all of the Caucasus.[59] In the opinion of George Churchill, the treaty was 'probably meant by the Soviet Government as a piece of propaganda...and they probably know that it will never be much more than a piece of paper...British interests are not directly affected by the treaty.'[60] Such calm acceptance of what one would have thought was a huge blow to Britain's position in Persia is perhaps indicative of the level of indifference the Foreign Office seemed to have towards that country by 1921. It also inevitably leads to a questioning of Curzon's motives in 1918–1919, when he had seemed so fiercely against allowing a Soviet presence within Persia. Had the foreign secretary simply been using the spectre of Bolshevism as a convenient excuse to justify extending Britain's influence within Persia? For it seems that once the possibility of British hegemony over Persia had been thwarted, Curzon was nonchalant about the threat of Bolshevism to Persia.

Or, perhaps, it was simply a case of sour grapes. Indeed, when in April 1921 the Bolshevik-inspired rebels in Gilan unexpectedly opened fire on the Cossack Division, the British Foreign Office seemed almost smug in its reaction. While the Soviet government denied it had any involvement in the events in north Persia,[61] Oliphant noted that 'the Russians are coming out in their true colours and the Persians will rue the day of their famous treaty'.[62] When, in May, Norman suggested that Britain use the Anglo-Soviet Trade Agreement to bring pressure to bear on the Bolsheviks regarding Persia, the Foreign Office declined.[63] The cynicism of that department towards the Persian government seemed to have now developed into something near malevolence. Having refused Britain's help, Persia was to be left to face the Bolsheviks on its own, while the Foreign

Office looked on. In his speech to the House of Lords in July 1921, Curzon characterised the Persian government as being now willing 'to accept the caresses of the Soviet Government'. 'Caresses', he noted wryly, 'which usually end up by strangling those to whom they are applied.'[64] In the same month Robert Lindsay in the Foreign Office noted that: 'The Bolsheviks are pursuing towards Persia their usual policy pursued towards Bokhara, Georgia, and Great Britain. They make a treaty, then set up some other Power – Azerbaijan, Soviet Armenia, or the Third International over whom they profess to have no control, to tear it up.'[65]

However, perhaps the Persian government was not in such a predicament as the Foreign Office believed. In late November 1921, Moscow addressed two letters to the Persian government, complaining that the Soviet–Persian Treaty had still not been ratified by the Medjliss.[66] The reply from Persia was that the delay was due to 'difficulties in certain clauses'.[67] As Reginald Bridgeman of the British Legation in Tehran noted in his telegram to the Foreign Office, 'it looks as if fate of Anglo-Persian agreement may overtake Russo-Persian [one]'.[68] Perhaps, then, it was the Persian government which had played Soviet Russia off against Britain, and was now having the last laugh.

Quid Pro Quo

One place in which the combined forces of Bolshevism, Islamism and nationalism can be clearly seen in 1921 is Afghanistan. In this year India was to conclude an official treaty with its neighbour, a project made particularly difficult as the Indian government found itself negotiating with both Kabul and London at the same time, as well as trying to outmanoeuvre Moscow as it looked to secure its own treaty with the emir. Indeed, it is through examining the Afghan debates of 1921 that some of the fundamental differences between London and Delhi can be seen. In essence, the divergence lay in what each government believed to be the best way of securing the future of the empire. For the Indian government, having a friendly and stable ally in Kabul was essential for two main reasons. First, the viceroy and his council were adamant throughout this period that a treaty of friendship with Afghanistan would be important to the stability of India, not only in that it would help quell the tribal unrest on its borders, but because it would remove some of the impetus of the pan-Islamic movement. Secondly, it was believed that by such a treaty, Britain would be able to counter any Soviet presence within Afghanistan and prevent its neighbour from becoming a conduit for the dissemination of Bolshevik propaganda and agents into India. Crucially, the Indian government believed these points to be intertwined and therefore of equal importance – so that the welfare of India was as reliant on having Afghanistan as a friendly Muslim neighbour as it was of having an Afghanistan free from Bolshevik dominance.

One such example of the critical role that country played in India's security is when M.N. Roy suggested a plan to Moscow in 1920 to march a Russian 'army of liberation' into India through Afghan territory. This audacious scheme was defeated, however, when the emir made it quite clear that he would not allow Russian troops to enter his country.[69] The ability of Afghanistan to be friend or foe was, therefore, something of which the Indian government was keenly aware, and in order to make friends, it was willing to acquiesce in whatever diplomatic games Kabul wanted to play.

For the Home government, however, uppermost in its concerns was that Britain should not appear to lose prestige in its dealings with Afghanistan. That a friendly Afghanistan was important to India was acknowledged in London, but did not appear to be as crucial a factor as it did in Delhi. The Home government was unwilling to pay the price of what it deemed was Britain's imperial dignity in order to gain the friendship of the Afghan emir. Indeed, it seems that, in 1921, the Home government looked upon its Afghan relations as something of a test-case for the strength of Britain's diplomatic influence in south Asia in general. This is particularly apparent when it came to the problem of Afghanistan's relationship with Soviet Russia. While, for the Indian government, the problems of pan-Islamism and Asian nationalism were just as (if not more) important than that of Bolshevism, for the Home government, combating Bolshevik influence within Afghanistan was paramount. In this way, Afghanistan was viewed as a diplomatic battleground by London; a show-down of the political strength of Soviet Russia versus that of the British Empire.

All of which helps to explain some of the discussion that took place between London and Delhi over the issue of an Afghan treaty of friendship. As may be recalled, the talks conducted between the Afghan and British representatives in Mussoorie in 1920 had been largely seen as a preliminary to the negotiation of an official treaty of friendship between the two nations. As such it was suggested by Amanullah at the end of 1920 that a British delegation travel to Kabul to resume talks. However, if the Home government had been sceptical about the Mussoorie conference, it disapproved entirely of this proposal. For London was aware that, in October 1920, an Afghan representative, Muhammad Wali Khan, had been despatched to Moscow to negotiate an agreement with the Soviet government.[70] In the eyes of some British officials, signing an agreement with Russia, while negotiating another with India, appeared too much like the traditional Afghan technique of playing one of its neighbouring countries off against the other (a definite legacy of the Great Game). To Whitehall, a mission sent to Kabul would risk being exposed 'to humiliation and misrepresentation'. Nevertheless, in the end the Home government was unwilling to overrule the Indian government and authorised the Kabul mission, should the viceroy insist on it.[71] (Although Chelmsford was somewhat hurt that his policy had 'not secured the whole-hearted support of His Majesty's Government').[72]

Afghan duplicity aside, one of the main concerns for Britain, when it came to a Soviet-Afghan treaty, was what practical gains the Soviet government could make from such an agreement. As Montagu noted, the Bolsheviks were not 'going to agree to pay the Afghans money from mere love of Afghanistan'.[73] The biggest worry for Britain was to be Article V of the treaty, which allowed Soviet Russia to open consulates close to the Indian frontier, including at Kandahar, for example.[74] It was undoubted that such establishments would become centres of Bolshevik intrigue directed south, towards India, and both Delhi and London agreed that these consulates should not be allowed to open.[75] For the Home government, the consulates were also an important sign of friendship developing between Soviet Russia and Afghanistan. For many British government figures imbued with Great Game thinking, it was simply inconceivable that Afghanistan could maintain equally friendly relations with both Russia and India. History dictated that one or other nation had to be dominant in Afghanistan; London's biggest fear was finding itself in the subordinate role.

It was this worry that led the Home government to demand, as a prerequisite to negotiating a treaty with Britain, that the Afghan government make a full disclosure of any agreement it had with Soviet Russia. Rather than wanting to know the details of what was contained within the document, the Home government saw this as a matter of principle.[76] As Montagu explained to Chelmsford, compliance with this demand was to be viewed as evidence of Afghan good faith towards Britain.[77]

The problem, however, lay with the idea that the British government was in a position to make such a demand of the Afghan government in the first place. While there were certainly advantages for Kabul in gaining a treaty of friendship with Britain, Afghanistan was by no means in a position of desperation. Not only did it now have Soviet Russia as an ally and potential source of funds and military supplies, but it was also busy making friends with the likes of Turkey and Persia; a Turko-Afghan treaty being concluded on 1 March 1921, followed in June by an agreement with Tehran.[78] Afghanistan also had less to fear from India following the First World War. The Afghan government could be relatively certain that the current weakness of its military meant the Indian government would only use force against its neighbour if extremely provoked. The ability to incite the tribes on India's borders to unrest against the Indian government was also a crucial advantage to Afghanistan. And, as the Afghan delegation pointed out to Dobbs, it was also aware that 'almost the whole world [is] hostile to Great Britain. All Musalmans are against you over the Khilafat question. You are in trouble in India.'[79]

Thus, Afghanistan could have confidence when it was negotiating with India in 1921:

All the Islamic world looks to us and considers us the leaders of Islam. We shall be taking a great burden on ourselves if we make friendship with you, and must have a substantial quid pro quo which will satisfy our people. You are in great need of our friendship, for if you make friends with us, India will turn towards you.[80]

Naturally, Dobbs tried to disabuse the Afghans of this belief by arguing that 'Afghanistan needs British friendship far more than Great Britain needs hers. You are a small country between two big Powers. You have to be very careful.'[81] Such public bravado between the two delegations was inevitable. In reality, Afghanistan and India probably had an equal need for the friendship of each other – a fact that the Home government failed to recognise but of which the Indian government was well aware. In the opinion of Delhi, Britain was faced with two choices (other than another Afghan war): to accept working alongside the Bolsheviks within Afghanistan, or to remain entirely detached from that country. As Chelmsford put it: 'The exclusive domination of Afghanistan, which we should doubtless much prefer, has been rendered impossible by development of events unless we go to war.'[82] It was the first course that the Indian government would much prefer, and as such would push for in 1921. As for Afghan duplicity, Chelmsford explained in March 1921 that 'as much as we may object to Amir's trying to get the utmost out of both sides without committing himself against either, it is not in our power to object effectively'.[83] This was the reality of the situation in Delhi's eyes and, as such, in its opinion, Britain could not afford to be sensitive or overly demanding when it came to its negotiations with Afghanistan.

Unfortunately for the Government of India, the Home government did not agree. Indeed, there were some in London who could still not accept that it was not within Britain's power to hold sway over Afghanistan's foreign relations. In February 1921, in response to a draft treaty Chelmsford proposed to offer the emir, Montagu suggested that the viceroy:

> should consider the possibility of adding some provision such as that it will be open to [the] Government of India to offer [the] Afghan Government, and for the Afghan Government to ask of the Government of India, advice in a friendly way in regard to foreign relations of Afghanistan.[84]

This, despite the persistent argument from the Indian government that it had absolutely no chance of gaining any such concession from Afghanistan. In spite of the viceroy's best efforts, London still either did not understand or refused to accept the changes that had overcome that nation since the Third Anglo-Afghan War. In all of their negotiations, Amanullah and his government were fiercely protective of their new-found independence in foreign relations and highly sensitive to any perceived encroachment upon it. Indeed, part of the reason that the Afghan delegation continually refused to disclose the details of its treaty with

Soviet Russia, as demanded by the Home government, was that this was deemed an affront to their country's independence in conducting its foreign affairs. As Chelmsford tried to explain, 'It is Afghanistan's determination to parade her complete independence and she will not be driven from this attitude by anything short of war.'[85] It is with this in mind that the viceroy argued that failure of the Afghans to disclose the terms of the Soviet–Afghan treaty should not result in a breakdown of Dobbs' negotiations. As he explained further, 'if we now attempt to base our policy on what is not any longer practical politics we shall not secure a Treaty. We shall be playing into the hands of the Bolsheviks, leaving them a free field and a very fruitful field for machinations directed against us.'[86]

Nevertheless, the India Office disagreed and, in March 1921, the matter was brought to the Cabinet. During the discussion 'stress was laid on the extent of the concessions we had offered the Amir, including the raising of the subsidy... and, above all, the surrender of our control over Afghan foreign policy, all of which justified us in insisting on a substantial *quid pro quo*'.[87] (The fact that the Home government saw the end of its control over Afghan foreign affairs as a 'concession' is telling: as if it had given up this privilege out of magnanimity and not necessity.) The decision was taken to instruct Dobbs not to sign any agreement with Afghanistan until the Cabinet had had a chance to consider the terms of the Soviet–Afghan Treaty.[88] For Chelmsford, this was highly irritating. What the viceroy had tried to point out was that the only way Britain could obtain the concessions it was insisting on was through force of arms and, since it was 'on India and Indian resources, financial and militarily, that the brunt would fall' of any such campaign against Afghanistan, the Indian government thus had the right to be listened to.[89] As Chelmsford complained to Montagu, the Indian government should be given more freedom in its dealings with Afghanistan, while those in London should trust those in Delhi to make the right decisions.[90]

Such concerns were soon no longer Chelmsford's, however, as in April 1921 Lord Reading replaced him as viceroy. The relationship between Montagu and Chelmsford had always been slightly strained. The secretary of state believed the viceroy was 'cold, aloof and reserved', describing him once as 'rather sloppy ice'.[91] For his part, Chelmsford often struggled to understand Montagu's erratic and depressive temperament.[92] As he explained to the secretary of state in 1918: 'We are built on different lines; you are full of imagination and impulse, I am prosaic and cautious.'[93] During their correspondence, Montagu would often complain of the misunderstandings and apparent lack of affinity between himself and his viceroy.[94] By 1921, this contrast in temperaments had led to such a deterioration in their relationship that Montagu was relieved to have Reading heading out to India in Chelmsford's place.[95]

Unfortunately for Chelmsford, Montagu was apparently not the only one to be happy at his leaving office. Among the population of India, the viceroy seems to have been generally unpopular.[96] The Indian commentator, Akshaya K. Ghose, for example, delivered a scathing attack upon him at the time of his retirement: 'A weak, tactless and incompetent ruler – for that is the verdict of History – Lord Chelmsford leaves India in April 1921. India will breathe a sigh of relief!'[97] Another (slightly more generous) contemporary believed that 'Chelmsford's lack of ideas of his own, his sound if cautious judgement, his coolness in all circumstances and his respect for orderly administration, contrasted sharply with Montagu's under-disciplined initiatives and constant state of excitement'.[98]

Yet the criticisms made of Chelmsford have often been contradictory. On the one hand, he is portrayed as a lack lustre viceroy – weak and unimaginative and dominated by his council. Some have described Chelmsford as a 'mediocrity', for instance,[99] while others have categorised him as merely an administrator and an agent rather than a policy maker.[100] Reading was also inclined to believe that Chelmsford 'was too disposed to tread conventional lines and was apparently apprehensive of any action for which there was no precedent...'[101] On the other hand, he was also blamed by some for all of the trouble to have beset India in this period, and for the violence and acts of repression that occurred during his tenure as viceroy. Thus, although apparently ruled by his council, it is Chelmsford that takes the fall for all of the Indian government's failures in these years – and is given no credit for its successes.

One has to feel some sympathy for Chelmsford. For it is undoubted that he faced one of the most difficult periods of British rule in India, caught as he was between the Conservatives in London, who opposed too many concessions to the Indian people, and those Liberals and Indian agitators who pushed for greater reform to the rule of the Raj. This is not to mention his having to continually battle with the Home government over Britain's Asian policy at large, while also desperately keeping a lid on Muslim and nationalist agitation and Bolshevik sedition. The post-war period was a time of high tension between those on the different ends of the political spectrum and if Chelmsford was inclined towards caution in his work, perhaps that was the necessary strategy, given his need to placate so many disparate groups. Chelmsford himself was aware of the accusation of weakness that were being made against him:

> I am told that people say that my Council run me. I am indifferent to that accusation...I think you will own that I had only to lift my little finger and I could have obtained dissent from the majority of the proposals to which you and I with certainly the bulk of my colleagues have given agreement.[102]

Some have tended to be more positive towards the viceroy than others, believing that Chelmsford governed astutely by looking for consensus among his colleagues.[103]

Some contemporaries were also generous about the viceroy. One report written in 1921, for example, summed up his tenure thus: 'To few Governor-Generals has it been given to accomplish so much towards the enduring welfare of their great charge; to fewer yet has the meed of praise and appreciation been so scantily rendered.'[104]

Nevertheless, whether it was justified or not, Montagu certainly appeared happier to have Reading as his viceroy, always referring to him by his first name, Rufus, in their correspondence (which he had not done with Chelmsford) and continually praising his work in India.[105] For his part, while he may have been more adept at coping with Montagu's particular personality, Reading did not actually differ greatly in his policies from that which had been followed by Chelmsford.[106] Hence, the Afghan negotiations continued along the same path as they had under the ex-viceroy's direction.

In fact, it was in this same month that Reading took office in Delhi that the Indian government heard encouraging news from Kabul. Since the Rawalpindi negotiations in 1919, the Indian delegation had been trying to uncouple Afghanistan from Soviet Russia, constantly intimating to the emir that the Bolshevik regime could not be trusted. In March 1921, Dobbs even presented Amanullah with information gathered by British intelligence demonstrating the duplicity of the Bolsheviks towards Afghanistan.[107] (Likewise, when news had reached Malleson in Meshed that the Afghans had sent letters and presents to the anti-Bolshevik rebels of Ferghana, he made sure to let the Soviet government know.)[108]

These attempts to drive a wedge between the two countries appeared to have finally succeeded when, on 12 April, Dobbs reported that the Afghans wanted to comply with Britain's wishes, but could only risk throwing over the Soviets if they could get reassurance of support against any backlash from Moscow.[109] Two days later, Dobbs repeated a conversation he had had with Amanullah, who had admitted plainly that he had tied himself up with the Bolsheviks because Britain would not make friendship quickly enough and that he was now in a mess.[110] By 20 April, the Afghan government was apparently very doubtful that it could ratify the agreement with Soviet Russia, since the latter was not sincere in its promise of not interfering in Khiva's and Bokhara's internal affairs.[111] For, while Soviet Russia had orchestrated the removal of Khan Abd Allah and Emir Amil, it had always maintained that it had merely been helping the Khivan and Bokharan people to attain freedom from their autocratic rulers. Thus, article VIII of the Russo-Afghan treaty had recognised 'The actual independence and freedom of Bukhara and Khiva, whatever form of government may be in existence there'. Yet, throughout 1921 the Bolshevik government would gradually gain greater authority over the regimes in the two new Soviet republics, so that by 1923 Bokhara and Khiva had gone from subordinate allies of Soviet Russia to 'thoroughly controlled satellites'.[112] Unfortunately for Amanullah the phrasing of article VIII did not afford him much recourse to prevent Bolshevik actions in Central Asia. By April 1921 then, Mahmud Tarzi, the Afghan foreign minister, was asking outright whether Britain would support Afghanistan should a rupture with Russia take place.[113]

The Home government immediately seized on this chance. On 22 April, Dobbs was instructed by Montagu to inform the emir that if he repudiated the treaty signed with Russia, and agreed to consult Britain before embarking on any more foreign agreements, Britain would give him the arms, money and assistance asked for. As the secretary of state explained to Reading:

> By such means as these we get our treaty of friendship, in the East we appear as the protector of an independent Moslem State against aggression and...we once again by the act of the Amir get a position of influence, if not of authority, over Afghan foreign relations.

Furthermore, Montagu noted, Curzon was also 'in full agreement with this view'.[114] By the end of April, Montagu reiterated his consent 'to *any* offer of money and arms, and assurance of support, which the Government of India would be prepared to give to secure [a] complete break with [the] Bolsheviks'.[115]

The new viceroy, however, was sceptical, believing Dobbs was 'unduly optimistic over [the] Afghans' willingness to throw over [the] Russian treaty'.[116] In a long telegram to Montagu, summarising the entire Afghan situation from his point of view, Reading explained the impossibility of completely purging Afghanistan of Bolshevik influence.[117] Even if Amanullah was to overthrow the Russian treaty, this would not necessarily mean the removal of the Soviet representative at Kabul, which would still allow the Bolsheviks to stir up anti-British feeling among the Afghan public. As he reiterated a few days later:

> I recognise that if we could make a clean sweep of the Bolshevik Treaty and of Bolshevik influence from Afghanistan, it would be a serious check for the Bolsheviks and a valuable diplomatic triumph...But it is essential to get a clear-cut idea what it is possible for us to buy.[118]

It would appear, then, that the new viceroy was apt to be as cautious when it came to the issue of Afghanistan and Bolshevik sedition as his predecessor had been. Montagu responded:

> In order to achieve the object of getting rid of both the Bolshevik Treaty and the Bolsheviks themselves we would agree to, and indeed urge, your going to the very limit of your financial capacity in this direction. ...we would urge you not to put too low a limit upon the

expenditure necessary for the production of a result so greatly to be desired.[119]

Despite Reading's doubts, the temptation to reinstate Britain's hegemony over Afghanistan was just too much for Montagu and the Home government. On 10 May, a meeting of the Cabinet decided 'that an effort should be made to offer Afghanistan sufficient inducement in money and arms to make her throw over the Bolshevik Treaty entirely'.[120]

Through the summer of 1921, then, Dobbs attempted to pin the Afghan government down to an 'exclusive agreement', as it became known, with offers of a subsidy, airplanes, telegraph equipment and munitions, in the event of Russia making an unprovoked attack upon Afghanistan.[121] However, the Afghan government procrastinated over this commitment, asking for the treaty with Britain to be signed and the munitions delivered before it cancelled the agreement with Russia.[122] In July, with still no exclusive treaty signed, Dobbs suggested that Amanullah could simply be playing a game: drawing out the negotiations until its treaty with Soviet Russia could be ratified and it had received Soviet aid, at which point it would break off with Britain.[123] Reading was a little more gracious towards the Afghan government, believing that the real reason behind its procrastination was its reluctance to face a definite break with Russia.[124] As the viceroy had noted, even if Soviet Russia did not attack Afghanistan militarily, pressure would undoubtedly increase on the emir should he sign an exclusive treaty, as the Bolsheviks would no doubt claim that he had sold out his country to Britain.[125] Whatever the reasons, by the end of July it had become clear that despite Dobbs' efforts 'there is now little hope of [the] Afghans accepting [an] exclusive treaty'.[126]

Reading began, instead, to advocate a *pis aller* ('last resort') agreement – a treaty which would prevent Bolshevik consulates being established near India's frontiers, but would not insist on Kabul making a complete break with Moscow. In return, Britain would still offer the emir munitions and a (albeit reduced) subsidy.[127] However, reluctant to lose the possibility of an exclusive treaty, on 5 August 1921 the Cabinet expressed its disapproval of Reading's suggestion, 'which, it was felt, conceded too much, obtained too little, and, if offered by Sir Henry Dobbs, would be the extreme limit of humiliation for the British Empire'.[128] During the meeting, attention was paid to 'well-informed' articles in the *Manchester Guardian* which indicated that the reluctance of Afghanistan to sign an exclusive treaty with Britain was less to do with fear of the Bolsheviks than with pan-Islamic pressure. In the Cabinet's opinion, therefore, the current Greek successes over Turkey would soon weaken the pan-Islamic movement and make the Afghan government more willing to sign an exclusive treaty.[129] That the Cabinet appeared more prepared to listen to a newspaper than the Indian government when it came to Afghanistan would be surprising were this any other Cabinet.

Nevertheless, when the Afghan government finally decided to ratify the Soviet treaty, in late August 1921, the issue of the exclusive treaty became a moot point.[130] The Home government now became willing to consider a *pis aller* agreement, but reverted back to the original proviso that the Afghans make full disclosure of their relations with Soviet Russia.[131] The disclosure of its dealings with Moscow was still a contentious matter with the Afghan government, however. Quite bluntly, the Afghan foreign secretary, Tarzi, refused Dobbs' demand to see the agreement, telling him instead that he could read its terms in the newspapers.[132] Anglo-Afghan relations appeared to be taking a turn for the worse.

For the Indian government, the inability of the Home government to temper its demands was extremely frustrating. The worst possible scenario in its eyes was for Dobbs to leave Kabul without any form of an agreement. As Reading explained to Montagu: 'If I am insistent it is because of my desire to avoid failure, which would stimulate Mohammedans and other extremists in India, and would necessitate continued heavy military expenditure, with all its opportunities for creating [a] troublesome position with [the] Legislature.'[133] Furthermore, for the Indian government, the pan-Islamic and nationalistic sentiment that was amassing in South Asia and being directed against the British empire was another crucial reason for fixing its relations with Afghanistan:

> We are supposed by Moslem India to be bent upon crushing Turkey...
> We are supposed to have turned against Persia after failing to impose
> our domination upon her... This being so, failure to make [a] treaty of
> friendship with Afghanistan would be regarded by Moslem India as
> further proof of a fixed policy of antagonism to independent Moslem
> nations.[134]

Desperate to try to convince London of the need to find a resolution to the situation, the viceroy even enlisted the help of his key officials, including the chief commissioner of the North West Frontier Province, Sir John Maffey, who entirely agreed with Reading's justifications for wanting a treaty of friendship with Afghanistan.[135] Montagu had no hesitation, however, in dismissing the Indian government's protests, arguing that he was simply unconvinced that a breach with Afghanistan would have such a negative impact on India, or that a *pis aller* treaty would have such positive effects.[136] When the Cabinet met again, on 3 November, to discuss the issue, it concurred with Montagu's judgement: no *pis aller* agreement was to be negotiated without disclosure of the Soviet-Afghan treaty.[137]

But why were Montagu and the Cabinet determined to follow a course of action so contrary to the advice of Delhi? When it came to the Soviet-Afghan treaty, for example, the Home government was actually well aware of its terms, not only from its own intelligence sources but from having been furnished with a copy by the Bolshevik diplomat, Leonid Krasin, during his stay in London to negotiate the trade agreement. This, then, was not about the practicalities of knowing if the treaty contained terms problematic to Britain. Rather, the Home government had decided to make the agreement a point of principle, an issue over which it quite simply refused to back down. In essence, these protracted debates between London and Delhi are a clear demonstration of what has been noted above – namely that each government placed a different value on Britain's relations with Afghanistan in this period. While, for the Indian government, stability within India and on its frontiers was paramount, for the Home government the issue with Afghanistan was clearly one of prestige. Indeed, Afghanistan appeared almost to be a testing ground for London to see whether Britain could still retain an authority in South Asia. Prestige was the currency of the British Empire – if Kabul could not be brought to heel, this could prove a bad omen to Britain's imperial future. As Reading noted quite aptly, in a letter to Montagu in August 1921: 'I wish...I had been better able to understand from the telegrams what was in the Cabinet's mind... The adjective "humiliating" I suppose gives the key.'[138]

Indeed, for the Home government, Afghanistan appeared to represent the last area in South Asia where it had a chance to remain a dominant force. In Persia, Britain's attempts to attain hegemony had failed; in India its rule was being daily challenged by the likes of Gandhi and others; even in Turkey, although the military situation in the ongoing Greco–Turkish War had recently swung in Greece's favour, the signing of a treaty between Moscow and the nationalist regime at Ankara was a further reminder of Britain's waning influence in this area of the world.[139] Worse still, it would seem that everywhere British officials looked not only was its own position faltering, but Soviet Russia was actually on the ascendancy.

So confident did Moscow appear by 1921 that it was flagrantly ignoring the terms of the trade agreement with Britain, much to the chagrin of men such as Curzon.[140] All was compounded by the embarrassing fallout following the despatch of the note of protest to the Soviet government in September 1921 over its agreement violation. When the Soviet reply came back, it unsurprisingly contained a denial of all that the British government had accused it.[141] Unfortunately for Curzon, it turned out that much of the evidence on which the note of protest had been based was actually rather shaky and that which was reliable was too sensitive to be made public.[142] The foreign secretary was said to be 'appalled' at the situation in which he had now been placed. Not only had his objections to the Soviet trade agreement been overruled in the first place, but now he faced 'the odium of having made public charges which I cannot sustain'.[143]

It could be postulated, then, that one reason the Home government was so stubborn over the Afghan negotiations was because, when faced with failure and humiliation elsewhere, it could not cope with the same results in Afghanistan. Much like with Persia, when the Afghans appeared to be rejecting the British proffer of friendship in the form of the exclusive treaty, London became intractable. This time, however, it was not simply Curzon proving difficult. Montagu was adamant that more could be extracted from Kabul than the Indian government would gain with the *pis aller* treaty. That the secretary of state was being influenced by the foreign secretary is clear from the statement noted above regarding Curzon's agreement with his course of action. Montagu had taken Curzon's side against Chelmsford when it came to the Persian agreement of 1919 – now he appeared to be doing the same over Afghanistan. And yet, considering his mistakes in Persia, it is surprising that the foreign secretary still appeared to command such authority over his colleagues. The *Times* newspaper certainly recognised the seeming contradiction here, criticising Curzon for his involvement in Afghan affairs:

> The Anglo–Persian Agreement fiasco should convince the British Cabinet, despite the influence of Lord Curzon, whose great knowledge of the East is out of date and tends to confirm his pro–consular attitude – an attitude unjustified now, when modern notions of self-determination have spread even to the pastoral ruggedness of Afghanistan.[144]

Why the head of the India Office did not recognise what the *Times* and the Indian government did, is perplexing.

Indeed, the *Times* was not the only one to question Curzon's apparent expertise in South Asian affairs. At the end of 1920, the decision had been taken by Cabinet to create a new Middle Eastern Department and to place it within the Colonial Office, rather than the Foreign Office.[145] Unsurprisingly, Curzon took this as a personal affront, and commenced on a battle of wills with the secretary of state for colonial affairs, Winston Churchill. Difficulties arose almost immediately over the exact remit of the new department, with Curzon complaining in a letter to his wife in February 1921 that he had spent the day arguing with Churchill in Cabinet over the Middle East: 'He wants to grab everything into his new Dept, and to be a sort of Asiatic Foreign Secretary. I absolutely declined to agree with this...'[146] Two days later, Churchill informed his own wife: 'Curzon will give me lots of trouble and have to be half flattered and half overborne. We overlap horribly. I do not think he is much good.'[147]

For the foreign secretary, matters became worse when Churchill began to insist on making speeches within and outside of Cabinet on issues relating to foreign affairs. As Curzon complained to Lloyd George, in June 1921: 'I have for some time been a good deal disturbed at Winston's unauthorised and sometimes not too helpful incursions into Foreign affairs which do not render my task or position any the more easy...'[148] While the prime minister agreed with Curzon 'that it is most improper and dangerous for any Minister [other than the foreign secretary] to make a pronouncement upon questions of foreign policy', there was little he could do to temper Churchill.[149] When Curzon complained directly to the colonial secretary,[150] he simply received the dismissive reply that Churchill always spoke 'with very great care on these matters'.[151] Curzon, however, was not prepared to let the issue rest, countering that he could not 'admit that the Minister of a Dept other than that of Foreign Affairs has any right without consultation with the FO to make speeches on Foreign Affairs, merely because he holds strong views upon them...'[152]

Such protests appeared to fall on deaf ears, however, since in November 1921, Curzon had cause yet again to complain of Churchill's behaviour: 'I find it very difficult to conduct foreign affairs at all under the conditions which are constantly created, not infrequently by yourself at Cabinet meetings.'[153] Such problems with Churchill compounded what was already a trying time for Curzon. The foreign secretary's speech to the House of Lords in July, in which he had confessed experiencing a feeling of 'disappointment, almost of despair' at the situation in Persia, certainly had an element of truth to it.[154] Given his self-promotion as an expert on Persia, the failure of the Anglo–Persian Agreement represented both a professional and personal blow.

By the end of 1921, then, Curzon's ego was feeling quite bruised. This may go some way to explaining the foreign secretary's sensitivity towards Churchill's actions that year, as well as the apparent mood of sulkiness towards all things Persia and his stubbornness when it came to Afghanistan. Nevertheless, Curzon rarely accepted fault for anything, but instead complained that 'the responsibility for all the catastrophes that impend in Persia is that of the War Office to begin with, the India Office in the second place, and the Cabinet in the third'. In a letter to his replacement in Tehran, however, Norman put forth a very different account of Curzon's actions in 1921. He reminded his successor how lucky he was:

> You have not been called upon to push through an impossible and insane policy, been loaded with the most virulent abuse because you could not do it, and been thwarted at every turn when you tried to save your official chief from the consequences of his own vanity and folly.[155]

The Year of the Treaty

This chapter started with questions surrounding the notion of change in Britain's foreign policy in 1921. Was this year a turning point for Britain? In the year of the treaty, did these numerous documents produced between Britain, Soviet Russia, Afghanistan and Persia actually change the dynamic within South Asia? In practical terms, yes. The signing of a treaty between Moscow and Tehran, for instance, meant that from 1921 onwards, a Bolshevik envoy would now receive full recognition from the Persian government – no longer were Lenin and his comrades international pariahs. The Anglo–Soviet Trade Agreement may not have been a watershed in relations between those two countries, but it did mark a begrudging acceptance by the British government that it could not continue to ignore the Soviet government.

In Afghanistan too, things were to change to an extent. Despite the unreasonable demands of the Home government, Dobbs was finally able to negotiate an agreement with the emir in November 1921 – one that even resolved the thorny issue of Soviet consulates.[156] Now that Afghanistan was an independent country in all its external affairs, it also insisted that following this treaty all its future relations with Britain were to be conducted through the Foreign Office in London, just as any other sovereign nation, as opposed to through Delhi. This meant that, at least superficially, from 1921 the Foreign Office was now to have control over Britain's Afghan policy. While care was taken by Montagu to set up a system whereby the India Office still retained a final (albeit surreptitious) say over Afghan affairs, it was inevitable that after 1921 the Indian government would lose some of the little freedom of action it had had in Afghanistan.[157]

Psychologically, however, there were many British officials who struggled to cope with these developments. Curzon, for example, resented the position Britain was now in with Persia, but found himself powerless to do anything about it. Rather than admit his mistakes and adjust his policies accordingly, Curzon expressed his frustration with bitter remonstration against those he felt had personally affronted him – the Persian government. When it came to Afghanistan, Montagu could not come to terms with the idea that Britain was no longer able to control that country's foreign relations. By insisting on unattainable concessions from Kabul, the secretary of state made the Indian government's work during the peace negotiations that much harder.

The trouble was that despite all the changes occurring in South Asia, London was still viewing the world with Great Game vision, and formulating policy based on a time when a perceived affront to the empire's prestige could be met with implacable hostility. While the Home government remained worried about imperial appearances, however, the Indian government appeared altogether more practical. In the opinion of Delhi, Britain could no longer afford to be so uncompromising as London advocated. Instead, British officials needed to swallow their pride and accept the little offences caused by the Persians and Afghans, for the sake of attaining stable relations with those two nations. By 1921, Britain could no longer rely on the threat of its military prowess to gain what it wanted in South Asia. London appeared to forget that Britain had won (and lost) its control over Afghanistan's foreign affairs following a military campaign. That it expected the Afghan government to relinquish its independence in external relations in 1921 without such a military threat was an unrealistic hope on the Home government's part. As Reading put it to Montagu, although there might be disappointment in the policies followed by the Indian government the 'pressure of facts seems inexorable'.[158]

Compounding the discomfort of those struggling to accept Britain's reduced standing was the constant reminder that, in contrast, Soviet Russia appeared to be going from strength to strength in South Asia. London's authority was receding in the face of Moscow's. The retreat from Enzeli in 1920, in the face of the Red naval invasion, demonstrated the apparent impotence of the British military compared to Soviet Russia; the creation of treaties between Moscow and Tehran and Kabul in 1921 heralded a decline in British imperial clout, when its own diplomatic efforts towards these two nations proved unsatisfactory. For, as much as the Foreign Office might have appeared nonchalant, it is hard to deny the political blow the Soviet–Persian Agreement represented to Britain, particularly when one compares the optimism of the Foreign Office in 1918–1919 regarding Persia, to its negativity in 1921.

Hence why, when it came to the Soviet–Afghan Treaty, London became almost obsessed with the need to use this as a test case to see how British persuasion fared against Russian proffers of friendship. It was Russian intrigue that, in the opinion of Whitehall, was ousting British influence from Persia and Afghanistan in 1921. In typical Great Game thinking, Russia was the one power which could cause humiliation for the British Empire, and hence was the true enemy; pan-Islamism and Asian nationalism were simply irritants. The Indian government instead tended to believe that it was the practical problem of having a pan-Islamic-nationalist-Bolshevik syndicate of mass popular discontent in South Asia that was the real threat to Britain's imperial position. Therefore, it was not so concerned with becoming entangled in shows of diplomatic strength with Russia.

The trouble for Curzon, Montagu and others in London, was that despite their desire to see their empire win out against the Bolshevik regime, times had changed since the Great Game. Whether they chose to recognise it or not, Persia and Afghanistan were no longer to be subservient to the empire. If Britain wanted to retain its authority in the region, it needed to change tactics from the pre-war period. The battle for influence in South Asia was now to be one of subtlety and persuasion – 'soft' power, as it were – rather than of imperial bluster and condescension. The power-play that had characterised Anglo-Russian rivalry during the Great Game was no longer applicable. The events of 1920 had demonstrated this. The Indian government had been perpetually trying to persuade the Home government of just this fact. When would London finally pay heed remains to be seen.

Chapter Five

A Gigantic Drum, 1922–1923

As the year 1922 dawned, Britain's position in southern Asia was a far cry from what Curzon had envisioned in 1918. Between 1919 and 1922 things had appeared to go from bad to worse for the foreign secretary. In Persia the 1919 agreement had proved a highly embarrassing failure, matched only by apparent British impotence in preventing the Bolshevik regime establishing its influence in the country. When it came to Afghanistan, Britain had also been unable to exert its authority to retain hold of Kabul's foreign relations or negotiate an exclusive treaty at the expense of Russia. The Anglo–Soviet Trade Agreement had been completed in spite of Curzon's objections, and his attempt to bring Moscow to task over its violations of the agreement had left him red in the face. Even Britain's policy towards Turkey had proved a mistake, contributing as it did to the impetus of the nationalist movement there. When Persia, Turkey and Afghanistan decided in 1921 to sign diplomatic agreements with Soviet Russia, it seemed that all of Curzon's worse fears had come true – Britain's patronage had been rejected for the friendship of the revolutionary upstarts now governing Russia. As Britain slunk away from its 1918 position of optimism, Curzon meanwhile reacted by throwing tantrums at the Persians, the Russians, the Indian government, Winston Churchill and anyone else who happened to cross him.

And yet, as this chapter will show, there were actually many reasons for London and Delhi to remain cheerful. While things may not have developed exactly as Curzon had planned, neither had they turned out as bad as the foreign secretary had predicted. For one thing, despite all his anti-Bolshevik rhetoric, the exposure of Afghanistan and Persia to Bolshevism proved far from fatal for the native governments. For although Whitehall had made its fair share of mistakes in its handling of Asian nationalism and Muslim discontent, the Soviet government had been committing its own blunders along the way. It has already been noted, for example, how the Baku Congress was not as successful a meeting of Muslim and Bolshevik minds as Moscow would have liked it to be.[1] The signing of the trade agreement between Russia and Britain in 1921 had also proved a blow to the morale of Asian revolutionaries who had hitherto looked with expectation to the Soviet government for support in their anti-imperialist crusade. By agreeing to the clauses regarding dissemination of propaganda, it appeared to some that the Bolsheviks had sacrificed revolution in southern Asia for the sake of trade with Britain. As two

Asian agitators lamented, the conclusion of the agreement had 'dealt a fatal blow at [sic] our work'.[2]

Furthermore, when it came to the treaties Soviet Russia had made with the various Asian nations, there was actually little significant gain to the Bolshevik cause. In fact, rather than being a sign of the Soviet government's increasing stature, the agreements of 1921 instead indicated 'the failure of Soviet propaganda to make any appreciable headway among the Muslims outside Soviet territory'.[3] The early Bolshevik hopes of being able to dispense with traditional diplomacy had proved wishful thinking, as year-on-year the world revolution failed to materialise. By 1921 the practicalities of international relations had forced the Soviet government to pay more attention to the matter of ambassadors, formal treaties and trade agreements; in the words of one writer, 'diplomacy was foisted upon a revolutionary regime'.[4] So began Bolshevik 'dual foreign policy' – the conducting of formal diplomatic relations with a country while using the Comintern to incite revolution among the people of that same nation.

However, while the Bolsheviks may have been more organised in their foreign affairs after 1921, they still faced two fundamental difficulties when it came to this dual policy in Asia: first was the incompatability of Communism and Islam. The second was the difficulty in getting Asian governments to play ball. Asian rulers appeared much more fair-weather in their diplomatic commitments. As the previous chapter has shown, the Bolshevik regime had quickly realised that having the Persian government sign an agreement and having the Medjliss ratify it were two different things. Even though they may have created treaties with Russia, Tehran, Kabul and Ankara had carefully 'avoided committing themselves to the principles of the Soviet social order'. They felt no qualms about breaching the terms of their agreements when desired.[5] These Asian nations had spent decades negotiating between their two powerful imperial neighbours, and were thus astute Great Game players. By 1922 and 1923, the survival instincts of the rulers of Persia and Afghanistan had become even more potent given their need to appease growing nationalist and pan-Islamic feeling among their people. Indeed, in a somewhat ironic twist, it was ultimately the intensification of these movements in the post-war years that actually helped prevent Bolshevism from taking hold in this region.[6] Rulers who had fought to remove a British imperial stranglehold on their country were not about to simply replace that with Soviet dominance. Reza Khan, Amanullah, Gandhi and Kemal Ataturk may not have been particular friends of Britain, but neither were they prepared to become bed-fellows of Lenin.

Excellent Medicine

While Russia was being frustrated in its Communist plan for southern Asia, by 1922–1923 Britain appeared to be developing some breathing space from the rampant nationalism and pan-Islamism that had taken hold of the region in the post-war period. In Persia, for example, affairs were starting to stabilise for Britain, due, in no small part, to a change in Whitehall's policy towards that country; a shift from the more forward policy of Curzon to something more akin to the Indian government's point of view. Marking this new phase in Britain's relations with Persia was the appointment of Sir Percy Loraine as ambassador to Tehran in January 1922. Unfortunately for him, Herman Norman had never been very popular with Curzon. One cannot help but feel sorry for the hapless diplomat, stuck in a rather hopeless position in Tehran and seemingly never able to set a foot right in Curzon's eyes. In contrast, Loraine was to prove very popular with the foreign secretary and would cultivate a reputation 'as a brilliant manager of British interests'.[7] In fact, Curzon had wanted to appoint Loraine as Counsellor under Norman, but he had ended up serving in Poland instead. However, Curzon's high regard for Loraine remained and when Norman relinquished his position the foreign secretary was quick to offer it to Loraine, making him one of the youngest appointees to such a sensitive post.[8] That Loraine was cousin to Lancelot Oliphant, the head of the Eastern Department in the Foreign Office, no doubt helped his position.[9]

Furthermore, although he differed in the policy he believed Britain should be pursuing in Persia, Loraine appeared to be attuned to Curzon's thinking. In August 1922, for example, Loraine wrote to the foreign secretary giving his impression of the entire Persian situation, which he summed up in an allegorical story. In this tale, Britain and Russia are cast as competitive beaus, vying for the position as the paramount love of Persia – a fickle woman happy to play her courtiers off against each other. Loraine characterises 'John Bull's' downfall as insisting on giving 'tiresome lectures and good advice' to 'Miss P.', when all the latter wants 'is that he should pay, and take charge again of the household expenses as well as giving handsome pin-money. Then, so long as some rather nominal appearances are kept up, he can do what he likes with the house'.

Of course, the allegory of 'Miss P.' and 'John Bull' entirely over-simplifies the relationship between Britain and Persia. It also conveniently lays the blame for Britain's current troubles with Persia solely at the door of the latter – for it is 'John Bull' who is trying to do the best for 'Miss P.', while she is simply disloyal and petulant. Yet this idea that Britain was being something of a martyr, suffering as it was for having tried to better things for Persia, appealed to the likes of Curzon. It was easier to believe this than admit that the Persian policy which he and his allies had pursued since 1918 had failed because of a fundamental misjudgement of the Persian situation. Even by 1922 Curzon still refused to recognise that he had made a miscalculation with the Anglo–Persian Agreement. Writing to Loraine in May 1922 Curzon insisted that it had been the Cabinet's decision to withdraw Britain's troops together with the ungratefulness of the Persian people which

Emir Amanullah (February 1919 – June 1926). One of Amanullah's first acts was to declare 'I put the Crown of the Islamic Kingdom of Afghanistan on my head in the name of the internal and external independence and freedom of Afghanistan'.

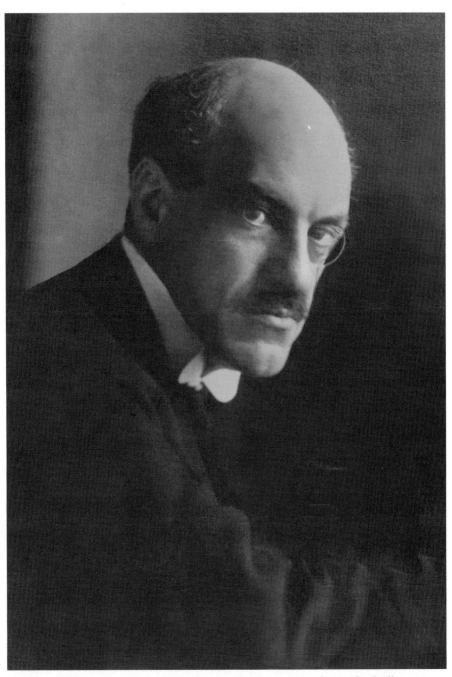

Edwin Montagu – the 'hypersensitive' secretary of state for India
(July 1917 – March 1922)

Lord Chelmsford, viceroy and governor-general of India, April 1916 – April 1921.
'To few Governor-Generals has it been given to accomplish so much towards the
enduring welfare of their great charge; to fewer yet has the meed of praise and
appreciation been so scantily rendered.'

Lord Curzon. As Foreign Secretary (October 1919 – January 1924) Curzon was finally able to enact his plans for British dominance in Persia.

The infamous crawling order enacted after the Amritsar Massacre. Indians were made to crawl on all fours past the spot where a British woman had been attacked in the days leading up to the massacre.

Henry Wilson. As Chief of the Imperial General Staff (CIGS), Wilson clashed frequently with Curzon over his policy in Persia.

Persian Cossack Brigade

Grigory Zinoviev addressing the Baku Congress

Delegates to the Second Congress of the Comintern, including Maxim Gorky,
Vladimir Lenin and Grigory Zinoviev.

Soldiers during the Third Anglo–Afghan War, 1919

Lord Reading, Montagu's much–preferred viceroy and governor-general of India
(April 1921 – April 1926).

had led to the failure of his Persian schemes.[10] As the self-proclaimed expert on Persia, Curzon was, of course, above reproach himself.

Together with being able to get on well with the foreign secretary, Loraine was also very much the right man at the right time. From the outset of his arrival in Tehran the new ambassador was to follow a policy of studied aloofness from Persia's political turmoil. In Loraine's opinion, the Persian people simply had to learn how to govern their nation properly, 'and if you want them to do that it's no use fiddling with them, and their affairs, still less intervening and pretending you don't'.[11] The idea of simply letting the Persians get on with things while Britain took a back-seat had, of course, long been advocated by the Indian government. Indeed, such language by Loraine is reminiscent of views put forward during the Eastern Committee debates on Persia in late 1918. Had Loraine tried to follow such a policy of detachment in 1919, however, no doubt he would have found himself at odds with Curzon. Yet by 1922, the foreign secretary was so disgruntled with the entire Persian situation that Loraine's haughty aloofness was well received in the Foreign Office. In the wake of the debacle which was the Anglo-Persian Agreement and a number of years of failed interference in Persia's internal affairs, it also seemed worth trying a change in tactic. After all, there appeared few other options for Britain by this time.

A further reason that Loraine tended to have London's approval was that, as noted, despite the prophecies of Curzon, Cox and Mallet in 1918, the retreat of Britain's influence in Persia did not portend the fall of that country to Bolshevism. Indeed, if one believed all the anti-Bolshevik rhetoric with which Curzon had surrounded his creation of the Anglo-Persian Agreement, one would be fairly surprised by the lack of progress the Bolshevik regime had made in Persia by 1922. As previously noted, the Soviet-Persian Agreement concluded in 1921 did not hail a particularly close friendship between the two signatories. Indeed, it in no way prevented the Persian government from actions which were in fact a complete violation of the terms of this treaty, including, for example, the seizure of Russian property within that country.[12] In January 1922 Loraine telegrammed home that the Bolsheviks had apparently become thoroughly sick of the Persians and their methods (perhaps also referring to the obfuscating of the latter when it came to having the agreement ratified by the Medjliss).[13] It also seemed that the Bolsheviks were regretting having given up all of Russia's previous privileges within Persia, realising all too late the bargaining value of these concessions when it came to dealing with the Persian government (a lesson from the Great Game they should have taken note of).[14] The new Bolshevik representative in Tehran, Theodore Rothstein, remarked to an American journalist that the Persians:

> ...will take money from everybody. From the British today from the Russians tomorrow or from the French or the Germans or anyone else.

> But they will never do anything for the money. You may buy their country
> from them six times over but you will never get it.[15]

By the end of the year this frustration had led Rothstein to address a letter to the shah complaining about the prime minister and stating that the Soviet legation could not work with a Persian government so hostile as the present one.[16] This letter was to cause a definite cooling in Soviet-Persian relations, much to the happiness of Loraine, who noted with satisfaction that the Russians 'can always be depended on to make gaffes'.[17] Too late did Rothstein realise he had overstepped the mark.[18]

The frustration with the Persian government was more than likely compounded by the little progress that was being made in advancing Communism within Persia. On his arrival in Tehran in April 1921, Rothstein had immediately begun agitating among the Persian population. One of his first acts had been to open the Russian embassy grounds, Atabak Park, to the public, thereby immediately increasing his legation's popularity among the Persian people.[19] Indeed, the appointment of Rothstein to Tehran is perhaps indicative of the seriousness with which the Bolsheviks now viewed relations with Persia. Compared to Bravin, Rothstein was a heavyweight diplomat; he had lived and studied in England and taken part in the labour movement there so he understood well how to deal with his British counterparts in Tehran.[20] He was also close to both Lenin and Trotsky and 'his voice carried weight in the highest quarters of the Soviet hierarchy'.[21] By the time Rothstein had arrived in Tehran, the Second Comintern Congress had also resolved some of the conflicting policies the Bolsheviks had hitherto been pursuing in Persia. All of which meant that, in contrast to Bravin, who had been given no credentials and no funding, Rothstein was well-financed and was able to expand his staff and open consulates in almost all the major cities of Persia.

And yet, in the opinion of the British military attaché in Tehran, Lieutenant-Colonel Saunders, the propaganda that Rothstein had been distributing 'has produced remarkably small results when one takes into consideration the numerous staff employed and large sums expended by him'.[22] Major Bray of the India Office concurred in this judgement, pointing out that 'the Bolsheviks have admitted that their Communist activities in Persia had not...met with great success'.[23] In fact, according to Bolshevik figures, by 1922 there were only 2,000 declared Communists within Persia.[24] As Loraine noted, 'bolshevism [sic] among the Persians themselves is losing its early glamour'.[25] It seemed that, despite his best efforts, Rothstein was faced with that perennial issue of the fundamental incompabatability of Communism and Islam.

It was not just from the Russian side that things were unsatisfactory. In January 1922 Oliphant noted how the Persians appeared disappointed that their agreement had not brought about better relations with the Soviet government.[26]

One person within the Persian government who was finding relations with the Bolsheviks particularly difficult was Reza Khan, minister of war and – since 1921 – arguably the strongest personality within the Persian government.[27] The British government had always held mixed views on Reza Khan. By replacing British control of the Cossack Division with Persian officers, and by involving himself in various governmental intrigues, Reza Khan had gained the suspicions of some British figures. Norman believed that the minister of war was 'an ignorant peasant' and 'not to be trusted',[28] while Armitage-Smith argued that the man was 'entirely in the hands of...Rothstein' who found it easy to manipulate the lower-born, lesser-educated Persian.[29]

Loraine was more positive about Reza Khan, however, believing him to be far more practical than most Persian political figures.[30] Victor Mallet, a legation staffer, was also well disposed towards the Persian minister:

> Our essential interests in Persia demand a stable and strong central government, able to resist Russian penetration and the spread of Communist propaganda, to keep order on the trade routes, in the oil fields district and in the provinces on the Baluchi and Afghan frontiers...It is towards such conditions that Reza Khan appears to be aiming. If in the efforts to obtain his objective, he occasionally falls foul of some minor British interest, it may be that at times it will be worth our while to give way...[31]

It was also quickly apparent that Reza Khan was just as determined to prevent a Bolshevik ascendancy over Persian politics as he was to remove any overt British influence. In a conversation with Loraine, Reza Khan explained his purpose was to do what the British had wanted to do themselves, namely to create a strong army, restore order and create a stable and independent Persia.[32] As one historian explains, 'Loraine backed Reza as a man who could achieve order in Iran and thus further British interests'.[33]

Above all, Reza Khan appeared to be a pragmatist. On a number of occasions he was to insist that he was not pro-Bolshevik as some accused him of being, since Bolshevism was ultimately incompatible with Islam.[34] Indeed, by early 1922 the war minister was complaining of the Communist activities of the Soviet legation in Tehran which he felt were destabilising Persian society.[35] Nonetheless, he was convinced that Persia could not afford to irritate its powerful neighbour, or to give the Bolsheviks any pretext for intensifying their activities. As Loraine explained, the Persians 'evidently suppose that Russia may at any moment recover her power, and, mindful of Persia's former sufferings at the hands of her northern neighbour, they anticipate...a swift vengeance'.[36] It is sometimes easy to forget that the period of the Great Game had left its impression not only on the minds of British officials but on Persians' as well.

A key factor of the Great Game is that Britain and Russia's competitiveness had ultimately prevented Persia from being absorbed by either nation. Indeed, prior to 1907 Persia had always looked upon Britain as its guardian in the face of Russian aggression. In Loraine's opinion, even the Anglo–Persian Agreement of 1919 had actually been viewed by some Persians as British protection of Persia against Russia. The Enzeli landings had quickly changed this.[37] However, even now in 1922, as relations with the Bolshevik regime were floundering, the Persian government looked to Britain for aid. As Loraine put it in a letter to Lindsay, the Persians 'go on hoping that someone will pull their chestnuts out of the fire so that they may take the profits if he succeeds, and he the blame if he don't [sic]. And there...you have the whole basis, theory and practice of Persian politics.'[38]

In order to sever this traditional fear of Russia, Loraine wanted to break the illusion of Moscow's capabilities. In a telegram to the Foreign Office in February 1922 he asked to be furnished with information which he could pass on to the Persian government exposing the Bolshevik government's weaknesses domestically, economically and militarily. Both Gregory and Lindsay, however, saw this as problematic. Many examples could also be found to show Russia's strength and power, while ultimately the whole scheme appeared too close to the promise made in the trade agreement to refrain from anti-Bolshevik propaganda.[39] Curzon agreed, telling Loraine that the Persian government would no doubt hear for themselves about Russia's internal problems.[40]

To some extent it suited Britain to have Persia fearful of Moscow anyway. As long as the Persian government remained apprehensive of the Bolshevik regime, and at odds with its representatives in Tehran, Britain was able to cast itself in the role of benevolent arbitrator. Should Persia realise Russia's bluff, it might give it unwarranted confidence in its own capabilities and further rebuff British proffers of aid. As Curzon wrote on a report by Loraine regarding the friction between the Persian government and the Soviet Legation:

> I consider these political crises inevitable and may prove excellent medicine for Persia until she recovers her senses. We should let them succeed each other with mathematical regularity but without showing slightest concern ourselves. One day Persia will knock again at the door of the British Legation.[41]

Again one gets the sense that the British foreign secretary was revelling somewhat in Persia's current difficulties with the Bolsheviks, seeing it almost as karmic retribution for having snubbed the Anglo–Persian Agreement.

By 1923 then, it would appear that things were on the up for Britain. When it came to Persia, Loraine declared in November that 'Russian shares politically are declining, and ours are undergoing a steady rise'.[42] Loraine's policy of non-interference and Rothstein's difficulties had combined to create a relatively comfortable position for Britain. A report by the Interdepartmental Committee on Eastern Unrest (IDCEU) in June 1923 reiterated the fact that the Bolsheviks were making little ideological headway in Persia.[43] Indeed, such was the growing confidence in London that when some suggested increasing British propaganda in Persia there was little enthusiasm for the idea. The sheer relentlessness of Rothstein's activities had made a few officials nervous enough to advocate a counter campaign. As one observer pointed out, such British propaganda need not be anti-Bolshevik, rather pro-British; defensive, not offensive, and involve the establishment of pro-British newspapers, and the support of local Mullahs to act as pro-British agents.[44] In his memorandum on Soviet propaganda in Persia, Saunders had agreed that to combat Rothstein's work, Britain would need to start subsidising newspapers and even open up its own press bureau. As Saunders pointed out, however, this would cost a considerable amount, and it was questionable whether the results would justify the expenditure.[45] In the opinion of R. Bridgeman, if Britain was to try to strengthen its position in Persia, it should do so through more subtle yet substantial forms of propaganda, such as founding local schools and hospitals. In Bridgeman's words, if money were to be spent, it should 'be spent *on* the Persians rather than *against* the Russians' – a far cry from the Russian-centric policies advocated by the likes of Cox in 1918.[46]

Unsurprisingly, Reading agreed with the idea of trying to cultivate Persian friendship rather than worrying about the Bolsheviks.[47] Indeed, the Indian government had been advocating just such a course of action since the end of the First World War. As it was, it had taken a number of years, a failed agreement, an embarrassing military rout, incompetent Bolshevik officials and the ascendancy of an astute British ambassador for the British government to finally seek a position within Persia which the Indian government had advocated from the outset.

Despite the growing confidence in their position in Persia, what was particularly worrying to British observers were the indications that Russia was growing ever closer to the new nationalist regime in Turkey, using Persia as something of a rendezvous point, and even involving Afghanistan in some of its intrigues.[48] As early as December 1921 Saunders had produced a report detailing the increased activity of the Kemalist party in Persia, and the involvement of the newly appointed Afghan minister to Tehran in these schemes.[49] Again he was supported in his judgement by a report from Major Bray, also showing the links between Rothstein, the Kemalist Pan-Islamic Committee and the Afghan minister.[50] As Loraine informed the Foreign Office, 'Turks, Russians and Afghans lose no opportunity of impregnating the Persians with anti-British feeling.'[51]

In a Cabinet meeting of 30 March 1922 the connection between Turkey and Russia was discussed. Churchill himself 'hoped the Cabinet would realise that our policy in regard to Turkey had resulted in achieving the impossible, namely the marriage of the Bolshevists [sic] and the Turks in spite of the entire conflict of principles between them'.[52] For, just as with Persia, Britain was a crucial factor in bringing Ankara and Moscow closer together. Traditionally, Russia's desire to have a warm water port and access to the Straits had caused conflict with the Ottoman Empire, and initially this tension between the two nations looked set to continue after the Russian Revolution (once Turkey had surrendered to the Allies at Mudros and the Treaty of Brest-Litovsk had thereby become null and void in Bolshevik eyes).[53] In 1920, for instance, nationalist Turkey and Soviet Russia had nearly come to blows over their rivalry for influence in Armenia and Georgia. However, the Treaty of Sèvres had made Kemal Ataturk more open to friendship with Russia (needing, as he did, support against the Allies) and thus led to the signing of the treaty between Ankara and Moscow in March 1921.[54] By its adherence to the Sèvres agreement, then, Britain had not only brought upon itself the animosity of the Muslim world, but had succeeded in creating an 'unnatural alliance between Turks and Russians...contrary to the teaching of history, and...opposed to all racial and religious instincts'.[55] By early 1923 there was further indication that the Soviet government was making efforts to bring about a pan-Islamic bloc 'consisting of Russia, Turkey, Persia, Afghanistan and possibly other Moslem States, the object being to enable Russia to exercise an influence over Moslem Nationalist movements'.[56]

Nevertheless, the agreement between Turkey and Soviet Russia had been a marriage of convenience, and once Kemal had improved his relations with the Allies (see below), then he would not be quite so keen to be in close collaboration with Moscow. That it was unlikely, however, that Turkey, Persia and Afghanistan would acquiesce in Russian interference in Muslim affairs was not as important to the Home government as the fact that the Soviet government was *trying* to bring about such an alliance. When combined with the increase in Bolshevik-sponsored agitation in India in 1922, and a variety of smaller irritations, these intrigues by the Soviet government took on greater meaning.[57] To London, it was becoming more and more apparent that Russia was not taking the terms of the trade agreement seriously. By May 1923, Curzon had reached the end of his patience, and gained Cabinet approval of a draft despatch to the Soviet government, detailing the various ways in which the trade agreement had been violated by the latter.[58] The 'Curzon Note', as it became known, included, among other things, complaint of Soviet subversive activities in Persia, Afghanistan and India. The note concluded with a demand that the acts of propaganda carried out in these countries be 'repudiated and apologised for', and that the officials responsible for them be disowned and recalled. Unless this and the other terms of the agreement were complied with within ten days of receipt of the communication, the trade treaty was to be terminated.[59] One historian has described the note as an example of 'Curzon's diplomatic style at its imperious best'.[60]

The Curzon note of 1923, however, was not dissimilar to that which had been sent to Moscow in 1921, the key difference being that the foreign secretary had learnt his lesson from that debacle and this time made quite certain that the 1923 complaint was based on irrefutable evidence, largely in the form of decrypted telegrams (portions of which Curzon could not resist taunting the Soviet regime with).[61] This time around too, although the Soviet government made some attempts at denying the charges laid by Curzon, it was ultimately conciliatory.[62] As the foreign secretary explained to Cabinet in June 1923, a series of communications had passed between the two governments, the result of which was 'that the Russian Soviet Government had given way on every point...'[63] Curzon believed himself 'to have won a considerable victory'.[64] The Bolsheviks had even moved to replace their representative in Kabul, Fedor Raskolnikov, who had proved so objectionable to Britain. They did refuse to recall B.Z. Shumiatskii, from Tehran, as Curzon had also demanded, but this was not in fact a crucial issue.[65] Indeed, in February 1923 Loraine had noted how Shumiatskii's 'tactless blundering has done more to revive [the] fear and detestation of the Russians than could have been accomplished by any other agency. With him as a political opponent, it's like taking candy from a baby.'[66]

As for Anglo-Soviet relations themselves, Thomas Preston, the British representative in Petrograd, believed that Curzon's note 'has resulted in our reaching a new phase in Anglo-Russian relations'. In Preston's opinion, 'The prestige of Great Britain in Russia has been...restored, and would seem to have reached its highest point since the evacuation of British troops from Russia in 1919.'[67] How far this was actually the case, and how far Preston simply supposed it to be true, is difficult to tell. One thing for sure is that Curzon's feelings towards the Bolshevik regime had not improved, nor were they likely to. The foreign secretary had made this perfectly clear in April 1922 when Loraine had asked whether he should participate in the Bolshevik celebrations of 1 May. It was decided by the Foreign Office staff that the ambassador 'should do the minimum consistent with courtesy'. Curzon reluctantly agreed: 'very well. But I abominate these flirtations with a declared enemy.'[68] For the foreign secretary the Bolsheviks would always be the 'enemy', no matter how many diplomatic agreements Britain signed with them. Yet, despite his best efforts, a Soviet presence in southern Asia was by now an established reality. All Curzon could now do in response was to adjust his expectations for Britain accordingly, and keep a sharp eye on those Bolsheviks.

Russians, Turks, Afghans and Indians

While things might have been settling down for Britain in Persia, 1922 was still an eventful year for officials in London. One of the most important occurrences at this time was the resignation of Edwin Montagu as secretary of state for India, highlighting as it did the broader struggle between London and Delhi over Britain's foreign relations. By 1922, this struggle was focused on the matter of Turkey. Indeed, Turkey was one subject the secretary of state for India and the viceroy could agree on. From the outset, Montagu and Chelmsford (and then Reading) had never missed an opportunity to impress upon the Cabinet the importance to India of having a stable relationship with Turkey. Caliphate agitation had remained steady in India, and the viceroy and secretary of state had no doubt that Britain's dealings with Turkey had been contributing to Muslim dissatisfaction with the empire. In February 1922, Reading made one more plea to London to take into account India's views. With the Conference of London proving unsuccessful in bringing about a resolution on the Turkish issue, there was still conflict between the Kemalist and Greek forces. In early 1922, Curzon was therefore preparing to head to Paris to try to bring about an Allied mediation between these two belligerents.[69] In view of this, the Indian government composed a telegram on 28 February once again explaining the intensity of feeling in India regarding the necessity of revising the Treaty of Sèvres. Reading pointed out that 'as the greatest power in the Mahomedan world, Great Britain must, no less than the other Allies, be sympathetic towards Moslem feeling and ready to take active steps on behalf of Islam'.

Although there was nothing particularly new in this plea from Delhi, the crucial point is that the viceroy asked to be allowed to publish the telegram, presumably to demonstrate to the Indian public his support for the Muslim cause.[70] On 6 March, without consulting the Cabinet, Montagu consented to publication.[71] Bypassing the Cabinet in this way and taking it upon himself to allow the Indian government to speak publicly on this matter was to prove a serious error on the part of the secretary of state. On 9 March when Lloyd George found out about the telegrams he summoned Montagu to his office and asked for his resignation:

> without being urged by any pressing necessity and without consulting the Cabinet, or the Foreign Secretary, or myself, or any of my colleagues, you caused to be published a telegram from the Viceroy raising questions whose importance extends far beyond the frontiers of India...Such action is totally incompatible with the collective responsibility of Cabinet...[72]

In the aftermath of his resignation, Montagu remained defiant, telling Reading 'I do not regret it. I believe I was right.'[73] On 11 March the ex-secretary of state gave a speech to his constituents in Cambridge where he argued that his sacking had been due to his opposition to Lloyd George's pro-Greek policy and to the erosion of Cabinet responsibility which the prime minister had presided over.[74] There was probably some truth to his claims. As Reading pointed out to Lloyd George, there was little if anything in the telegram which he had asked to publish that was new and had not already been approved for publication in previous communications.[75] While Montagu may have made a mistake not consulting the Cabinet, one cannot help feeling that this would not have been enough to have forced his resignation if it had not been for the general level of animosity that appeared to be growing within government and Parliament against him. Instead it is likely that the incident proved to be the straw that broke Lloyd George's back. Montagu's incessant criticism of the Cabinet's Turkish policy was irritating to the prime minister, and despite the fact that both men were members of the Liberal Party, there was no love lost between the two. As Montagu had complained to Reading in September 1921:

> All the time I feel that it is a thousand pities for India that the Prime Minister has not a little more confidence in his Secretary of State, and how bad a thing it is for India that the Secretary of State has so little confidence in the Prime Minister...[76]

It was not just Lloyd George who had a problem with Montagu, however. Unfortunately for him, the Liberal, Jewish, secretary of state had never been popular with the Conservative party. His appearance in front of the House of Commons in July 1920 in which he denounced the action of General Dyer in the Amritsar Massacre had demonstrated just this.[77] Montagu did not appear to be a good debater, nor was he adept at winning people over to his point of view (a skill particularly crucial in a coalition government). As one historian has put it, the secretary of state's 'hypersensitive temperament...was ill-suited to his political role'.[78] His joint authorship of the Indian reforms of 1919 also meant that 'An idea was prevalent that...he was an exponent of an anti-British policy in India'.[79] As trouble developed in India during this period, much of the good-will felt by Britain towards the Indian people following the war began to dissipate. As Montagu explained to Reading in February 1922:

> The fact of the matter is, Rufus, that people here are fed up with India, and it is all I can do to keep my colleagues steady on the accepted policy, let alone new instalments of it. The Indians are so unreasonable, so slow to compromise, so raw in their resentments, and the insults to the Prince of Wales have made fierce feeling in this country.[80]

As well as a growing backlash against the Montagu-Chelmsford reforms, there was also a belief among some that by his constant emphasis of the Caliphate issue, Montagu had lent that movement a level of legitimacy and publicity.[81] Fairly or unfairly, the verdict was in on Montagu's tenure as secretary of state for India.[82]

Unfortunately for him, Montagu's actions after his resignation only served to further his unpopularity. Together with his criticisms of Lloyd George, the ex-secretary of state could not help attacking Curzon for his alleged role in the affair. According to Montagu, Curzon had known about the publication of the viceroy's telegram at a Cabinet meeting the following day, and had said nothing: 'But what did Lord Curzon do? He maintained silence in the Cabinet and contented himself that evening with writing to me one of those plaintive, hectoring, bullying, complaining letters which are so familiar to his colleagues.'[83] On 14 March Curzon used the House of Lords as the stage to defend himself against Montagu who had:

> vilified the colleague whose advice in relation to India, Foreign and Frontier affairs he has not seized [sic – ceased?] both to solicit and to receive in unstinted measure in most weeks of recent years and endeavoured to sift some portion of the responsibility for his lamentable indiscretion on to my shoulders.

Curzon was being truthful when he claimed that Montagu had frequently turned to him for advice regarding India and Afghanistan; Montagu's communications with Chelmsford and Reading often mentioned Curzon's opinion on matters. One contemporary even believed that the foreign secretary 'terrorised' the secretary of state.[84] And yet, despite his apparent irritation with Curzon's constant 'hectoring', Montagu generally seemed ready to listen to the ex-viceroy. As time progressed, he even appeared to value Curzon's judgements more than that of Chelmsford or Reading – his acquiescence to the 1919 Anglo-Persian Agreement despite the protests of the Indian government is one such example. In fact, Montagu was apt to believe the views of numerous other sources both in India and in Britain over that given by the Indian government itself, something Chelmsford found particularly irritating. Indeed, generally speaking the India Office underrated the Indian government.[85] Montagu might lament the fact that the prime minister had no confidence in him, but he in turn appeared to lack confidence in his viceroys. Given the constitutional position and physical distance of the Indian government to the Home government, Delhi needed an ally in London if it was to make sure its views were listened to. Unfortunately, Montagu failed to be that ally.

Curzon's reaction to the publication of Reading's telegram is also very telling and is clear from the letter he wrote to Montagu the following day:

> That I should be asked to go into Conference at Paris while a subordinate branch of the British Government 6,000 miles away dictates to the British Government what line it thinks I ought to pursue in Thrace seems to me quite intolerable...For if the Government of India, because it rules over a large body of Moslems, is entitled to express and publish its views about what we do in Smyrna or Thrace, why not equally in Egypt, the

Soudan, Palestine, Arabia, the Malay Peninsula or any other part of the Moslem world. Is Indian opinion always to be a final court of Moslem appeal[?][86]

Not only does this give an insight into Curzon's thoughts on the Indian government's input on foreign policy but, again, it goes some way to explaining why Delhi was ignored in these post-war years. In the foreign secretary's view Reading's opinion was both unwelcome and inappropriate. And unfortunately for the viceroy it was not only Curzon who thought so. Hardinge too argued that 'If India is to dictate our policy in Europe the F.O. had better shut up shop.'[87] Apparently being ex-viceroys did not equal greater sympathy from Curzon and Hardinge towards the Indian government. It has already been shown how Curzon had himself lamented being ignored by the Home government when he was out in India. How short his memory appeared to be.

The fact that both Curzon and Hardinge used the term 'dictate' is also interesting – the Indian government was actually 'dictating' very little when it came to British foreign policy in the years after 1918. Likewise the remarks by Curzon are indicative of a failing on his part to grasp the importance of the pan-Islamic issue in the post-war period. One contemporary 'likened the Islamic world to a gigantic drum, the reverberations from one end of which could be heard at the other'.[88] The idea that peace with Turkey was a European issue and therefore did not concern the Indian government demonstrates how short-sighted the Foreign Office was. Ultimately the Foreign Office failed to grasp the connections between the various problems facing the British Empire in this period. It refused to see the links between its treatment of Turkey and of Muslim agitation in India, and ignored the Indian government when such warnings were given.[89] The international nature of the Caliphate movement and of nationalist agitation eluded London. The Indian government was more astute in realising the changing world post-First World War. It was just unable to make the Home government understand this.

It was in the same year as Montagu's resignation that Lloyd George would exit from British politics, also as an indirect result of Britain's relations with Turkey. The Chanak Crisis had proved the last straw for those Conservatives who were unhappy with Lloyd George's leadership and on 19 October 1922, after a meeting at the Carlton Club, leading Tories decided that they would run independent of the Liberal party in the next general election.[90] Their vote of no confidence in the prime minister effectively ended both the coalition and Lloyd George's career in government, and in the eyes of some writers, precipitated a new phase in Britain's foreign affairs.[91] The creation of the 'Garden Suburb' and the Prime Minister and the Cabinet Secretariats were seen to represent Lloyd George's prime-ministerial style and, in particular, his contempt for traditional channels of diplomacy. It was certainly true that few tears were shed in the Foreign Office at news of the prime minister's downfall. J.D. Gregory explained to Percy Loraine, 'how much we have suffered under the old system',[92] while Robert Lindsay wrote of his hope that 'the F.O. on the N. side of Downing St.' (i.e. the Garden Suburb) would now be closed.[93]

Nonetheless, while there may have been no love lost between the Foreign Office and Lloyd George, this did not necessarily mean that his removal from office marked a seismic change in Britain's foreign relations. For one thing, Curzon still remained in the Foreign Office. By the 1920s the foreign secretary may have been feeling increasingly impotent, particularly when he saw the ambitious plans he had conceived of in 1918 had failed to come to fruition.

However, Curzon was never one to willing go quietly into the night. His note to the Soviet government in 1923 was one example of the important role he continued to play in British foreign relations in these years. The negotiations with Turkey in Lausanne was another. After the Chanak Crisis a peace had finally been achieved on 11 October 1922 when the Armistice of Mudanya was signed by the Allies and nationalist Turks.[94] The following month a conference opened in Lausanne, Switzerland between the belligerents. Being the main architect of the conference and the chief Allied negotiator, Curzon was afforded an international stage for his diplomatic talents.[95] After many months of wrangling, the Treaty of Lausanne was signed in July 1923, finally bringing to an end the years of conflict between the Allies and Turkey.[96]

One of the most important results of Lausanne for the Muslim population throughout southern Asia was the recognition of the sovereignty of the new Republic of Turkey. The Turks had resisted the Allies and the punishing terms of Sèvres and had emerged successful from their nationalist struggle – 'All over the country [sic – region], the South Asian Muslims celebrated this occasion with great joy.'[97] However, for Muslim onlookers, the victory was to prove bitter-sweet. After the Armistice of Mudanya in 1922, the Kemalist government entered Constantinople and rapidly regained control of the city's administration from the Allies. The republican Grand National Assembly under Kemal Ataturk were now *de facto* rulers of Turkey and thus the sultan, Mehmed VI, quietly left the country. On 1 November the Sultanate was abolished by the assembly, followed a few days later by the election of the ex-sultan's cousin, Abdul Mejid, as Caliph – a democratised Caliphate for the newly democratic Turkish Republic.[98] In one stroke, the new Turkish government had removed centuries of tradition.

It had also undermined the whole foundation of the Caliphate movement which argued that the Caliph was not just a spiritual leader but a temporal one too.[99] From November 1922, any power the Caliph/Sultan once held now rested with the Turkish Assembly. One would have thought that, given how vehemently the Caliphate movement had protested against any hint of interference with the Caliph by the Allies, the Kemal government's actions would have been met with outcry. Instead, on 4 December, Reading reported that most Indian Muslims appeared confused and some distrusted the newspaper reports on the decision.[100] They simply 'could not accept that the Turks, who appeared to be fighting for the elevation of the caliphate, were instrumental in destroying it'.[101] Some even hoped that the Turks were only trying to save the Caliph from the burden of ruling the country so that he would have more time to concentrate on Muslim matters.[102] In December 1922, the Caliphate Committee expressed its acceptance of Turkey's actions and its continued support of the Kemalist government.[103] By February 1923 the viceroy was able to report that the issue of the Caliph had caused little bad feeling against the new Turkish government.[104] This, of course, was all good news to the Indian government. The admittance, however, that the dissolution of the Caliph was actually of little practical consequence brought scoffs from the Foreign Office. Curzon argued that this mistake on India's part now meant that the Foreign Office was justified 'in not attaching the slightest value to any future representation of the Govt. of India in European politics'.[105]

Despite Curzon's mocking, the reaction of Indian Muslims to the actions of the Turkish Assembly is not so surprising when the matter is considered further. For one thing, the fact that the new Kemalist government itself chose to abolish the Sultanate, rather than having it forced upon it by the Allies, is a crucial factor in Muslim reaction. Indeed, the Caliphate movement had never really been about the issue of the Caliph *per se*. The plight of Turkey and the Caliph had instead been seen by Muslims as an embodiment of the erosion of Islamic power by the Christian western nations. The fact that the new Turkish government under Kemal had successfully challenged the Allies and the terms of the Treaty of Sèvres, was a welcome demonstration of Islamic power to Indian Muslims that helped soften the blow of the dissolution of the Sultanate/Caliphate.[106] Indeed, for the average Muslim the complexities of the Caliphate issue was probably more than they could appreciate, but it had been a convenient rallying point for anti–British agitation. The Foreign Office itself had previously argued this when it had been trying to undermine the Indian government's fear of the Caliphate problem.[107] However, as already noted, what London failed to grasp is that regardless of the legitimacy of the form which Muslim agitation took, the result was still the same for the Indian government. As Reading pointed out in January and repeated in February of 1923, while the dissolution of the Caliphate had been reasonably well received in India, the government still had to be careful what it said on the matter, lest it be accused of complicity in the Turkish decision and re-inflamed Muslim opinion.[108] Even after the complete abolition of the Caliphate in 1924, Turkey still received the loyalty of Indian Muslims.[109] Islamic Turkey had more leeway when it came to Muslim issues than did Christian, imperial Britain.

The muted reaction of Indian Muslims to Turkey's actions can also be explained somewhat by the fact that the Caliphate movement was on the wane anyway by this time. In particular, the division between Muslim and Hindu agitators had been growing since 1921. For while the non-co-operation and Caliphate movements had collaborated in protest against the West they had never really merged into an integrated struggle. This was, in part, due to disagreements about the use of violence and the question of civil disobedience.[110] In trying to bring together two disparate movements, Gandhi had repeatedly to defend his position to both Muslim leaders and Hindu activists.[111] As early as May 1921, Reading had predicted that 'the Hindu-Moslem combination...rests upon insecure foundations'.[112] Later that year in August, a confrontation between the Indian government and Caliphate protestors in Malabar resulted in an uprising which developed into the committing of atrocities by Muslims against Hindus, including forcible conversion and murder.[113] News of the Moplah rebellion, as it became known, caused serious upset among the general Hindu population, and Gandhi had to struggle to keep the Hindu-Muslim alliance alive.[114] By January 1922 Reading was reporting how the extremist pan-Islamic language of some of the Caliphate leaders was also causing concern to more moderate Hindus.[115]

The relative failure of the non-co-operation movement by mid-1922 caused further disenchantment among the population.[116] In November 1921 a *hartal* (general strike) had been called in response to the arrival of the Prince of Wales in India, and there were a number of violent outbreaks throughout the country.[117] By 4 February 1922 the movement reached a peak when a mob of around 2,000 agitators attacked government buildings in Chauri Chaura in the United Provinces, killing and mutilating the bodies of police and government officials trapped inside.[118] To those watching from London, the Indian government's hitherto lenient attitude towards Gandhi and his followers was to blame for this current crisis. In a Cabinet meeting two days later, 'General regret was expressed at the delay which had taken place in arresting Gandhi, a policy which the Cabinet had favoured more than three months ago.'[119] Feeling the pressure, Montagu was now far less supportive than he had been in 1920. Consequently the secretary of state fired off a telegram demanding those principally involved in the non-co-operation movement – including Gandhi – be promptly dealt with. As Montagu pointed out to Reading (somewhat obviously), the situation could not be dealt with simply with the issuing of a communiqué: 'There is no doubt that you are confronted by a movement designed and supported with a view to overthrowing your Government and it is of the essence of such a situation that whatever measures are essential for dealing with it must be taken promptly.'[120] Unsurprisingly Reading took offence at the strong terms of this telegram. While the viceroy realised the Home government must be anxious at the situation, 'We must at the same time offer our respectful protest against the implication that so far we have failed to realise the gravity of the present situation as to think that it could be met merely by the issue of a communiqué.'[121]

The debate on how to deal with the non-co-operation movement had effectively become a battle of wills between London and Delhi. Although Montagu had initially supported the viceroy, others in the Home government had never been happy with how the Indian government had chosen to deal with Gandhi, calling several times for the viceroy to simply arrest the Indian leader. In January 1922 Montagu had informed Reading that the British public was apparently becoming more and more perplexed by the fact that Gandhi remained at liberty, despite his seditious activities.[122] However, as the viceroy had tried to explain to the secretary of state, were he to arrest the Indian leader now, 'another will take his place and carry on in Gandhi's name, with the additional stimulus that Gandhi, the saint, is in prison'.[123] The Indian government had a strong belief that if left largely alone, the non-co-operation movement would eventually run its course. In the meantime it refused to make a martyr of its leader.[124] As Reading respectfully pointed out to Montagu, while he understood London's concerns, 'the determination of the situation ought to rest upon my view of the effect in India and not so much in debate at Home'.[125] Indeed, the Indian government had already given Sir George Lloyd, the Governor of Bombay, permission to arrest Gandhi before Montagu's demanding telegram had actually arrived.[126] However, on 8 February, following public outcry at the events in Chauri Chaura, Gandhi called a halt to the non-co-operation movement. The Indian government now decided to gamble and postpone Gandhi's arrest, much to Lloyd's chagrin.[127]

Ultimately, the viceroy was to be awarded for his patience. In the days after Chauri Chaura, as public opinion turned and moderates began to withdraw their support from the movement and its leaders, conditions now turned in favour of the Indian government.[128] By the beginning of March, it felt confident enough to re-issue the order for Gandhi's arrest.[129] Reading had been patient, and timed his actions perfectly, so that when the arrest finally took place, there was virtually no public response.[130] As one contemporary noted, 'the fiery emotionalism of Non-co-operation has for the time spent itself'.[131] Yet again, the Indian government could feel vindicated that in its battle with the Home government it had been proved right.

By the end of 1922 then, with Gandhi in prison, the collapse of the non-co-operation movement and the effective end of the Caliphate issue, the Indian government was able to breathe a little easier, and Reading could report that 'for the present the outlook is thus more favourable than it has been at any time during the last three years'.[132] The Indian government had 'managed to come out relatively unscathed' from these troubled years.[133] Nonetheless, the viceroy and his men could never afford to become complacent in this post-war period of tension and upheaval when there were so many disgruntled groups ever-ready to exploit any perceived British weakness. Indeed, just as Muslim and Indian nationalist agitation appeared to be calming down, intelligence reports began to note a resurgence of Bolshevik activity (which would ultimately precipitate the Curzon Note of 1923).[134] For the Foreign Office, this was seen as a direct result of Russia's involvement in the Genoa Conference of April 1922. The Soviet government had been invited to participate in the conference discussions which centred mainly on economic issues – a further attempt by Lloyd George to 'civilise' the Bolsheviks (the first had been the trade agreement) by impressing fiscal responsibility upon them.[135] In a speech made to the House of Commons on 3 April 1922, the prime minister argued that, with the New Economic Policy, Lenin had effectively abandoned the principles of Communism anyway and that by attending Genoa Russia would have to 'recognise all conditions imposed and accepted by civilised communities as the test of fitness for entering into the comity of nations'.[136] Such claims were largely wishful thinking on Lloyd George's part, however, for it appears that the invitation to the Soviet government merely served to increase its confidence in its international position, as did the Rapallo Treaty which it signed with Germany during the conference.[137] As Gregory in the Foreign Office reported, the Soviet government was touting the invitation to the conference 'first as being tantamount to *de jure* recognition, and secondly as a complete victory of the Soviet Government over the Governments of the West'.[138]

It was as a result of this boost in confidence that the Bolshevik authorities appear to have once again begun its propaganda activities, particularly its support of anti-British nationalist movements.[139] Following protests by Curzon during the Anglo–Soviet trade agreement talks and his note of 1921, the Soviet government had been forced to temporarily pare back some of its more overt propaganda efforts, including the school for revolutionaries which had been set up in Tashkent by the Indian Communist M.N. Roy.[140] Despite this closure of Roy's school, however, there was always scant hope that the Bolshevik regime was going to completely give up its agitation among the people of Asia, and in April 1921 the Communist University of the Toilers of the East (KUTV) was founded in Moscow. Most of the students of Roy's were transferred to the Russian capital, although soon the university would set up departments in Tashkent, as well as Baku and Irkutsk.[141] Thus by December 1922, the new secretary of state for India, Lord Peel, was warning Reading of Bolshevik-sponsored sedition in India: 'The danger is increasing.'[142] Peel seems to be referring particularly to the growing activity of Roy, who since April had been in Berlin from where he kept up a continual stream of agitation against the Indian government. Despatching propaganda into India such as the newspaper *The Vanguard of Indian Independence*, and the pamphlets *India in Transition, India's Problem and Its Solution* and *What Do We Want?*, Roy was also devising various plans to send into India a number of the students from the KUTV.[143] It was probably these activities which Peel had in mind when he informed Reading in December 1922 of indications that the Bolsheviks were succeeding in smuggling literature and agents into India.[144]

Reading's reply to Peel's warning was calm and reassuring: 'We are fully alive to the necessity for exercising the closest watch over all Bolshevik activities directed against this country.' As the viceroy explained further, together with the provincial Criminal Intelligence Departments, there existed at Peshwar and Quetta Intelligence Bureaus which were specifically charged with the detection of Bolshevik agents. The Department of Central Intelligence (DCI) co-ordinated the work of these agencies and kept local governments fully informed of developments. The Indian government was also happy that its existing laws were more than adequate for prosecuting any of those who were found guilty of conspiracy against it, either inside or outside of India. As for the activities of Roy in particular, Reading believed that while his propaganda might excite a small number of people, the revolutionary in no way had the supporters and resources to carry out a proper Communist campaign on Indian soil.[145]

Indeed, although it remained ever vigilant, the Indian government was relatively confident in its ability to cope with Soviet and émigré revolutionary activity. A large part of this confidence was owed to the Indian intelligence services. For one thing, by 1918 the Indian government already had a strategy in place to combat possible German insurrection in Asia – this meant that when it faced Bolshevik agitation after the war it was prepared. As one historian explains:

> Despite some initial uncertainty about the power of Communism to win support in India, the British very soon found out that the threat of Communist subversion there was not nearly as serious as the German intrigues during the war which had caused serious difficulties... When they faced the Bolshevik threat, the British benefited from the experience they had gained in the earlier struggle against the Germans.[146]

Intelligence bases outside of India – in Meshed, Kashgar, the Far East, North America and Europe – also meant that by the early 1920s the Indian government had a reasonable understanding of Bolshevik and Indian revolutionary activity.[147] The apparatus put in place by the Indian government (as described above and in Chapter Three) was also very successful in its attempts to capture any anti-British literature and agents sent into India. The majority of the students from the school at Tashkent and the KUTV were either quickly arrested or 'found the police so hot on their trail that they fled the country without having carried out their mission'.[148] Others were largely incompetent and some had simply taken advantage of the Bolshevik willingness to clothe and feed them – one graduate of the Tashkent school had reportedly succeeded in smuggling a large sum of money into India meant for the purpose of Communist propaganda. Instead, the man had used the money to build himself a house.[149]

Together with the vigilance of its border officials, another reason the Indian government was so successful at detecting any revolutionary infiltration into the country was that it was kept well informed intercepting Roy's mail. Indeed, his letters had 'been an unfailing source of information of proved accuracy as to the movements of men, money and literature'.[150] The British government had also been regularly decoding encrypted Soviet and Comintern communications[151] and monitoring Communist radio traffic,[152] while the Indian police force were adept at infiltrating any germinating Communist organisations within India. It was through such vigilance that by 1923 Roy's main agents in India had all been arrested and tried in what became known as the Cawnpore Conspiracy.[153] Indian intelligence reports also emphasised the fact that India was just not ready for Communism: 'Roy's main adversary was not just the Indian police, but also Gandhi. Gandhi from 1919 onwards had gained such a commanding position over the Indian nationalist movement that it proved almost impossible for the Communists to gain a foothold within it.'[154]

Indeed, it would not be until 1925 that an Indian Communist Party would be founded on Indian soil.[155] Just as the nationalism of Reza Khan and emir Amanullah had kept Bolshevism at bay in Persia and Afghanistan, so too did Gandhi do the same in India. Thus, in contrast to MI5 and Special Branch in Britain, who were 'gripped by a deep anxiety' in regards to Bolshevism, the DCI proved a calming influence on the Indian government.[156] One historian has demonstrated how the IDCEU in London suffered from 'imperial paranoia', seeing isolated incidents of anti-British agitation as part of a vast conspiracy against the empire.[157] Another has argued that individuals in intelligence and defence in London often inflated the Bolshevik threat, as opposed to in India where there was 'recognition that the threat might easily be contained, given the ineptitude and greed of many Communist agents'.[158] This confidence in its understanding of, and ability to combat, Bolshevism goes a large way to explaining why the Indian government was less obsessed by the Soviet Russian threat during the post-war years than the Home government was.

When it came to Afghanistan, things were also gradually moving in Britain's favour and just as with Persia, much of this appeared to be as a result of waning Bolshevik influence. The main problem with Soviet-Afghan relations throughout this period was, effectively, that each wanted to be the champion of Islam in Central Asia. Soviet Russia wanted to harness Muslim discontent in the region and use it, initially to bring down imperialist Britain, but also to extend Communism through Asia. For this cause, the Bolshevik regime was ready to subvert its more overt Marxist ideals and make alliances with revolutionary Muslim groups, such as the Jadids and Young Bukharans. For his part, Amanullah was ambitions to make his mark on the world stage and developing an image as protector of Muslims was one such way. The first attempt by Amanullah to harness pan-Islamism had been supporting the *hijrat*. Another opportunity appeared to present itself with the dissolution of the Caliph. In February 1922 Reading was warning London that there was a danger the emir would put forward a claim to be the new Caliph. An aggrandised Afghanistan with its leader presuming to be head of Islam, however, would cause untold problems for the Indian government.[159] Whether Amanullah seriously considered becoming the next Caliph is difficult to say, although it appears he had the support of some of his subjects.[160] Either way, as Dobbs pointed out: 'Afghanistan will keep her eyes fixed on her Indian and Central Asian frontiers, ready to move forward in one or other direction on a certitude of real weakness.'[161]

Luckily, the emir seemed to have learnt his lesson from 1919 regarding invading India. Instead, a more promising venture appeared to lie in extending Afghanistan's influence into Central Asia. For one thing, affairs were not going entirely in Soviet Russia's favour by 1922. The treatment of Muslims by the Tashkent Soviet in the early days of its existence had considerably soured relations between the two. Muslims had been excluded from the Soviet, and when they had then tried to set up their own government in Kokand, the Tashkent regime had attacked and destroyed it.[162] The Kokand massacre had been followed by an eruption of Muslim discontent centred in the Fergana region and the creation of the Basmachi resistance. The Basmachi were roaming bands of Muslim men who opposed the presence of Russians in Central Asia.[163] After the invasions of Khiva and Bokhara, the ranks of the Basmachi swelled and were joined by the emir of Bokhara and a couple of prominent Jadids, all of which raised the standing of the movement among the local population.[164] By 1921 then, the rebellion had become a refuge for all those who were opposed to Soviet Russia's presence in Central Asia, thereby proving a constant source of irritation and embarrassment to the Bolshevik government who were trying so hard to maintain a pro-Islam image. Indeed, the Basmachi resistance and the invasions of Bokhara and Khiva demonstrate just how problematic Moscow's foreign policy could be. Even after the Second Comintern Congress had apparently solved the *theoretical* issues about collaboration with nationalists and pan-Islamists (and tempered some of the initial extremism displayed by local activists), this did not remedy the *practical* problems the Bolsheviks faced in trying to extend their influence into Central and South Asia. For, try as the Bolsheviks might to temper their ideology and pander to nationalist sentiment, many Asian Muslims were not to be fooled; ultimately the Russian Soviet government was a foreign Communist power whose belief system was fundamentally incompatible with Islam. Furthermore, Moscow's dual policy of conducting diplomatic relations with Afghanistan while simultaneously deposing neighbouring native rulers was a risky one, as it threatened to alienate emir Amanullah and push him towards the British.

As it was, Amanullah faced a dilemma. As the new British ambassador in Kabul, Colonel Humphrys, explained, the emir could not afford to alienate Soviet

Russia by becoming too involved in the affairs of the likes of Bokhara, yet he also could not outright abandon this region for fear of being regarded as a traitor to Islam. The idea of being the saviour of those Muslims who rejected Soviet rule was also a tempting proposition. In Humphry's opinion, Amanullah had in fact become obsessed with the issue of Bokhara.[165] The presence of emir Alim, who had fled to Afghanistan in 1921, was also a constant reminder of the plight of that country. How far this obsession was truly motivated by religious affinity, however, is questionable. The Indian government certainly believed that it was Afghan ambitions for northern expansion (since southern expansion was largely out of the question) which really inspired this interest in Turkestan. Despite some half-hearted protests on the Afghan side, the plight of Khiva and Bokhara had certainly not prevented the creation of the Soviet-Afghan treaty of 1921.

Indeed, it soon became apparent that Amanullah intended on resolving the conflict between his ambitions towards Turkestan and his weakness in relation to Russia by turning to Britain. In his report following his return from Kabul, Dobbs noted that the real reason the emir had tried to gain an exclusive treaty with the Indian government had been in the hope that should a conflict arise with Soviet Russia, Britain would come to Afghanistan's aid.[166] As Humphrys put it, the emir's solution to his dilemma when it came to Bokhara was to try 'to induce the British Government to pull his chestnuts out of the fire'.[167] With the exclusive treaty proving a non-starter, another way the emir hoped to involve Britain in the situation in Turkestan was to get the British government publicly to recognise Khiva and Bokhara as independent states. Neither the British Foreign Office nor the Indian government, however, were prepared to jeopardise Britain's own relations with Soviet Russia and possibly precipitate a conflict in Central Asia for the sake of two nations wholly unconnected to the British Empire's welfare.[168]

Complicating the situation in the region in 1922 was the presence of the Turkish revolutionary, Enver Pasha. Originally a close friend of the Bolshevik regime, Pasha had been celebrated at the Baku Congress as a 'representative of Moslem hostility to the Western powers and particularly England'.[169] Having failed in his endeavours to rival Kemal Ataturk for power in Turkey, Enver Pasha had arrived in Turkestan in late 1921, ostensibly as a Bolshevik envoy to conciliate Muslim insurgents. It was quickly apparent, however, that the Turk had not gone to Bokhara to service the Soviet government but to fulfil his own desire for glory. Styling himself as leader of the Basmachi rebellion, Enver Pasha turned against his erstwhile Communist sponsors and began to help organise resistance against the Bolshevik presence in Turkestan.[170]

To Afghanistan, Enver Pasha appeared to provide the leadership and stimulus needed to challenge Soviet Russia in Bokhara and elsewhere and the emir struck up a correspondence with the Turk, an action which inevitably brought protest from the Soviet government.[171] Again, Afghanistan tried to protect itself by garnering British support. In an interview with Humphrys in April 1922, Tarzi asked if it were not possible to use Enver Pasha as an instrument to promote the joint interests of Afghanistan and Britain and create a stable Bokhara. The Afghan Foreign Minister believed that Enver Pasha could remove the Bolsheviks from Bokhara if he was supplied with some 60,000 rifles.[172] In the opinion of both Humphrys and Reading, however, Britain should steer clear of the Bokhara situation. As the viceroy pointed out, Enver Pasha in particular was an ambitious adventurer, and was not to be trusted.[173]

In an effort to try to win over Britain to his plans, Amanullah had even begun to try to appease the Indian government by cracking down on anti-British intrigue within his country. In February 1922, for example, the emir summoned many of the Indian revolutionaries who were resident in Kabul and warned them to refrain from anti-British activity or risk being expelled from Afghanistan.[174] Economic and political considerations also required the emir to ease back on his more militant attitude towards India, as he simply could not afford to completely alienate Delhi.[175] Perhaps unsurprisingly, this period of courtship with Britain coincided with a period of decline in Afghan relations with Soviet Russia. As one British source noted in February 1922, 'There appears no doubt that the Russians [in Kabul] are now subjected to all the petty restrictions and annoyances with which the British Mission was formerly favoured.'[176] Before he was recalled by his government following Curzon's note, the Bolshevik representative in Kabul, Raskolnikov, was busy making himself unpopular - information reached the Foreign Office of a 'strong resentment felt by the Afghan Government at the disloyal activity of Monsieur Raskolnikoff, who is alleged to be intriguing with seditious persons with the object of encouraging disaffection within the country'.[177] Thus, just as in Persia, Bolshevik influence appeared on the wane.

Afghanistan was a fickle friend, however, and such goodwill towards Britain was not to be forever assured. By 1923, following a series of irritations and petty annoyances caused by Afghan behaviour, relations between the two countries would decline to the point where London was threatening to recall its Legation from Kabul.[178] Matters were not helped by the fact that Humphrys had quickly developed a dislike for Amanullah on his arrival in Afghanistan. The British minister looked down upon the emir, and opposed the nationalist and modernising forces prevalent in Kabul in the post-war period.[179] Nonetheless, Anglo-Afghan relations had a history of these ups-and-downs, and the Indian government had become particularly adept at dealing with its neighbour's vacillations. Importantly, the Indian government was also able to recognise the old Afghan trick of trying to play Russia and Britain off against each other, and was sensible enough to refuse to become involved in the emir's Turkestan adventures. By 1923 then, Anglo-Afghan relations were in a relatively stable position. Just as the trade agreement with Russia did not preclude Britain experiencing irritations with that country, so too did India's relationship with Afghanistan continue to see its peaks and troughs even following the treaty of 1921. However, as with the Soviet trade agreement, the treaty with Afghanistan did bring a level of resolution to some of the issues between India and its neighbour, not least because it provided the Indian government with much needed clout. From 1921 Britain could always threaten to rescind the treaty and its concessions whenever Amanullah decided to become unreasonable.

Build, Build, Build

By the end of 1923 it appeared that Britain's foreign relations in South Asia had come full circle, almost to pre-First World War days. The ambitious optimism of the immediate post-war months had dissipated and the reality of the situation in the region had set in. Curzon's temerity had been replaced with the Indian government's sensibility and by 1923 Britain's standing had improved from the low to which it had sunk in 1920–1921. In Persia, Loraine's policy of detachedness proved effective damage control after the embarrassment of the failed Anglo-Persian Agreement and the Enzeli debacle. After months of failing to come to grips with the Turkish question, the settlement at Lausanne and the creation of the new Turkish Republic finally resolved many problems for Britain, not least of which was the settlement of the Caliphate issue. The removal of this *cause célèbre* simultaneously resulted in a cooling down of pan-Islamic agitation and a weakening of the Hindu–Muslim revolutionary bond in India. Even in Afghanistan relations appeared to have settled into something of their old routine, with the Afghan ruler busily courting first one and then the other of his neighbours for his own gains. By 1923 then, affairs in South Asia had stabilised.

And while part of this improvement in Britain's foreign relations can be attributed to the pragmatism of the likes of Loraine and Reading, undoubtedly this change was also helped along by the relative failure of the Bolshevik regime to attain their goals in Persia and Afghanistan. Despite all the anti-Bolshevik rhetoric of 1918–1919, by 1922 it was clear that Lenin and his colleagues were struggling just as much as Britain was with pan-Islamism and nationalism. Superficially Moscow was still capable of stirring up trouble for Britain through its anti-imperialist propaganda and sponsoring of men such as M.N. Roy. However, it was becoming increasingly apparent that beneath all this bluster, the Bolsheviks were struggling to recruit to the Communist cause. On a diplomatic level, Asia's rulers were proving almost as disloyal and adept at self-preservation as the Bolsheviks themselves were, while at the grass-roots, the failure to create many fully-fledged Communists out of the milieu of Asian revolutionaries was limiting the extent to which the Bolsheviks could really infiltrate the region. While the emir of Afghanistan or the shah of Persia would always find flirting with the Soviet government (and thus irritating the British) an enjoyable pastime, there remained an invisible barrier of caution surrounding these rulers. Decades of British and Russian intrigue in this region of the world had taught these nations to be wary of allowing either of their powerful neighbours to get too close, whatever placations and promises the new leaders in Moscow might give.

The failure of the Soviet government to make great revolutionary headway in South Asia by 1922-23 was particularly important as it meant that when the likes of Loraine advocated a detached policy in Persia, London was more inclined to listen than it had been in 1918. Despite Curzon's previous claims, Britain's failure to extend its influence in this region had not portended the Bolshevik apocalypse. There therefore seemed no harm in now following a policy in Persia and Afghanistan that appeared to involve less effort and less risk than what Britain had been doing hitherto. Curzon's sulkiness over the failure of the Anglo-Persian Agreement also helped ensure a change of direction in Foreign Office policies. Not that Curzon ever fully relinquished his ambitions in this region of the world (just as he could never bring himself to feel positive towards Bolshevik Russia). In May 1922, for example, he could not resist instructing Loraine to 'slowly Build Build Build' when he could.[180] But as stubborn as he was, Curzon had to admit by 1923 that pursuing a more limited role in Persia was actually working to Britain's advantage. It was just unfortunate for Britain that the foreign secretary had not been made to realise this sooner. For, as demonstrated, there was nothing in Loraine's Persian policy which the Indian government had not been advocating for years, and which it was already doing in Afghanistan – being as little involved in the country's internal affairs as was necessary to simply retain a British presence. The foreign secretary's peculiar inability to listen to the advice coming from Delhi had cost Britain valuable prestige points in the years after 1918. At least this was beginning to be rectified. Indeed, by 1923 Britain's relations in South Asia had settled down to something akin to the pre-war years, with London accepting both the limitations of the empire's capabilities and the inevitable presence of Russia in this region.

The End of An Epoch

This work opened with a number of research questions, not least of which was why the Indian government's opinions were ignored when it came to formulating Britain's foreign policy in South Asia in the years after the First World War. Why was it that, even though relations with Persia and Afghanistan were intimately related with the security of India, Delhi's point of view was marginalised? Why was it not recognised that perhaps officials in India might be better placed than those in London to understand the problems facing Britain's imperial position in this region of the world? As noted in the Introduction, the answer to this hinges on the issue of who was formulating Britain's foreign policy in this period. Montagu summarised the situation himself in 1919 in a letter to Chelmsford. In response to the viceroy's complaints about being ignored, Montagu explained: 'it so happens that you are interested in matters in which...Lord Curzon plays a very important part. That is really the *whole secret*.'[1] As we have seen, despite what some authors have said, the Foreign Office still dominated the formulation of Britain's foreign policy in the post-1918 period. As foreign secretary, this meant Curzon would always have a large amount of control over Britain's foreign relations – with his experiences in South Asia and his personality traits, Curzon in fact came to dominate Anglo-Asian affairs. Unfortunately, this meant that in the years after 1918 the Indian government faced a formidable obstacle to having its voice heard in London. Curzon had a certain way of viewing the world, and the fact that the Indian government disagreed with this view meant it was destined to be ignored by the stubborn foreign secretary.

As for what influenced Curzon's thinking, the answer is relatively simple. The foreign secretary was an old-fashioned imperialist who believed that the prestige of the British Empire was best protected by maintaining a physical dominance over India's neighbouring states, thereby creating a buffer against Russia – for in Curzon's opinion Russia was always the premier enemy of the empire. This was the Great Game mentality described in Chapter One – a mode of thought which continually viewed Russia with hostility and suspicion; which over-emphasised the supreme threat of Russia to Britain's imperial interests in South Asia; which saw Persia and Afghanistan as mere pawns; and which insisted on the use of the 'iron hand' to extend Britain's influence in the region. Crucially, the Great

Game mentality therefore blinded Curzon to the growth of nationalism and pan-Islamism in South Asia in the years after the First World War.[2] And it is this which brought the foreign secretary into conflict with the Indian government. Curzon saw the world as he thought it ought to be – and perhaps as it was prior to 1914. He did not see it as it was. The foreign secretary's inability to recognise why the agreement had failed is a clear indication of just how little he understood the changes which had overcome Persia since his travelling days.

The trouble was that Curzon's obsession with Russia had had a long gestation – formulated during his early travels, and solidified while he was viceroy. It meant that it was hard for him to see anything else as a comparable threat. Which leads to another question posed in the beginning of this work – how far was the foreign secretary actually fearful of Bolshevism taking hold in South Asia? Was his anti-Bolshevik rhetoric based on ideological antipathy? Or to put it another way, was Curzon anti-Bolshevik or actually anti-Russian? And more importantly, does it actually matter? In 1918–1919, there certainly appeared to be some confusion in London over who was the real threat to Britain's interests in Persia: the remnants of the tsarist regime in the form of the Cossack Division and the Russian Legation, or the new revolutionary government in Moscow. Indeed, despite Curzon's anti-Bolshevik rhetoric, in these early years it was certainly the Cossack Division which could cause more immediate problems for Britain in Persia, given that the Bolshevik regime was distracted by the Russian civil war. A cynic could argue that Curzon realised he would have been unable to push through his Persian plans if he had couched them in imperialistic terms. In these months after the conclusion of the First World War there was great reluctance for Britain to be extending its responsibilities further than it had to. But Bolshevism provided a convenient justification – Britain needed to protect the Persians from this destructive ideology (or so Curzon claimed).

The great fear which Bolshevism could incite in Britain was demonstrated in 1924 by the case of the Zinoviev Letter. The 'greatest Red Scare in British political history' was precipitated by the publication in British newspapers of a letter ostensibly written by Zinoviev to the British Communist party instructing them to prepare for the coming of a revolution in Britain.[3] The publication happened just four days before the general election of 29 October 1924 and is generally seen as the reason for the Conservatives' victory in the polls that month.[4] The Soviet government denied authorship of the letter but it was not until 1999 that the truth of the matter was revealed when it was shown that the letter was a forgery, written most probably by White Russians in Berlin in an attempt to disturb the relationship between Britain and Russia.[5] How far the Foreign Office of the time suspected the authenticity of the letter remains unknown – the years after the Russian revolution saw a veritable avalanche of documents of dubious origin making their way into Britain, all purporting to provide information on the

Bolshevik regime, or indeed claiming to be written by the Soviet government itself. The note of 1921, for example, which Curzon had presented to Moscow detailing Bolshevik transgressions of the trade agreement had been proven to be based on bad intelligence. The important point is that in 1924 the fear and suspicion which Soviet Russia could ignite amongst the British public was enough to apparently influence a general election. If Curzon wanted support for his Persian plans, using Bolshevism to scare his colleagues into action appeared a good idea.

In the end Curzon's scaremongering actually did not matter. For the likes of Montagu, it was financial considerations which persuaded him to support the creation of the Persian agreement. But Curzon's use of anti-Bolshevik rhetoric for his own means does go some way to explaining some of his behaviour towards Persia after 1919. Given his doomsday warnings in 1918, Curzon appeared very complacent in 1920 when discussing the potential for a Bolshevik invasion of Persia. In the months that followed the Enzeli landings, as Soviet Russia gradually increased its presence within that country, Curzon remained relatively placid. If he had truly been that concerned about the threat which Bolshevism posed to Persia and to South Asia at large, one would have expected greater agitation from the foreign secretary. Instead, Curzon wanted to create the Anglo-Persian agreement in order to make his mark on the region and extend Britain's imperial influence while he was able to take advantage of Russia's weakness. Curzon was a Great Game player by nature, and whether Russia was ruled by a Tsar or by Communists, the most important thing was for Britain to exert its authority in South Asia. After he had managed to conclude the 1919 agreement, Curzon cared very little for what happened to Persia. The country was 'a means to an end', not a legitimate end in itself. And when that agreement was wholeheartedly rejected by the Persian people, Curzon's reaction was simply to sulk. All of which gives an insight into Curzon's Great Game mentality. For the foreign secretary, Persia was a prize up for grabs. If he could not win it, he certainly wasn't going to invest his energy into the country for the sake of the Persians themselves.

So why did the Indian government appear so much more relaxed about the apparent threat of Bolshevism to Britain's imperial interests than many officials in London? For even though Curzon's scare tactics had not worked particularly well in regards to the Anglo-Persian Agreement, throughout this period Whitehall did appear generally more distracted by the issue of Bolshevism than Delhi did – surprising, given that for so many decades the Indian government had always been the ones obsessed about Russia's intentions towards South Asia. The answer is unclear. Probably it was at least partly due to the different intelligence assessments made by the Home and the Indian governments. Officials in India seemed to have greater confidence in their ability to cope with Communist agitation in the country, and their success at disrupting the work of M.N. Roy and his allies helped boost this self-assurance. In the post-war period there were also other concerns which appeared more pressing to the Indian government than Bolshevism. While Moscow was struggling to recruit to its ideological cause, the likes of Gandhi and the Ali brothers were having no such trouble. It was the *hartals* of the non-co-operation movement and the Caliphate *Hijrat* which were causing the real, practical problems for the viceroy and his men, not the bluster of the Bolsheviks and their incompetent fellow travellers.

In contrast, domestic labour unrest and disturbances such as that which occurred in Glasgow in January 1919, appeared to bring the Bolshevik threat to Whitehall's doorstep, while their intelligence reports only served to confirm their fears. The Indian government also seemed to have something of a better understanding of how Bolshevism functioned. Rather than viewing the new Russian government by the same parameters of the tsarist regime, Chelmsford and Hamilton Grant, for example, appeared to grasp the idea that the Bolshevik ideology was most successful when popular discontent supplied it with fertile breeding ground. Hence the warnings not to upset the Persians or the Afghans by forcing unpopular diplomatic agreements on them. Perhaps the simple answer as to why the Indian government did not hold the same Great Game mentality as Curzon is that the day-to-day exposure which its officials had with South Asians made it more attune to the changes which had overcome the region since the First World War. Russia was the threat of yesterday, even if it did have a new ideological form. The problem of today was how to manage the pan-Islamic and nationalist fervour taking hold of Persia, Afghanistan and India.

The difficulty for the Indian government was that Curzon was not the type of man to listen to others. And herein lay the crux of the matter. That Curzon followed a Great Game mentality was not itself a unique fallacy. Indeed, there were others within the British government who shared aspects of his world view. Cox and Mallet had, of course, encouraged the creation of the 1919 Persian agreement; Hardinge and Eyre Crowe had also on occasion questioned the Indian government's apparent interference in what they deemed to be Foreign Office affairs; and Winston Churchill was perhaps an even greater Russophobe than the foreign secretary himself. That the Indian government might disagree with the Home government over issues of foreign affairs was also not an unusual occurrence. Minto had objected to the creation of the 1907 Anglo-Russian convention, while Curzon had had his own battle with London over Kitchener's reforms to India's military. Instead, Curzon's cardinal sin was to not recognise that in some circumstances it might be worth listening to others, even if what they were saying was not what he wanted to hear. By refusing point blank to pay the slightest attention to Delhi, to concede in even the smallest way that the viceroy's contributions to the formulation of foreign policy was valid, it meant that the foreign secretary was ignoring valuable expert opinion.

The trouble was that Curzon's travels, writings and time as viceroy had not only given him a Great Game mentality, but had also provided him with an unwarranted confidence in his own knowledge of South Asia. Despite the fact it had been a number of years since he had been in Persia, Afghanistan or India, throughout the post-war period the foreign secretary insisted that he knew best – in fact that he knew better than those officials currently in India. Curzon also possessed a 'competitive or even combative instinct', which meant that rather than remaining open-minded to alternative points of view, he was apt to see this as a personal challenge and aimed to silence those who disagreed with him.[6] This explains why he did not simply ignore the Indian government, but actually went as far as degrading its expertise as in the case of the Anglo-Persian Agreement, or mocking and belittling it as with the Caliphate issue. Indeed, Curzon made his feelings on the Indian government perfectly clear in his letter to Montagu in 1922 prior to the secretary of state's resignation. That he believed Delhi was trying to 'dictate' to London about Muslim affairs is indicative of his belligerent attitude towards the Indian government, as well as his sensitivity – boarding on paranoia – of having his authority questioned by others. Stubborn, combative and narrow-minded, Curzon was also highly ambitious. As one biographer has put it, 'The goal at which he [Curzon] ever aimed can be described compendiously as achievement'.[7] Curzon's tenure as viceroy had ended ignominiously and for a number of years afterwards he had been left out in the cold from government business. This meant that by the time Curzon had ascended to a position of authority in 1918 he was looking to rehabilitate his image. The demise of imperial Russia appeared to provide the perfect opportunity for him to make his mark on South Asia, and thus the Indian government's scepticism and constant criticism of his chosen course of action was highly inconvenient.

The Indian government's position was made worse by the fact that there were few in London who were willing to challenge Curzon when it came to South Asia. His travels and writings had given him a self-proclaimed expertise on the region which meant that others often deferred to his opinion. Curzon also frequently referred to the fact that he was an ex-viceroy whenever his advocated policies were questioned. Within the Home government Curzon's knowledge of South Asia probably was unrivalled. Even if his arguments were wrong, there were few who were in a position to dispute this with him. As one historian puts it, in the post-war period 'A prime minister who knew nothing about the East was matched by a foreign secretary who knew everything about it except how to deal with it...'[8] His position of authority within government, his apparent knowledge of the region, and his forceful personality meant that Curzon was adept at getting his way when it came to South Asia, often over-riding the objections of others. And when all else failed, he could always threaten to resign, as with the attempts to reform the Eastern Committee, or during the debates about removing Britain's troops from Persia. Curzon's difficult personality was in fact one reason that he had been passed over as prime minister in 1923.[9]

Given its subordinate position and its physical distance, if the Indian government was to have its voice heard it needed an advocate in London – and one who was strong enough to stand up to an overbearing foreign secretary. Unfortunately for Delhi, Montagu was to prove an inadequate ally. When it came to the Persian agreement, for example, the secretary of state allowed himself to be persuaded by Curzon rather than listening to his own viceroy. Luckily, in Afghanistan and India, the viceroy had more control and Curzon's attempts to impose his Persian-style policies in Afghanistan were rebuffed. Curzon's calls in 1918 to make the emir an official ally in the war, and his latter belief that India could retain some control of Afghanistan's foreign relations demonstrate that he not only got the Persia situation wrong, but entirely misread Afghanistan too.

However, even then Montagu failed to defend the Indian government's actions to the Cabinet. In his letters to Chelmsford, Montagu often complained that he felt the viceroy behaved unfairly towards him – making it known to the Indian public every time the secretary of state disagreed with the viceroy.[10] However, given what has been discussed, it seems hardly surprising that the Indian government often bridled at the lack of India Office support. The personal difficulties between Montagu and Chelmsford also did not help matters, and the secretary of state was not in office for long after Reading's appointment. Montagu's unpopularity with the Conservative party was a further problem for India. Despite all of his flaws, Curzon was extremely valuable to Lloyd George and to the coalition. Though he did not attract many friends, Curzon was a well-respected, prominent figure within the British political elite and an experienced statesman. Montagu was a Jewish Liberal, who appeared to take criticism very personally and often got far too emotional – a weakness for any politician.[11] His performance during the House of Commons debate on General Dyer demonstrates his failings as a political operator, especially when compared to the speeches made by Churchill and Curzon.

Unfortunately for both the Indian government and for Britain's international standing, things only finally started to change for the better after Curzon's policies proved a failure. Events in Persia, Afghanistan and India would show how potent the forces of nationalism and pan-Islamism were in the post-war years, and just how much the British foreign secretary was out-of-touch with the current climate in the region. It was only by 1922 that the British government at last abandoned the ambitious policies once advocated by Curzon for the more modest but realistic aims of the Indian government – even if it was actually Sir Percy Loraine who now represented this change of policy, rather than Delhi. Nevertheless, even after seeing his plans for South Asia collapse, still Curzon could not admit that he had been wrong. When it came to the agreement with Persia in 1919, for example, he attributed its failure to the ungratefulness of the Persian people, and the insincerity of the Persian government. It was because the Cabinet had decided to withdraw all of Britain's troops from the country and because Herman Norman was incompetent – in short it was everyone else's fault but his. When the Red Army landed at Enzeli, Curzon insisted he was not to blame, despite refusing to allow the British troops to withdraw earlier, thereby avoiding an embarrassing rout. When Muslim agitation was soothed by the Treaty of Lausanne, the foreign secretary could not admit that perhaps Britain had hitherto mishandled the Turkish – and by extension, the pan-Islamic – question. Instead, Curzon simply took it as a sign that Delhi had been exaggerating Muslim unrest. Even in the face of overwhelming evidence, Curzon was unable to open his mind to the possibility that the Indian government had been right in what it said in 1918 and to recognise that perhaps he had underestimated the strength of the nationalist and pan-Islamic feelings of the day. The foreign secretary simply could not be shifted from his stubborn adherence to a Great Game mentality.

The reason, then, that the advice of the Indian government was ignored when the Home government was forming its foreign policy towards South Asia is simple: Curzon. The foreign secretary's Great Game mentality, his stubbornness, narrow-mindedness and ambition combined with his self-professed expert status and position of authority within the British government to make him an obstruction for the Indian government. The fact that Delhi had no reliable advocate in London to support its position meant that it was doomed to being disregarded in this period. Only once Curzon's forward policies had proved futile did the Indian government's more pragmatic ideas find support. Even then, however, Delhi was still not afforded the credit for its foresight when it came to Britain's relations with South Asia. Ultimately, it is hard not to feel that had London simply followed the advice of Delhi in the first place, it could have avoided many headaches during this period. As it is, it was lucky for Britain that the Bolshevik government also had fundamental problems with its Asian policy in the years after 1918. Indeed, it is interesting to note that both Britain and Russia were essentially trying to achieve the same ends in Central and South Asia – that of extending their own influence in the region at the expense of the other – albeit through different means. But both Moscow and London appeared to fall foul of pan-Islamic and nationalist feeling. Propaganda efforts such as the Baku Congress and the KUTV might alarm some British officials, but ultimately they were simply a lot of hot air.

For despite all of these Bolshevik efforts 'revolution in Asia – in the short term – proved even more illusory than revolution in Europe'.[12] While nationalist leaders might find it convenient to have a potential ally against imperial Britain, it did not mean that they were willing to replace one domineering foreign power with another.[13] The quality of the Asian recruits was also a real problem for Moscow in these early years after the October revolution. Most of those students of the KUTV, for example, were either incompetent or simply taking advantage of the

Bolshevik willingness to feed and clothe them. Some revolutionaries, such as Barakatullah, were simply looking for any support in their struggle against the British. A high number were impractical intellectuals.[14] The one thing which the Bolshevik government did have going for it was its pragmatism, and its ability to learn and adapt to the current situation. For example, when it came to its failed first attempt at invading Bokhara in March 1918 'Lenin drew the theoretical lesson of this event when he wrote that it was necessary to move cautiously in the matter of revolution' in the Muslim world.[15] Unlike the British foreign secretary, the Russian leader was willing to be flexible in how he approached the Asian question.

* * *

In December 1923 the Conservative party lost the general election and the very first Labour government was ushered into power in Britain. One of the first acts of the new prime minister, Ramsey MacDonald, was to extend official recognition to the Soviet government in February 1924.[16] If the Labour government was trying to differentiate itself from the previous two administrations, it could not have chosen a more appropriate way of doing so. The world had moved on from the days when Karl Bravin was ignored and maligned by the Persian government. Soviet representatives now resided in Tehran, Kabul, Ankara and even London. And yet, MacDonald's actions were not entirely unforeseen, nor were they a result of some sort of socialist solidarity, as might be expected. Economic pragmatism had dictated Britain's conclusion of the Soviet Trade Agreement in 1921, and so it did in 1924 with the issue of formal recognition. The trouble with the agreement of 1921 is that it had not stimulated trade between the two countries to the extent that had been hoped for. British business still felt wary of dealing with Russia when no British consulates existed there to help protect their interests. Thus, formal diplomatic relations needed to be established.[17]

After 1923, the majority of those who had directed Britain's foreign policy since the First World War were no longer in government. Curzon, Lloyd George, Montagu, Chelmsford, Hardinge and Churchill – all had left office one way or another by 1924. It is true that the Labour government did not last for long, and that by the end of the year the Conservative party was back in power (helped by the Zinoviev scandal). Nevertheless, by this point Lloyd George and Montagu had been forced to resign, while Chelmsford and Hardinge had retired. Churchill was one of the few who not only remained in government, but of course went on to greater things after the 1920s. By the time of the Second World War, Churchill would come to have his own problems with the Soviet government – and perhaps, just like Curzon, Churchill's feelings towards Stalin and his regime were also influenced by his previous experiences of Russia.

As for Curzon, his period of supremacy over Britain's foreign relations ended in 1923 when he left the Foreign Office. He had already faced bitter disappointment when, upon Bonar Law's retirement in May 1923, he had been passed over for prime minister in favour of Stanley Baldwin. In 1930, during the unveiling of a statue in London in Curzon's honour, Baldwin would in fact pay homage to the man he believed was indeed more experienced than he when he took the position as prime minister seven years earlier. Despite his bitterness, however, at having been usurped by 'a man of inferior claims', Curzon begrudgingly agreed to continue as foreign secretary under Baldwin until the appointment of the Labour government. However, on the Conservatives' resumption of government, Curzon was yet again disappointed when instead of being allowed to resume his position at the Foreign Office, Baldwin made him Lord President of the Council instead – a role he had occupied eight years previously. Although he acknowledged Curzon's achievements, Baldwin believed that foreign policy needed 'a fresh start'.[18] Despite his incredible talents of administration and his indefatigable work ethic, of which nearly all contemporaries acknowledged, Curzon had not only been denied the highest office of the country, but was effectively demoted. It was a hugely disappointing end to a career which had started with such promise.[19] Less than four months later, on 20 March 1925, Lord George Nathaniel Curzon – probably the greatest of the Great Game players – died of a bladder haemorrhage. As one of his biographers has put it, 'It was the death of a man, but it was also the end of an epoch.'[20]

Notes

Introduction

1. As quoted in Hopkirk, *Setting the East Ablaze: Lenin's Dream of an Empire in Asia*, p. 102 (hereafter *East Ablaze*).
2. As quoted in Nicolson, *Curzon: The Last Phase 1919–1925: A Study in Post-War Diplomacy*, p. 38.
3. Pearce, 'The 26 Commissars', *Sbornik* (1981), pp. 54–66 (hereafter '26 Commissars'); Hopkirk, *On Secret Service East of Constantinople*, pp. 366–70 (hereafter *Secret Service*); Stalin, 'The Shooting of the Twenty-Six Baku Comrades by Agents of British Imperialism', http://www.marxists.org/reference/archive/stalin/works/1919/04/23.htm [8/8/13] and Ellis, 'Operations in Transcaspia, 1918–1919, and the 26 Commissars Case', *St. Antony's Papers*, No. 6 (1959), pp. 131–50 (hereafter 'Operations').
4. Dunsterforce was a small military formation under the command of General L.C. Dunsterville, sent from Baghdad to Baku in the summer of 1918. See: Arslanian, 'The British Decision to Intervene in Transcaucasia during World War I', *Armenian Review* Vol. 27 (1974), pp. 146–59 (hereafter 'British Decision'); Arslanian, 'Dunsterville's Adventures: A Reappraisal', *International Journal of Middle East Studies*, Vol. 12 (1980), pp. 199–216 (hereafter 'Dunsterville's Adventures'); Teague-Jones, *The Spy Who Disappeared: Diary of a Secret Mission to Russian Central Asia in 1918*.
5. Gupta, *Comintern and the Destiny of Communism in India, 1919–1943* and Spector, *The Soviet Union and the Muslim World, 1917–1958*. See also Hopkirk, *East Ablaze*; Persits, *Revolutionaries of India in Soviet Russia: Mainsprings of the Communist Movement in the East*; Imam, 'The Effects of the Russian Revolution in India, 1917–1920', *St. Antony's Papers*, No. 18 (1966), pp. 74–97 (hereafter 'Effects') and Druhe, *Soviet Russia and Indian Communism, 1917–1949*.
6. Bunyan and Fisher, *The Bolshevik Revolution, 1917–1918: Documents and Materials* (Stanford: Stanford University Press, 1934), pp. 467–9.
7. Gupta, op. cit., p. 53.
8. White, 'Soviet Russia and the Asian Revolution, 1917–1924', *Review of International Studies*, Vol. 10 (1984), pp. 219–20 (hereafter 'Soviet Russia').

9. Throughout this work 'Home government' will refer to the British government based in London, while 'Indian government' will refer to the system of governance in India headed by the Governor-General/Viceroy which ruled the British Raj and held suzerainty over the Princely States. For information on Britain's rule in India see Ashton, *British Policy Towards the Indian States, 1905–1939* and Roberts, *British Rule in India, Volume II: India Under the British Crown, 1856–1947.*

10. McKercher, 'Old Diplomacy and New: the Foreign Office and Foreign Policy, 1919–1939' in Dockrill and McKercher, eds, *Diplomacy and World Power: Studies in British Foreign Policy, 1890–1951,* p. 79.

11. Lowe and Dockrill, *The Mirage of Power: British Foreign Policy 1902–1922,* p. 335–336. Warman, 'The Erosion of Foreign Office Influence in the Making of Foreign Policy, 1916–1918', *The Historical Journal,* Vol. 15 (1972), pp. 133–59.

12. Warman, op. cit., p. 135.

13. As quoted in Johnson, 'Preparing for Office: Lord Curzon as Acting Foreign Secretary, January–October 1919', in Johnson, ed., *The Foreign Office and the British Diplomacy in the Twentieth Century,* p. 57.

14. Maisel, *The Foreign Office and Foreign Policy, 1919–1926,* p. 84.

15. Warman, op. cit., p. 142.

16. Bennett, *British Foreign Policy in the Curzon Period, 1919–1924,* p. 4 (hereafter *Curzon Period*)

17. Maisel, op. cit., pp. 68–9.

18. The head of the Cabinet Secretariat, Sir Maurice Hankey, complained that he was often blamed for actions which were in fact taken by the Prime Minister's Secretariat: Naylor, *A Man and an Institution: Sir Maurice Hankey, the Cabinet Secretariat and the Custody of Cabinet Secrecy,* p. 50.

19. *Ibid.,* p. 27.

20. For details of Lloyd George's general prime ministerial style, see Morgan, 'Lloyd George's Premiership: A Study in 'Prime Ministerial Government'', *The Historical Journal,* Vol. 13 (1970), pp. 130–57.

21. Maisel, op. cit., pp. 73–4.

22. Steiner & Dockrill, 'The Foreign Office Reforms, 1919–21', *The Historical Journal,* Vol. 17 (1974), p. 147. Crowe would become permanent under-secretary of state in 1920 following after Hardinge.

23. Maisel, *op. cit,* pp. 76–7.

24. Sharp, 'Adapting to a New World? British Foreign Policy in the 1920s', in Johnson, op. cit., p. 76.

25. Lord Beaverbrook, *The Decline and Fall of Lloyd George.*

26. Bennett, 'Lloyd George, Curzon and the Control of British Foreign Policy 1919–1922', *Australian Journal of Politics and History,* Vol. 4 (1999), p. 470 (hereafter 'Lloyd George').

27. Naylor, op. cit., pp. 76–88.
28. Warman, op. cit., p. 138.
29. More on which in Chapter Four.
30. Bennett, 'Lloyd George', pp. 476–8.
31. Morgan, op. cit., p. 147; Bennett, 'Control', p. 477; Johnson, op. cit., p. 55; Nicolson, op. cit., p. 34.
32. In 1911, during his time as viceroy, Hardinge had reversed the partition of Bengal, which had been the brainchild of Curzon when he was in India. Curzon apparently never forgave Hardinge. A few years later, in 1917, Curzon had asked Hardinge for his resignation following a critical report on the Mesopotamia Campaign that had occurred under Hardinge's viceroyalty – 'I had known Curzon too long to relish having to serve under him at the Foreign Office'. Lord Hardinge of Penhurst, *Old Diplomacy*, pp. 243–4 and Maisel, op. cit., p. 41.
33. Goldstein, 'British Peace Aims and the Eastern Question: The Political Intelligence Department and the Eastern Committee, 1918', *Middle Eastern Studies*, Vol. 23 (1987), pp. 419–36 (hereafter 'Peace Aims').
34. The most common complaint made against Lloyd George is that of his conduct at the Paris Peace Conference and the various other conferences which occurred in the aftermath of the war. As Hardinge observed, the problem with the prime minister was not only his own lack of knowledge but his inability to listen to the advice of experts: 'If ever he consulted his own Delegation and their advice was not such as he desired, he would take and act upon the opinion of anybody whose views might coincide with his own, whether they really knew anything of the subject or not.' Hardinge, op. cit., p. 241.
35. McKercher, op. cit., pp. 90–1.
36. In 1922 the GC&CS and Secret Intelligence Service officially came under Foreign Office control: Maisel, op. cit., p. 6.
37. Bennett, 'Control', p. 475.
38. Gilmour, *Curzon*, p. 513; Johnson, op. cit., p. 55.
39. Glenny, 'The Anglo-Soviet Trade Agreement, March 1921', *Journal of Contemporary History*, Vol. 5, No. 2 (1970), pp. 63–82 and Ullman, *Anglo-Soviet Relations, 1917–1921: Volume Three, The Anglo-Soviet Accord* (hereafter *Anglo-Soviet Accord*).
40. The Mesopotamia Administration Committee had become the Middle East Committee in August 1917, before becoming the Eastern Committee on 21 March 1918. Permanent members of the committee included General Smuts, Arthur Balfour, Edwin Montagu and Sir Henry Wilson (CIGS). Other frequent attendants included General MacDonough (the Director of Military Intelligence), Hardinge, Sir Mark Sykes, Lancelot Oliphant of the Foreign

Office, J.E. Shuckburgh of the India Office and occasional experts. Maisel, op. cit., pp. 205–6.

41. The National Archives, (hereafter TNA)/CAB27/24, Curzon Note on Memorandum 'The War in the East', 1 Aug. 1918.
42. Goldstein, 'Peace Aims', p. 424.
43. Fisher, *Curzon*, pp. 116–17. Mark Sykes was a diplomatic adviser with a special expertise in the Middle East.
44. TNA/CAB23/23, Cabinet 82, 31 Dec. 1920. More on which in Chapter Four.
45. The Eastern Committee would become the Interdepartmental Conference on the Middle East (IDCE), followed by the Interdepartmental Committee on Bolshevism as a Menace to the British Empire and then the Interdepartmental Committee on Eastern Unrest (IDCEU). See Fisher, 'The Interdepartmental Committee on Eastern Unrest and British Responses to Bolshevik and Other Intrigues Against the Empire During the 1920s', *Journal of Asian History*, Vol. 34 (2000), pp. 1–34 (hereafter 'Interdepartmental Committee').
46. The Union of Democratic Control was one particularly vocal group which lobbied for the creation of a standing parliamentary committee on foreign relations and for all treaties to be submitted to Parliament before their conclusion. See: Swartz, *The Union of Democratic Control in British Politics During the First World War* and Bishop, *The Administration of British Foreign Relations*, pp. 131–8 and 160–1.
47. Prior to 1919, anyone wanting to work for the Foreign Office had to be nominated by the foreign secretary and be interviewed by a board of selection before they were even allowed to sit the entrance exam. This, of course, meant that the candidate had to be known personally by the foreign secretary or someone acquainted with him. Larner, 'The Amalgamation of the Diplomatic Service with the Foreign Office', *Journal of Contemporary History*, Vol. 7 (1972), p. 107.
48. *Ibid.*, pp. 107–10.
49. Craig, 'The British Foreign Office from Grey to Austen Chamberlain', in Craig and Gilbert, eds, *The Diplomats 1919–1939*, pp. 21–2.
50. Cromwell and Steiner, 'Reform and Retrenchment: The Foreign Office Between the Wars', in Bullen, ed., *The Foreign Office, 1782–1982*, pp. 85–6.
51. As quoted in Maisel, op. cit., p. 19.
52. Steiner and Dockrill, op. cit., p. 140.
53. Cromwell and Steiner, op. cit., pp. 85–108; Steiner and Dockrill, op. cit., pp. 131–56; Steiner, 'The Foreign and Commonwealth Office: Resistance and Adaption to Changing Times' in Johnson, ed., *The Foreign Office and the British Diplomacy in the Twentieth Century*, pp. 13–30 (hereafter 'Resistance').
54. Larner, op. cit., pp. 124–126; Cromwell and Steiner, op. cit., pp. 86–7; Steiner and Dockrill, op. cit., p. 144.

55. McKercher, op. cit., p. 82.
56. As quoted in *ibid.*, p. 82.
57. Neilson, *Britain and the Last Tsar. British Policy and Russia, 1894–1917*, pp. 48–50 (hereafter *Last Tsar*).
58. McKercher, op. cit., pp. 80–1. T.G. Otte discusses the concept of 'political generations' and their differing perceptions of Britain's foreign relations. See: Otte, *The Foreign Office Mind: The Making of British Foreign Policy, 1865–1914* (hereafter *Foreign Office Mind*).
59. Crowe, 'Memorandum on the Present State of British Relations with France and Germany', 1 Jan. 1907, in Gooch and Temperley, eds, *British Documents on the Origins of the War*, Vol. III, pp. 397–420.
60. McKercher, op. cit., p. 85.
61. Joll, *1914: The Unspoken Assumptions*, p. 6.
62. Steiner, 'Elitism and Foreign Policy: The Foreign Office Before the Great War', in McKercher and Moss, eds, *Shadow and Substance in British Foreign Policy, 1895–1939*, pp. 19–56.
63. Otte explores the nature of the Foreign Office mind further in his work on the pre-war period: Otte, *Foreign Office Mind*.
64. The role of the foreign secretary in the creation of foreign policy and the complexity of understanding how individuals within government influenced each other is explained further by Michael Hughes: Hughes, *British Foreign Secretaries in an Uncertain World, 1919–1939* (hereafter *Uncertain World*).
65. For example: Darwin, 'The Fear of Falling: British Politics and Imperial Decline Since 1900', *Transactions of the Royal Historical Society*, Vol. 36 (1986), pp. 27–43 (hereafter 'Fear of Falling'); Cross, *The Fall of the British Empire, 1918–1968*; Hyam, *Britain's Imperial Century 1815–1914*, 2nd ed; Dilks, ed., *Retreat from Power: Studies in Britain's Foreign Policy of the Twentieth Century, Vol. One, 1906–1939* (hereafter *Retreat*).
66. For an insight into this preoccupation with economic decline, see Supple, 'Fear of Failing: Economic History and the Decline of Britain', in Clarke and Trebilock, eds, *Understanding Decline: Perceptions and Realities of British Economic Performance*, pp. 9–29.
67. In August 1917 the new secretary of state for India, Edwin Montagu, declared to the Cabinet in a speech written by Curzon, that British policy should henceforth be ensuring 'the progressive realisation of responsible government in India as an integral part of the British Empire'. To this end, in 1919 the Montagu-Chelmsford reforms were enacted, which had at their heart the idea of giving greater control to the Indian people over their affairs. Ashton, *British Policy Towards the Indian States 1905–1939*, p. 52 and Roberts, *British Rule in India, Volume II: India Under the British Crown, 1856–1947*, pp. 583–4.

68. Cain and Hopkins, *British Imperialism: Crisis and Deconstruction, 1914–1990*, pp. 4–5 and 298.

69. *Ibid.*, p. 5.

70. Ferris, '"The Greatest Power on Earth": Great Britain in the 1920s', *The International History Review*, Vol. 13 (1991), p. 734 (hereafter 'Greatest Power').

71. Jeffrey, 'Sir Henry Wilson and the Defence of the British Empire, 1918–22', *The Journal of Imperial and Commonwealth History*, Vol. 5 (1977), pp. 270–293 (hereafter 'Wilson'); Jeffrey, *The British Army and the Crisis of Empire, 1918–1922* (hereafter *British Army*); Jeffrey, '"An English Barrack in the Oriental Seas"? India in the Aftermath of the First World War', *Modern Asian Studies*, Vol. 15 (1981), pp. 369–86 (hereafter 'English Barrack').

72. On 13 April 1919, Brigadier-General Reginald Dyer opened fire on a crowd of Indians who had gathered at the Jallianwala Bagh in Amritsar, killing 379 people and wounding over 1,200 (according to official estimates. Indian estimates are much higher). Dyer's actions caused outrage and controversy within both India and Britain. For further details of the incident, see: Wagner, *Amritsar 1919: An Empire of Fear and the Making of a Massacre*.

73. Nicolson, op. cit., p. 52.

74. McLean, *Britain and Her Buffer State. The Collapse of the Persian Empire, 1890–1914*, p. 132 (hereafter *Buffer State*).

75. Ferris, 'Greatest Power', p. 743.

76. Quoted in Kennedy, *The Realities Behind Diplomacy: Background Influences on British External Policy, 1865–1980*, p. 223. Author of the statement is unclear.

77. Gallagher and Seal, 'Britain and India between the Wars', *Modern Asian Studies*, Vol. 15 (1981), p. 388.

78. British Library (hereafter BL) MSS/Eur/E238/11 (Reading Collection (hereafter RC)), Telegram from Montagu to Reading, 14 Feb. 1922.

79. Darwin, 'Imperialism in Decline? Tendencies in British Imperial Policy between the Wars', *Historical Journal*, Vol. 23, No. 3 (1980), p. 679 (hereafter 'Imperialism').

80. Major-General Wilfred Malleson had been sent from India in June 1918 to Meshed in Persia with instructions to monitor events in the area and, if necessary, to sabotage any Turko-German advance that might ensue in the aftermath of the Treaty of Brest-Litovsk. However, Malleson soon exceeded his remit when he began to officially cooperate with the Menshevik and SR Transcaspian Government in Ashkhabad. See: Ullman, *Anglo-Soviet Relations, 1917–1921: Volume One, Intervention and the War*, pp. 311–15 (hereafter *Intervention*) and Ellis, *The Transcaspian Episode, 1918–1919* (hereafter *Transcaspian*).

81. For example, *A Collection of Reports on Bolshevism in Russia* (London: HMSO, 1919), contained eye-witness accounts of Bolshevik atrocities from various people who had managed to escape from that country and make it to Britain.

82. Thompson, 'Allied–American Intervention in Russia, 1918–1921', in Black, ed., *Rewriting Russian History: Soviet Interpretations of Russia's Past*, pp. 319–380. See also: Thompson, 'Lenin's Analysis of Intervention', *American Slavic and Eastern European Review*, Vol. 17, No. 2 (1958), pp. 151–60; Goode, *Is Intervention in Russia a Myth?*; Woodward, 'British Intervention in Russia during the First World War', *Military Affairs*, Vol. 41 (1977), pp. 171–5.

83. Brand, 'British Labour and Soviet Russia', *South Atlantic Quarterly*, Vol. 48 (1949), pp. 327–40; Graubard, *British Labour and the Russian Revolution, 1917–1924*; Macfarlane, 'Hands off Russia: British Labour and Russo-Polish War, 1920', *Past and Present*, Vol. 38 (1967), pp. 126–52; Cowden, *Russian Bolshevism and British Labour, 1917–1921*; White, 'British Labour in Soviet Russia, 1920', *The English Historical Review*, Vol. 109 (1994), pp. 621–40 (hereafter 'British Labour'); Challinor, *The Origins of British Bolshevism*.

84. Glenny, op cit.; Ullman, *Anglo-Soviet Accord*; White, *Britain*.

85. In her article on the subject, Jennifer Siegel explains that in these early days of the revolution (1918–1919), there was limited intelligence coming out of Russia and that which the British were receiving was often unreliable or contradictory. In such circumstances it was difficult to make informed judgement on the situation in Russia. Siegel, 'British Intelligence on the Russian Revolution and Civil War – A Breach at the Source', *Intelligence and National Security*, Vol. 10 (1995), pp. 468–85 (hereafter 'Breach'). Not until the 1920s would better intelligence become available.

86. Gregory, *On the Edge of Diplomacy*, p. 127; Hughes, *Inside the Enigma: British Officials in Russia, 1900–1939*, pp. 117–18 (hereafter *Enigma*).

87. Other forms of information on Bolshevism in these early months after the October revolution included Bolshevik public statements and newspapers, the reports of various Allied subjects returning to their countries, accounts of Russian émigrés fleeing the Communists and intercepted Bolshevik wireless communications. Siegel, 'Breach', p. 470. Indeed, in these early years of the Russian revolution, the Soviet government proved very inept at protecting their communications. In 1920 the Commissar for Foreign Affairs, Georgii Chicherin sent cipher keys by post to his deputy, Maxim Litvinov, in Copenhagen. He then wired to let Litvinov know of the letter and how to retrieve the keys which were written in chemical ink! Madeira, '"Because I Don't Trust Him, We are Friends": Signals Intelligence and the Reluctant Anglo-Soviet Embrace, 1917–1924', *Intelligence and National Security*, Vol. 19 (2004), pp. 32–41.

88. *Report (Political and Economic) of the Committee to Collect Information on Russia; Russia: the Official Report of the British Trades Union Delegation to Russia and*

Caucasia, Nov. and Dec., 1924 and *Report of the British Labour Delegation to Russia, 1920.*

89. One exception was Georgii Chicherin's *Two Years of Foreign Policy: The Relations of the Russian Socialist Federal Soviet Republic with Foreign Nations, from November 7, 1917, to November 7, 1919.* Although even then, Chicherin says little about Asia.
90. Stanwood, 'Revolution and the "Old Reactionary Policy": Britain in Persia, 1917', *Journal of Imperial and Commonwealth History*, Vol. 6 (1978), p. 113 (hereafter 'Britain in Persia').
91. Popplewell, *Intelligence and Imperial Defence: British Intelligence and the Defence of the Indian Empire, 1904–1924*; Fisher, 'Interdepartmental Committee'; Ferris, '"The Internationalism of Islam": The British Perception of a Muslim Menace, 1840–1951', *Intelligence and National Security*, Vol. 24 (2009), pp. 57–77 (hereafter 'Internationalism') and Madeira, op. cit.

Chapter 1: Curzon, Russia and the Great Game

1. John William Kaye helped to make the term famous when he used Conolly's papers as sources for his work on Afghanistan in this period. Kaye, *A History of War in Afghanistan.*
2. Meyer and Brysac, *Tournament of Shadows: The Great Game and the Race for Empire in Central Asia*, p. xxiii.
3. Together with Meyer, Brysac and Hopkirk, other works of interest on the Great Game include the multi-volume work by Martin Ewans which brings together contemporary writings on this subject: Ewans, ed., *The Great Game, Volumes I–VIII.* Also, Wynn, *Persia in the Great Game: Sir Percy Sykes Explorer, Consul, Soldier, Spy.*
4. Hopkirk, *The Great Game: On Secret Service in High Asia*, pp. 15–20 and 26–37 (hereafter *Great Game*).
5. Meyer and Brysac, op.cit., pp. 3–26.
6. Ingram, 'Great Britain's Great Game: An Introduction', *The International History Review*, Vol. 2 (1980), p. 167 (hereafter 'Introduction').
7. Meyer and Brysac, op. cit., pp. 94–104.
8. Ingram, 'Introduction', p. 167.
9. Hopkirk, *Great Game*, p. 383.
10. *Ibid.*, pp. 384–5.
11. Meyer and Brysac, op. cit., pp. 192–8.
12. Although Britain's position in Afghanistan would never be entirely assured. For one thing, there was a tendency for the local representatives of the Tsar's government to follow their own policies on the ground and this was the case throughout Asia. The Afghans themselves were also not particularly

happy with Britain's restrictions on their ability to conduct foreign relations. In 1915, for example, there was little India could do to stop a German mission travelling to Kabul to try to conduct relations with the emir (see Chapter Two for further details).

13. Sazonov, *Fateful Years 1909–1916. The Reminiscences of Serge Sazonov*, p. 22.

14. On the night of 21 October 1904, the Russian Baltic Fleet mistook British fishing trawlers at Dogger Bank for Japanese vessels. Three British sailors died, and a number were wounded, in the attack: Lieven, *Russia and the Origins of the First World War*, p. 28.

15. Middleton, *Britain and Russia. An Historical Essay*, p. 79.

16. Williams, 'The Strategic Backround to the Anglo-Russian Entente of August 1907', *The Historical Journal*, Vol. 9 (1966), p. 369.

17. For an excellent work on the true extent of Germany's eastern ambitions, see McMeekin, *The Berlin-Baghdad Express: The Ottoman Empire and Germany's Bid for World Power 1898–1918* (hereafter *Berlin-Baghdad*). For further information regarding the situation in the Persian Gulf, see Busch, *Britain and the Persian Gulf, 1894–1914* and Kelly, 'The Legal and Historical Basis of the British Position in the Persian Gulf', *St. Antony's Papers* (1958), pp. 119–40.

18. See Grant, ed., *The Kaiser's Letters to the Tsar*.

19. Lieven, op. cit., p. 28.

20. Neilson, *Last Tsar*, pp. 30–1.

21. Seeger, ed., *Memoirs of Alexander Iswolsky*, pp. 43–5.

22. By lending its support to the Austrian-Hungarian annexation of Bosnia and Herzegovina, Germany was attempting to demonstrate the strength of the Central Powers compared to the weakness of the Triple Entente: Neilson, *Last Tsar*, p. 306.

23. By 1909, Russia was pressing Britain for a conversion of the Convention into a formal alliance: Nicolson, *Sir Arthur Nicolson Bart, First Lord Carnock. A Study in the Old Diplomacy*, pp. 313–14.

24. *Ibid.*, pp. 269–75.

25. Neilson, *Last Tsar*, pp. 322–3.

26. Churchill, *The Anglo-Russian Convention of 1907*, p. 349.

27. Sazonov, op. cit., p. 23.

28. Middleton, *Britain and Russia*, p. 92.

29. Siegel, *Endgame*.

30. While the British shied away from the term 'sphere of influence', this was undoubtedly what the convention created. For further information regarding the negotiations and details of the convention, see Gooch and Temperley, eds, *British Documents on the Origins of the War 1898–1914. Vol. IV, The Anglo-Russian Rapprochement 1903–1907*.

31. Kazemzadeh, *Russia and Britain in Persia. A Study in Imperialism, 1864–1914*, pp. 507–8 (hereafter *Russia and Britain*).
32. The American minister in Tehran claimed that it was commonly believed 'that the "Bear" had gotten the "Lion's" share': Greaves, 'Some Aspects of the Anglo-Russian Convention and Its Working in Persia, 1907–1914 – I', *Bulletin of the School of Oriental and African Studies, University of London*, Vol. 13 (1968), p. 80.
33. Churchill, op. cit., p. 325.
34. McLean, 'English Radicals, Russia and the Fate of Persia 1907–1913', *The English Historical Review*, Vol. 93, No. 367 (1978), p. 346 (hereafter 'English Radicals'). For full information regarding the reception of the Convention in Parliament, see *Hansard Parliamentary Debates*, 4th Series, Vol. 183, 29 Jan. – 11 Feb. 1908. Also, *Hansard Parliamentary Debates*, 4th Series, Vol. 184, 12 Feb. – 26 Feb. 1908.
35. McLean, *Buffer State,* p. 104.
36. McLean, 'English Radicals', p. 345.
37. Ross, 'Lord Curzon and E.G. Browne Confront the 'Persian Question'', *The Historical Journal*, Vol. 52 (2009), pp. 402–5.
38. McLean, 'English Radicals', p. 340.
39. *Ibid.*, p. 346.
40. Neilson, *Last Tsar*, p. 325.
41. Greaves, op. cit., p. 80.
42. Klein, 'The Anglo-Russian Convention and the Problem of Central Asia, 1907–1914', *The Journal of British Studies*, Vol. 11 (1971), p. 138 (hereafter 'Convention').
43. Klein, 'British Intervention in the Persian Revolution, 1905–1909', *The Historical Journal*, Vol. 15 (1972), p. 739 (hereafter 'Persian Revolution').
44. Sir George Barclay as quoted in Kazemzadeh, *Russia and Britain*, p. 511.
45. Sareen, *India and Afghanistan: British Imperialism vs. Afghan Nationalism, 1907–1921*, pp. 21–7.
46. Habberton, *Anglo-Russian Relations Concerning Afghanistan, 1837–1907*, pp. 68–81.
47. Klein, 'Persian Revolution', pp. 731–52.
48. *Ibid.*, p. 741.
49. There was a certain concern that Persia could end up as a base for 'revolutionary forays' against the Russian government: *Ibid.*, p. 740.
50. Created in 1879, the Cossack Division was a Persian force that was organised, trained and officered by Russians and which served as a personal guard to the shah: Kazemzadeh, 'The Origin and Early Development of the Persian Cossack Brigade', *American Slavic and East European Review*, Vol. 15, No. 3 (1956), pp. 351–5 (hereafter 'Origin').

51. Sweet and Langhorne, 'Great Britain and Russia, 1907–1914', in Hinsley, ed., *British Foreign Policy under Sir Edward Grey*, p. 239.
52. McLean, *Buffer State*, p. 137.
53. Kazemzadeh, 'Russia and the Middle East', in Lederer, ed., *Russian Foreign Policy. Essays in Political Perspective*, p. 494.
54. Klein, 'Persian Revolution', pp. 746–8.
55. *Ibid.*, p. 746.
56. Sweet, op. cit., p. 239.
57. A note was even drawn up between Britain and Russia, and presented to the Persian government, which emphasised their respect for the independence of the Persian nation: Churchill, op. cit., p. 313.
58. *Ibid.*, p. 316.
59. *Ibid.*, p. 319.
60. Grey, *Twenty-Five Years 1892–1916*, p. 169. For Shuster's point of view on Persia, see Shuster, *The Strangling of Persia*.
61. This is not to say that this mentality did not then manifest itself in physical forms such as with the building of railways or the despatch of intelligence officers. Rather, it is to say that these things did not define the Great Game and therefore we need to look elsewhere to better understand this concept of Anglo-Russian rivalry.
62. Interestingly, the notorious KGB mole H.A.R. Philby was given his nickname 'Kim' by his father, in homage to the Kipling character. Indeed, Philby was born in India in 1921, his father a civil servant of the Raj whom the Soviets erroneously believed to be a British secret service agent. Meyer and Brysac, op. cit., pp. xxiv–xxv.
63. Gleason, *The Genesis of Russophobia in Great Britain*, pp. 1–3 and 280.
64. Neilson, *Last Tsar*, pp. 84–109.
65. *Ibid.*, pp. 84–5.
66. Ashton, *British Policy Towards the Indian States, 1905–1939*, p. 3.
67. de Lacy Evans, *On the Practicability of an Invasion of British India*, front page. Emphasis in original. Peter the Great's project is explained further on.
68. Curzon, *Russia in Central Asia in 1889 and the Anglo-Russian Question*, pp. 320–321 (hereafter *Russia*).
69. Yapp, 'British Perceptions of the Russian Threat to India', *Modern Asian Studies*, Vol. 21, No. 4 (1987), pp. 647–65.
70. Prestona, 'Sir Charles MacGregor and the Defence of India, 1857–1887', *The Historical Journal*, Vol. 12, No. 1 (1969), pp. 58–77.
71. Williams, op. cit., pp. 360–363.
72. Hopkirk, *Great Game*, pp. 26–30.
73. A squadron of Orenburg Cossacks was dispatched in January 1801 but was recalled when Paul was deposed and killed in March: Yapp, op. cit., pp. 664–5.

74. That McNeill, an ardent Russophobe, was appointed minister to Tehran is indicative of the nature of Anglo–Russian relations at the time. Habberton, op. cit., p. 9.

75. Hopkirk, *Great Game*, pp. 163–4.

76. McLean, *Buffer State*, p. 14.

77. Hopkirk, *Great Game*, p. 20.

78. As quoted in Meyer and Brysac, op. cit., p. 121.

79. A term borrowed by Meyer and Brysac for their book on the subject: Meyer and Brysac, *op. cit.*, p. xviii.

80. Beaverbrook, op. cit., p. 46.

81. Moore, 'Curzon and Indian Reform', *Modern Asian Studies*, Vol. 27 (1993), p. 722.

82. BL/MSS/Eur/E264/4 (MC), Letter from Montagu to Chelmsford, 15 June 1918.

83. Meyer and Brysac, op. cit., p. 285.

84. Jones, 'Lord Curzon of Kedleston, 1859–1925: An Appreciation', *International Affairs*, Vol. 37, No. 3 (1961), p. 337.

85. Hardinge, op. cit., p. 244.

86. Earl of Ronaldshay, The Life of Lord Curzon, *Volume Three*, p. 5.

87. Dilks, *Curzon in India, Vol. I*, pp. 27–28 (hereafter *Curzon*).

88. Bosworth, 'The Hon. George Nathaniel Curzon's Travels in Russian Central Asia and Persia', *Iran*, Vol. 31 (1993), p. 127.

89. *Ibid.*, pp. 127–8.

90. Dilks, *Curzon*, pp. 30–1.

91. Curzon, *Russia*, p. 13.

92. *Ibid.*, pp. 34–62.

93. Bosworth, op. cit., pp. 128–9.

94. Dilks, *Curzon*, p. 162.

95. Nicolson, *Curzon*, p. 52.

96. Curzon, *Russia*, pp. 13–14.

97. McLean, *Buffer State*, p. 43.

98. Meyer and Brysac, op. cit., p. 283.

99. Ross, op. cit., pp. 393–4.

100. *Ibid.*, p. 394.

101. Curzon, *Russia*, p. 356.

102. Curzon, *Persia and the Persian Question*, pp. 3–4 (hereafter *Persia*).

103. Ross, op. cit., pp. 391–2.

104. Ibid., pp. 270–3.

105. For example, the chapter on Curzon in H. Tinker's work on the viceroys is entitled 'Curzon: The Most Viceregal Viceroy': Tinker, *Viceroy: Curzon to Mountbatten*, p. 19.

106. Meyer and Brysac, op. cit., p. 294.
107. *Ibid.*, pp. 294–5.
108. Dilks, *Curzon*, pp. 41–2.
109. Tinker, op. cit., p. 19.
110. Lord Salisbury took over both the premiership and Foreign Office in 1895, relinquishing the latter in 1900, and the former in 1902.
111. Not to be confused with the Charles Hardinge mentioned above, who was 1st Baron Hardinge of Penhurst and Viceroy of India 1910–1916.
112. Michael Hughes has argued something similar, believing that the attributes which made Curzon a good viceroy actually hindered him when he became foreign secretary. Hughes, *Uncertain World*, p. 15.
113. McLean, *Buffer State*, pp. 31–2.
114. Dilks, *Curzon*, pp. 157–8.
115. Dilks, *Curzon in India, Vol. II*, pp. 57–58 (hereafter *Curzon, Vol. II*).
116. McLean, *Buffer State*, pp. 47–9.
117. Dilks, *Curzon, Vol. II*, p. 74.
118. *Ibid.*, pp. 74–101.
119. Meyer and Brysac, op. cit., p. 306.
120. Dilks, *Curzon, Vol. II*, p. 81.
121. *Ibid.*, p. 76.
122. Hughes, *Diplomacy before the Russian Revolution: Britain, Russia and the Old Diplomacy, 1894–1917*, p. 41 (hereafter *Diplomacy*).
123. Dilks, *Curzon, Vol. II*, p. 257.
124. Gilmour, op. cit., p. 510.
125. Churchill, op. cit., p. 329.
126. Fisher, *Curzon and British Imperialism in the Middle East, 1916–1919*, p. 10 (hereafter *Curzon*).
127. For more on Britain's relations with Persia and Afghanistan in the nineteenth century see Yapp, *Strategies of British India: Britain, Iran and Afghanistan, 1798–1850* (hereafter *Strategies*).

Chapter 2: The Iron Hand and the Velvet Glove, 1918–1919

1. Jeffrey, *British Army*, p. 1.
2. *Ibid.*, p. 31.
3. *Ibid.*, p. 1.
4. For more on the Paris peace conference see Macmillan, *Peacemakers: The Paris Conference of 1919 and Its Attempt to End War*.
5. Nicolson, op. cit., p. 2.
6. Fisher, *Curzon*, p. 124.
7. Fisher, 'Interdepartmental Committee', p. 33.

8. TNA/CAB27/37, Indian Desiderata for Peace Settlement. Note by Political Department, India Office, 4 Dec. 1918.

9. Gallagher and Seal, op. cit., p. 394.

10. The South Persia Rifles were formed in 1916 to counter German influence in Persia. Led by Sir Percy Sykes, the SPR consisted of a few British officers and Indian troops and a number of local recruits. See: Sykes, 'South Persia and the Great War', *The Geographical Journal*, Vol. 58, No. 2 (1921), pp. 101–16.

11. TNA/CAB27/24, Minutes of Eastern Committee Meeting, 24 June 1918.

12. TNA/CAB27/24, Memorandum 'The War in the East', 5 July 1918. William Olson notes that throughout the nineteenth century such a set up essentially led to Britain having two foreign policies towards Persia: a British one and an Indian one. Olson, *Anglo-Iranian Relations During World War I*, p. 2.

13. TNA/CAB27/24, Memorandum 'The War in the East', 5 July 1918.

14. TNA/CAB27/24, Minutes of Eastern Committee Meeting, 4 July 1918.

15. TNA/CAB27/24, Memorandum 'The War in the East', 5 July 1918.

16. TNA/CAB27/24, Foreign Office Note on Memorandum 'The War in the East', 17 July 1918.

17. TNA/CAB27/24, War Office Report on Memorandum 'The War in the East', 15 July 1918.

18. TNA/CAB27/24, Curzon Note on Memorandum 'The War in the East', 1 Aug. 1918.

19. TNA/CAB27/24, War Office Report on Memorandum 'The War in the East', 15 July 1918 and TNA/CAB27/24, Foreign Office Note on Memorandum 'The War in the East', 17 July 1918.

20. Maisel, op. cit., pp. 205–6.

21. Mejcher, 'British Middle East Policy 1917–21: The Inter-Departmental Level', *Journal of Contemporary History*, Vol. 8, No. 4 (1973), p. 81.

22. Maisel, op. cit., p. 206.

23. Fisher, *Curzon*, p. 111

24. TNA/CAB27/24, Curzon Note on Memorandum 'The War in the East', 1 Aug. 1918.

25. Maisel, op. cit., p. 210.

26. TNA/CAB27/24, Minutes of Eastern Committee Meeting, 13 Aug. 1918.

27. TNA/CAB27/24, Minutes of Eastern Committee Meeting, 13 Aug. 1918. Threatening to resign when he was unhappy was a favoured tactic of Curzon: 'Curzon was always sending me letters of resignation. He would send them by a messenger afflicted with a club-foot. A second more nimble messenger would thereafter be despatched with a second letter.' Lloyd George, as quoted in Nicolson, *Curzon*, p. 214.

28. TNA/CAB27/39, Dissolution of the Eastern Committee, 10 Jan. 1919. Fisher, 'Interdepartmental Committee', p. 2.

29. Maisel, op. cit., p. 212.

30. Stanwood, *War*, p. 24.

31. Mejcher, op. cit., pp. 96–101.

32. Nicolson, op. cit., p. 121.

33. TNA/CAB27/24, Minutes of Eastern Committee Meeting, 30 Dec. 1918.

34. TNA/CAB27/24, Eastern Committee Meeting, 24 June 1918; TNA/CAB27/24, Eastern Committee Meeting, 4 July 1918.

35. Presumably Cox was referring to America since it was predicted to play a large role in the future League of Nations.

36. Ghani, *Iran and the Rise of Reza Shah: From Qajar Collapse to Pahlavi Power*, p. 28. For more on Cox see Graves, *The Life of Sir Percy Cox* and Townsend, *Proconsul to the Middle East: Sir Percy Cox and the End of Empire* – although Townsend's chapter on Persia is very brief.

37. TNA/FO371/3263/196918, Chelmsford to Foreign Office, 27 Nov. 1918.

38. TNA/FO371/3263/197283, Cox to Foreign Office, 29 Nov. 1918. William Olson believes that Cox was just as dismissive of the opinion of the Indian government as Curzon was, and together both 'were ready to override all opposition that interefered with their vision for a Persian settlement'. Olson, 'The Genesis of the Anglo-Persian Agreement of 1919', in Kedourie and Haim, eds., *Towards a Modern Iran: Studies in Thought, Politics and Society*, p. 206.

39. For discussion on the historiography of pan-Islamism, see Lee, 'The Origins of Pan-Islamism', *The American Historical Review*, Vol. 47, No. 2 (1942), pp. 278–87.

40. Naeem Qureshi, *Pan-Islam in British Indian Politics: A Study of the Khilafat Movement, 1918–1924*, p. 62.

41. Aziz, *Britain and Muslim India: A Study of British Public Opinion vis-a-'vis the Development of Muslim Nationalism in India, 1857–1947*, pp. 76–94.

42. 'There is no doubt that, at the turn of the century, Turkey had come to occupy a place in the minds and hearts of large sections of the Muslim community': Nanda, *Gandhi, Pan-Islamism, Imperialism and Nationalism in India*, p. 108.

43. Kemal Öke, *The Turkish War of Independence and the Independence Struggle of the South Asian Muslims: "the Khilafat Movement", 1919–1924*, p. 72.

44. This will be discussed further in Chapter Three.

45. British Library, India Office Records, Political and Secret Department (hereafter BL/IOR/L/PS) 11/142/5466/1918, Memorandum by the India Office on The Future of Russian Central Asia, 3 Dec. 1918.

46. H. Sabahi has noted the Indian government's attention to the 'rising tide of nationalism in the region' and its sensitivity to Muslim feeling at this time. Sabahi, op. cit., p. 7.

47. TNA/FO371/3263/191541, Malleson to Chief of General Staff, 3 Sept. 1918.

48. In these early days the Tashkent Soviet included Mensheviks and Left SRs as well as Bolsheviks. Carrére D' Encausse, *Islam and the Russian Empire: Reform and Revolution in Central Asia*, p. 148.

49. Mawdsley, *The Russian Civil War*, pp. 236–237; Carr, *The Bolshevik revolution, 1917–1923, Vol. I*, pp. 330–1 and Swain, *Russia's Civil War*.

50. Dailami, 'Bravin in Tehran and the Origins of Soviet Policy in Iran', *Revolutionary Russia*, Vol. 12 (1999), pp. 63–82 (hereafter 'Bravin').

51. Volodarsky, *The Soviet Union and its Southern Neighbours Iran and Afghanistan, 1917–1933*, pp. 12–15.

52. BL/IOR/L/PS/11/130/170/1918, Marling to Foreign Office, 12 Jan. 1918; TNA/FO371/3858/13066, Lieutenant-Colonel Grey, Indian Agent Khorasan, to Government of India, 27 Sept. 1918. All of Bravin's communications with Russia were being intercepted and read by the British. Chaqueri, *The Soviet Socialist Republic of Iran, 1920–1921: Birth of the Trauma*, p. 147 (hereafter *Birth of a Trauma*).

53. TNA/FO248/1213, Bravin to Chicherin, 19 June 1918.

54. Dailami, 'Bravin', p. 74.

55. Von Laue, 'Soviet Diplomacy: G.V. Chicherin, Peoples Commissar for Foreign Affairs, 1918–1930', in Craig and Gilbert, op. cit., p. 235.

56. Blank, 'Soviet Politics and the Iranian Revolution of 1919–1921, *Cahiers du Monde russe et soviétique*, Vol. 21 (1980), pp. 173–94.

57. Bravin was a supporter of the Jangalis ('Forest People'), a group of revolutionary Persians based in the north of the country at Gilan and led by Kuchik Khan who, since 1914, had agitated for a continuation for the Constitutional Revolution which had begun in 1905 in Persia, but had been suppressed in 1911 by Tsarist Russia. Dailami, 'Bravin', pp. 75–8. In July 1920 at the Second Congress of the Comintern this issue of whether the Bolsheviks should support 'bourgeois nationalist' movements would be the central feature. For more, see Chapter Three.

58. During 1921 the Soviet government would negotiate a number of treaties with different nations, including Persia, Afghanistan, Turkey and Britain (see Chapter Four). Meanwhile, Bravin would be recalled from Tehran in June 1918 and sent to Kabul. His replacement, I.O. Kolomytsev would have just as little success in Persia as Bravin, and was forced to leave in November 1918 when the Soviet legation was attacked by the Cossack Division. In August 1919 Kolomytsev would be murdered by the Whites as he tried to return to Persia. Volodarsky, op. cit., pp. 21–4. Not until April 1921, when Theodore Rothstein arrived, would the Soviet government have a professional representative in Persia.

59. TNA/FO371/3858/4506, Report by Colonel George Churchill on conversation with Samad Khan, 31 Dec. 1918.

60. TNA/FO371/3263/189123, Cox to Foreign Office, 15 Nov. 1918. Oliphant was an assistant clerk who had been employed in both Constantinople and Tehran. He now ran the War Department within the Foreign Office and would become the head of the Eastern Department.
61. TNA/CAB27/24, Minutes of Eastern Committee Meeting, 19 Dec. 1918.
62. TNA/CAB27/24, Minutes of Eastern Committee Meeting, 19 Dec. 1918.
63. Goldstein, 'Political Intelligence Department', p. 420.
64. TNA/FO371/3263/211466, Memorandum by L. Mallet, 21 Dec. 1918.
65. TNA/FO371/3858/150, Memorandum by Sir Hamilton Grant, 20 Dec. 1918.
66. Unwilling to allow Persia to become a passage for German and Turkish troops into Central Asia and India, British and Russian forces occupied large parts of the country during the conflict. For more see: Fatemi, *Diplomatic History of Persia 1917–1923: Anglo-Russian Power Politics in Iran*, pp. 2–9 (hereafter *History of Persia*) and Moberly, *Operations in Persia 1914–1919*.
67. BL/IOR/L/PS/10/735/1000/18, Telegram from Viceroy to the Secretary of State for India, 2 Nov. 1918.
68. Stanwood, 'Britain in Persia', p. 149; Ross, op. cit., p. 270.
69. TNA/CAB27/24, Minutes of Eastern Committee Meeting, 30 Dec. 1918.
70. TNA/CAB27/24, Minutes of Eastern Committee Meeting, 30 Dec. 1918.
71. BL/IOR/L/PS/10/780/18/1919, Payments for Maintenance of Cossack Division, Pts 1 & 2. Interdepartmental Conference on Middle Eastern Affairs, 22 Feb. 1919.
72. TNA/FO371/3858/13186, Cox to Foreign Office, 21 Jan. 1919.
73. '...the Russian officers who control the [Cossack] force regard themselves as guarantors of the interests in Persia of the future Russian Government which, they expect, will pursue the old Russian policy in Persia.' TNA/CAB27/38, Memorandum regarding the policy of His Majesty's Government towards Persia at the Peace Conference, 17 Dec. 1918.
74. TNA/FO371/3263/191994, Cox to Foreign Office, 20 Nov. 1918.
75. The Russians in Persia 'are like the Bourbons, in as much as they have learnt nothing and forgotten nothing': TNA/FO371/3263/202308, Malleson to Chief of General Staff, 20 Sept. 1918. See also, TNA/FO371/3858/30241, Malleson to Cox, 13 Oct. 1918; Cox to the Government of India, 17 Oct. 1918; Cox to the Government of India, 17 Oct. 1918; Cox to the Government of India, 22 Oct. 1918; TNA/FO371/3858/30240, Cox to the Government of India, 17 Nov. 1918; TNA/FO371/3858/30240, Cox to the Government of India, 29 Nov. 1918.
76. TNA/FO371/3859/40590, Chief of General Staff to Malleson, 6 Dec. 1918.
77. Volodarsky, op. cit., p. 5.
78. TNA/FO371/3263/191994, Cox to Foreign Office, 20 Nov. 1918.
79. TNA/CAB27/24, Minutes of Eastern Committee Meeting, 30 Dec. 1918

80. BL/IOR/L/PS/10/734/1000/18, Telegram from Sir C. Marling to Foreign Office, 24 April 1918.
81. TNA/FO371/3263/210529, Memorandum by Sir C. Marling, 20 Dec. 1918.
82. TNA/FO371/3858/30240, Cox to the Government of India, 29 Nov. 1918.
83. TNA/FO371/3263/211466, Memorandum by L. Mallet, 21 Dec. 1918.
84. TNA/FO371/3858/1841, Shuckburgh to Foreign Office, 3 Jan. 1918.
85. BL/IOR/L/PS/11/142/5383/1918, Minute by India Office [author unclear], 22 Dec. 1918.
86. TNA/FO371/3263/197385, Minute by Oliphant, 30 Nov. 1918.
87. TNA/FO371/3858/1841, Minute by Oliphant, 4 Jan. 1918.
88. TNA/FO371/3860/65465, Chelmsford to Foreign Office, 26 April 1919.
89. TNA/FO371/3990/63630, Telegram Chief Commissioner North-West Frontier Province to Delhi, 23 Feb. 1919.
90. Gallagher and Seal, op. cit., pp. 387–414.
91. BL/MSS/Eur/E264/4 (Chelmsford Collection (hereafter CC)), Letter from Chelmsford to Montagu, 30 Sept. 1918.
92. TNA/FO371/3263/212539, Letter from India Office to Foreign Office, 27 Dec. 1918.
93. TNA/FO371/3263/201353, Minute on telegram from Cox to Foreign Office, 7 Dec. 1918.
94. BL/MSS/Eur/E264/4 (CC), Letter from Chelmsford to Montagu, 12 Dec. 1918.
95. TNA/CAB27/24, Foreign Office Note on Memorandum 'The War in the East', 17 July 1918.
96. BL/MSS/Eur/E264/4 (CC), Letter from Chelmsford to Montagu, 12 Dec. 1918. The expedition of October–November 1915 to capture Baghdad had led to a severe defeat of the Indian Army at the hands of Turkish troops and the loss of thousands of lives. In June 1917, the report of the Mesopotamia Commission gave a powerful indictment of the entire campaign and caused the subsequent resignation of the then secretary of state for India, Austen Chamberlain. For more information see Goold, 'Lord Hardinge and the Mesopotamia Expedition and Inquiry, 1914–1917', *The Historical Journal*, Vol. 19, No. 4 (1976), pp. 919–45.
97. TNA/FO371/3860/77565, Interdepartmental Conference On Middle Eastern Affairs, 7 May 1919.
98. TNA/FO371/3860/68201, Shuckburgh to Foreign Office, 3 May 1919.
99. TNA/CAB27/24, Minutes of Eastern Committee Meeting, 30 Dec. 1918.
100. Curzon to his wife, 17 August 1919. See Ronaldshay, op. cit., p. 217.
101. TNA/FO371/3862/113492, Agreement between the Governments of Great Britain and Persia, 8 Aug. 1919.
102. TNA/FO371/3862/114911, Memorandum by Curzon, 12 Aug. 1919.

103. The *Times*, 16 Aug. 1919.

104. *Daily Telegraph*, 16 Aug. 1919.

105. *Manchester Guardian*, 16 Aug. 1919.

106. Stanwood, *War*, pp. 74–5.

107. TNA/FO371/3863/122515, Cox to Foreign Office, 29 Aug. 1919.

108. TNA/FO371/3862/118250, Curzon to Lindsay, 18 Aug. 1919; TNA/FO371/3863/127878 Cox to Foreign Office relaying American communiqué, 10 Sept. 1919; TNA/FO371/3863/128532, Curzon to Mr Davis, 13 Sept. 1919. For more on American and French reaction to the agreement, see Fatemi, *History of Persia*, pp. 54–72.

109. TNA/FO371/3863/123784, Cox to Foreign Office, 1 Sept. 1919.

110. Pearce, *The Staroselsky Problem 1918–1920: An Episode in British–Russian Relations in Persia*, p. 13 (hereafter *Staroselsky Problem*) and Dailami, 'The Bolsheviks and the Jangali Revolutionary Movement, 1915–1920', *Cahiers du Monde russe et soviétique,* Vol. 31 (1990), p. 44 (hereafter 'Bolsheviks').

111. TNA/FO371/3864/135600, Lord Derby to Foreign Office, 30 Sept. 1919.

112. TNA/FO371/3864/137710, Cox to Foreign Office, 1 Oct. 1919.

113. Pearce, *Staroselsky Problem*, p. 45.

114. TNA/FO371/3864/137710, Cox to Foreign Office, 1 Oct. 1919.

115. Sareen, *India and Afghanistan: British Imperialism vs. Afghan Nationalism, 1907–1921*, pp. 10–11.

116. TNA/CAB27/24, Minutes of Eastern Committee Meeting, 24 June 1918. In September 1915 a Turko-German contingent (the Niedermayer Mission) arrived in Kabul with the aim of persuading the Afghan emir to join the war on the side of the Central Powers. Emir Habibullah deftly managed to stall the Germans and Turks with promises of support which he never intended on fulfilling. Arghandawi, *British Imperialism and Afghanistan's Struggle for Independence, 1914–1921*, pp. 94–105.

117. TNA/CAB27/24, Note by C.I.G.S. on British Policy in Afghanistan and Turkestan, 21 June 1918.

118. TNA/CAB27/24, Minutes of Eastern Committee Meeting, 24 June 1918.

119. Habibullah lamented: 'The intervention of Turkey in the war has caused my position to become indescribable; I am between the devil and the deep sea, with a friend on the one hand and a brother in faith, weak and in need of help, on the other hand, asking me for help against the first friend'. BL/IOR/L/P&S/10/202. Kabul Diary, 31 May 1916. See also Gregorian, *The Emergence of Modern Afghanistan: Politics of Reform and Modernization, 1880–1946*, pp. 221–4.

120. TNA/CAB27/24, Minutes of Eastern Committee Meeting, 4 July 1918.

121. The anti-British/pan-Islam sentiment had grown so strong within Afghanistan by 1919 that there is some reason to believe this was the motivation behind the emir's assassination. Heathcote, *The Afghan Wars, 1839–1919*, p. 169.

122. TNA/FO371/3990/63630, Telegram from British Agent in Kabul to Delhi, 23 Feb. 1919. Telegram from Secretary of the Government of India to Teheran, 4 March 1919.
123. Amanullah had always been a leading figure of the modernist–nationalist faction of the royal court – a group which advocated a strong Afghanistan could only be achieved through modernisation and independence. Gregorian, op. cit., p. 220.
124. Poullada, *Reform and Rebellion in Afghanistan, 1919–1929*, p. 234.
125. On his accession Habibullah too had tried to free himself of British constraints, initially refusing to re-negotiate the treaty which his father had concluded with India. Traditionally any agreements between India and Afghanistan were specific to a particular emir – when an Afghan ruler died, his successor had to negotiate his own settlement. This was a subtle (and patronising) way of Britain influencing Afghanistan's governance – it meant each new emir had to gain British approval before being deemed a legitimate ruler. Gregorian, op. cit., pp. 206–8.
126. 'I put the Crown of the Islamic Kingdom of Afghanistan on my head in the name of the internal and external independence and freedom of Afghanistan... No Foreign Kingdom has any right of protection and control over you [the Afghan people].' TNA/FO371/3990/91692, Copy of proclamation by Amir Amanullah, forwarded to the Foreign Secretary of India by the Chief Commissioner of Baluchistan, 28 April 1919.
127. Sims-Williams, 'The Afghan Newspaper Siraj al-Akhbar', *British Society for Middle Eastern Studies*, Vol. 7, No. 2 (1980), pp. 118–22.
128. TNA/FO371/3990/98423, Leaflet from Amir discussing unrest in India, 7 May 1919.
129. TNA/FO371/3991/134685, A Brief Narrative of the Hostilities with Afghanistan in 1919, 29 Sept. 1919. For more on the actual war see: Heathcote, op. cit., pp. 177–195 and Molesworth, *Afghanistan, 1919: An Account of Operations in the Third Afghan War*. On a slight aside, one of the junior officers of the RAF for whom the bombing campaign in Afghanistan proved formative was Arthur Harris – later to be 'Bomber' Harris, head of RAF Bomber Command during the Second World War. Heathcote, op. cit., p. 195.
130. 'Malleson reports low class elements in Meshed hostile to British and Pan-Islam-cum-Bolshevik propaganda reported greatly on increase in Afghanistan, Persian and Turkestan districts'. BL/IOR/L/PS/10/809/1061/1919 'Telegram from Viceroy to the India Office', 16 May 1919.
131. BL/IOR/L/PS/10/809/1061/1919 'Telegram from Chief of General Staff to Director of Military Intelligence', 30 May 1919.
132. TNA/FO371/3990/117730, Telegram from Viceroy to Secretary of State for India relaying intercepted Russian telegram from Tashkend to Moscow, 23 May 1919.

133. TNA/FO371/3990/89581, Extract from *Isvestiia* of interview with Professor Barakatulla, 6 May 1919.
134. Ansari, op. cit., p. 515.
135. TNA/FO371/3990/89581, Extract from *Isvestiia* of interview with Professor Barakatulla, 6 May 1919.
136. Druhe, op. cit., pp. 20–2.
137. Ansari, op. cit., p. 519.
138. BL/IOR/L/PS/10/809/1061/1919, Telegram from Mr Dobbs to Sir Hamilton Grant, 1 July 1919.
139. TNA/FO371/3991/13110, Record of Indo–Afghan Peace Conference. Second Meeting, 29 July 1919.
140. Imam, 'Effects', p. 81.
141. TNA/FO371/3990/77273 'Report by Indian Political Department to the Foreign Office on Afghanistan Situation', 17 May 1919.
142. TNA/FO371/3991/13110, Record of Indo-Afghan Conference. First Meeting, 26 July 1919.
143. TNA/FO371/3991/166259, Letter from Sir Hamilton Grant to Indian Government, 6 Sept. 1919.
144. TNA/FO371/3991/131110, Record of Indo-Afghan Peace Conference. Second Meeting, 29 July 1919.
145. Reetz, *Hijrat: The Flight of the Faithful: A British File on the Exodus of Muslim Peasants from North India to Afghanistan in 1920*, p. 24.
146. TNA/FO371/3991/126609, Telegram from Chief British Representative of the Indo-Afghan Peace Conference to the Indian government, 29 July 1919.
147. BL/IOR/L/PS/10/809/1061/1919, Telegram from Mr Dobbs to Sir Hamilton Grant, 1 July 1919.
148. For greater detail on the nature of Bolshevik foreign policy see Debo, *Survival and Consolidation: The Foreign Policy of Soviet Russia, 1918–1921* (hereafter *Survival*); Debo, *Revolution and Survival: The Foreign Policy of Soviet Russia, 1917–1918* (hereafter *Revolution*); Uldricks, *Diplomacy and Ideology: Origins of Soviet Foreign Relations, 1917–1930* and O'Connor, *Diplomacy*. Fischer's, *The Soviets in World Affairs, Vol. 1* is an older work but still of value.
149. BL/MSS/Eur/D523/3 (Montagu Collection (hereafter MC)), Letter from Montagu to Chelmsford, 11 June 1919.
150. TNA/FO371/3990/95062, Telegram from the Viceroy to the Secretary of State for India, 26 June 1919.
151. BL/IOR/L/PS/10/809/1061/1919, Note by Secretary of the Military Department on Memorandum 'Afghanistan. Question of Future Relations', 23 June 1919.
152. General Skeen, *Lessons in Imperial Rule: Instructions for British Infantrymen on the Indian Frontier*, 5th edition, pp. v-xii.

153. 'We are undoubtedly anxious about our military capacity at the present moment to go through with this war satisfactorily', MSS/Eur/E264/5, Letter from Chelmsford to Montagu, June 18 1919.

154. BL/IOR/L/PS/10/809/1061/1919, Telegram from Secretary of State for India to Viceroy, 16 July 1919.

155. BL/IOR/L/PS/10/809/1061/1919, Telegram from Viceroy to Secretary of State for India, 30 June 1919.

156. BL/IOR/L/PS/10/809/1061/1919, Telegram from Viceroy to Secretary of State for India, 12 July 1919.

157. BL/IOR/L/PS/10/809/1061/1919, Telegram from Viceroy to Secretary of State for India, 12 July 1919.

158. Sakhawaz, 'The Role of Afghan Intellectuals in Modernisation and Independence from Britain', www.goftaman.com/daten/en/articles/article47 [accessed 11/11/11].

159. Gregorian, op. cit., pp. 225–226. Sir Percy Sykes even believes that Habibullah might not have been assassinated had he actually been able to gain Afghanistan's freedom from British hegemony: Sykes, *A History of Afghanistan*, p. 265.

160. Gregorian, op. cit., p. 229.

161. As had been the case with the Niedermayer Mission: Delhi had no real choice other than to ignore the fact that Habibullah had technically violated his agreement with India by talking to the Germans and Turks.

162. BL/IOR/L/PS/10/809/1061/1919, Telegram from Sir Hamilton Grant to Major-General Sir George Roos-Keppel, 20 June 1919.

163. BL/IOR/L/PS/10/809/1061/1919, Telegram from Sir George Roos-Keppel to Sir Hamilton Grant, 24 June 1919.

164. BL/MSS/Eur/E264/5 (CC), Letter from Chelmsford to Montagu, 4 June 1919.

165. TNA/FO371/3991/150698, Telegram from Chief Delegate of Indo-Afghan peace to Viceroy, 8 Aug. 1919.

166. BL/IOR/L/PS/10/809/1061/1919, Treaty with Afghanistan, 8 Aug. 1919.

167. BL/MSS/Eur/D523/3 (MC), Letter from Montagu to Chelmsford, 11 Sept. 1919.

168. BL/IOR/L/PS/10/813/1229/1919, North-West Frontier Provincial Diaries (1919–1920), No.35 week ending 30 Aug. 1919.

169. TNA/FO371/3991/166259, Report from the Foreign and Political Department on Indo-Afghan Peace, 2 Oct. 1919.

170. BL/MSS/Eur/D523/3 (MC), Letter from Montagu to Chelmsford, 7 Nov. 1919.

171. For example, the Bolshevik 'Appeal to the Moslems of Russia and the East', which incited the people of Asia to rise up against British imperial rule. Bunyan and Fisher, op. cit., pp. 467–9.
172. Darwin, *Britain, Egypt and the Middle East: Imperial Policy in the Aftermath of War, 1918–1922*, p. 159 (hereafter *Britain*).
173. 'Unless we drive Afghanistan into the arms of the Bolsheviks, we have, I believe, little or nothing to fear from Bolshevik influence in Afghanistan', TNA/FO371/3991/166259, Letter from Hamilton Grant to Simla, 6 Sept. 1919.
174. Olson, op. cit., p. 225.
175. BL/MSS/Eur/E264/5, Letter from Chelmsford to Montagu, 8 Oct. 1919.
176. TNA/FO371/3990/84239, Letter from Viceroy to the Amir of Afghanistan, 3 June 1919.

Chapter 3: A Nice State of Affairs, 1920

1. Curzon gained sole control of the Foreign Office when Balfour retired as Foreign Secretary in October 1919.
2. TNA/FO371/4909/C8788, *Times* article on Lord Curzon's speech to the Central Asiatic Society, 14 Oct. 1920.
3. Darwin, *Britain*, p. 30.
4. For more on this see: Macfarlane, op. cit., pp. 126–52.
5. Mowat, op. cit., pp. 24–5.
6. *Ibid.*, pp. 38–9.
7. Darwin, 'Fear of Falling', p. 27.
8. The Triple Alliance comprised the National Union of Mineworkers, the National Transport Workers' Federation and the National Union of Railwaymen: Mowat, op. cit., p. 42.
9. Jeffrey, *British Army*, p. 28.
10. The Imperial War Museum (hereafter IWM) HHW/1/35/1, Sir Henry Wilson, diary 22 Jan. 1920.
11. Darwin, *Britain*, p. 33.
12. Gilbert, *Companion, Vol. IV, Part 2*: Cabinet memorandum by Churchill on Army Estimates, 7 Feb. 1920, pp. 1030–1 and Jeffrey, *British Army*, p. 23.
13. Jeffrey, *British Army*, p. 13.
14. Gilbert, op. cit., Cabinet memorandum by Churchill on Army Estimates, 7 Feb. 1920, p. 1032.
15. 'What is essential is concentration of forces in the theatres vital to us viz:- England, Ireland, Egypt, India, Mesopot: in that order'. IWM/HHW/1/35/7, Sir Henry Wilson diary, 15 July 1920.

16. Gilbert, op. cit., General Radcliffe to Sir Henry Wilson, 9 Feb. 1920, pp. 1036–7.
17. TNA/CAB24/106, Mesopotamian Expenditure, 1 May 1920.
18. Gilbert, op. cit., Letter from Churchill to Sir Hugh Trenchard, Chief of the Air Staff, 2 March 1920, pp. 1044–6.
19. IWM/HHW/1/35/5, Sir Henry Wilson diary, 1 May 1920.
20. Swain, op. cit., pp. 117–30.
21. Malleson and his troops had been withdrawn in the spring of 1919, freeing the way for these Bolshevik successes in Transcaspia. Mawdsley, op. cit., pp. 236–7.
22. More on which below.
23. TNA/CAB23/20, Cabinet 1, 6 Jan. 1920.
24. BL/MSS/Eur/E264/12 (CC), Telegram from the Foreign and Political Dept. to Montagu, 21 Feb. 1920.
25. Carr, op. cit., p. 535.
26. A reference to the Caliphate issue which will be discussed later in this chapter.
27. BL/MSS/Eur/F112/217 (Curzon Collection (hereafter Curzon)), Letter from Montagu to Curzon, 5 Jan. 1920. Churchill for his part also took exception to having to financially support the troops stationed at Meshed: Gilbert, op. cit., Cabinet memorandum by Churchill on Army Estimates, 7 Feb. 1920, pp. 1033–4.
28. TNA/FO371/4904/C11, Summary of Events in North West Persia, 21 May 1920.
29. TNA/FO371/4904/C11, Summary of Events in North West Persia, 21 May 1920.
30. BL/MSS/Eur/E264/12 (CC), Telegram from the Foreign and Political Dept. to Montagu, 21 Feb. 1920.
31. TNA/FO371/4904/C11, Summary of Events in North West Persia, 21 May 1920.
32. Gilbert, op. cit., Cabinet memorandum by Churchill on Army Estimates, 7 Feb. 1920, pp. 1033–4.
33. TNA/CAB23/20, Cabinet 11, 18 Feb. 1920.
34. BL/MSS/Eur/E264/12 (CC), Telegram from Curzon to Chelmsford, 22 March 1920.
35. Emphasis in original. IWM/HHW/1/35/5, Sir Henry Wilson diary, 19 May 1920.
36. TNA/ADM233/18/WN483, Soviet Russia and Persia – invading force unauthorised and to be recalled, 23 May 1920.
37. The *Times*, 14 July 1920. TNA/FO371/4905/C6004, Telegram from Norman to the Foreign Office, 10 Sept. 1920.
38. Volodarsky, op. cit., p. 35.

39. TNA/ADM233/18/WN483, Congratulatory message to the sailors of the Red Commercial Fleet of the Caspian Sea, 23 May 1920.
40. Dailami, 'The Bolshevik Revolution and the Genesis of Communism in Iran, 1917–1920', *Central Asian Survey* (2007), pp. 51–82 (hereafter 'Genesis').
41. Blank, op. cit., p. 182.
42. For more see Chaqueri, *Birth of a Trauma*.
43. TNA/FO371/4904/C11, Summary of Events in North West Persia, 21 May 1920.
44. BL/MSS/Eur/F112/215 (Curzon), Letter from Churchill to Curzon, 20 May 1920.
45. BL/MSS/Eur/F112/218 (Curzon), Letter from Wilson to Curzon, 20 May 1920.
46. IWM/HHW/2/20B, Letter from Curzon to Wilson, 20 May 1920.
47. TNA/CAB23/21, Conference of Ministers, 18 June 1920.
48. IWM/HHW/1/35/5, Sir Henry Wilson diary, 21 May 1920. TNA/CAB23/21/30, 21 May 1920.
49. BL/MSS/Eur/F112/215 (Curzon), Letter from Churchill to Curzon, 20 May 1920.
50. TNA/CAB23/21, Conference of Ministers, 18 June 1920.
51. IWM/HHW/1/35/6, Sir Henry Wilson diary, 18 June 1920. Alfred Milner was secretary of state for the colonies.
52. BL/MSS/Eur/F112/215 (Curzon), Letter from Churchill to Curzon, 22 May 1920.
53. TNA/FO371/4909/C11905, Memorandum by Armitage Smith, 22 Nov. 1920.
54. Katouzian, 'The Campaign against the Anglo-Iranian Agreement of 1919', *British Journal of Middle Eastern Studies*, Vol. 25 (1998), pp. 5–46.
55. Qajar Prince Parviz-Mirza, quoted in Volodarsky, op. cit., p. 27.
56. Fatemi, *History of Persia*, p. 13.
57. TNA/FO371/4908/C4966, Memorandum by George Churchill, 9 July 1920.
58. BL/MSS/Eur/E264/13 (CC), Telegram from Curzon to Norman, 19 July 1920.
59. BL/MSS/Eur/E264/13 (CC), Telegram from Curzon to Norman, 31 July 1920.
60. TNA/FO371/4909/C6531, Telegram from Norman to the Foreign Office, 15 Sept. 1920.
61. TNA/FO371/4906/C10290, Curzon telegram to Norman, 5 Nov. 1920.
62. TNA/FO371/4910/C12949, Telegram from Norman to the Foreign Office, 2 Dec. 1920. The Anglo-Persian Agreement was formally denounced by the Medjliss on 22 June 1921.
63. BL/MSS/Eur/E264/6 (CC), Letter from Chelmsford to Montagu, 8 Dec. 1920.

64. BL/IOR/L/PS/10/780/18/1919, Foreign Office to Cox, 20 Dec. 1920.
65. BL/IOR/L/PS/10/780/18/1919, Foreign Office to Cox, 31 May 1920; IOR/L/PS/10/780/18/1919, Foreign Office to Norman, 19 June 1920 and IOR/L/PS/10/780/18/1919, Norman to Foreign Office, 27 June 1920.
66. BL/IOR/L/PS/10/780/18/1919, Norman to Foreign Office, 5 July 1920.
67. TNA/FO371/4904/C56, Telegram from Norman to the Foreign Office, 17 June 1920.
68. TNA/FO371/4905/C2920, Telegram from Norman to Curzon, 3 Aug. 1920.
69. Pearce, *Staroselsky Problem*, pp. 63–8.
70. Chaqueri, *Birth of a Trauma*, pp. 185–6.
71. Ironside had supervised the withdrawal of British troops from Archangel and then from Ismid. Importantly, he had combat experience against Soviet troops. Ghani, *Iran and the Rise of Reza Shah: From Qajar Collapse to Pahlavi Power*, p. 107.
72. TNA/FO371/4906/C10166, Telegram from Norman to the Foreign Office, 26 Oct. 1920.
73. Pearce, *Staroselsky Problem*, pp. 68–70. In removing Staroselskii, Ironside and Norman (whether by design or by accident) opened the way for Reza Khan to take control of the Division and later on enact a *coup* against the Persian prime minister, Sepahdar-e Azam. For more detail see Ghani, op. cit., pp. 153–92.
74. TNA/FO371/4907/C12838, Minute by Edmund Overy, 4 Dec. 1920.
75. TNA/FO371/4904/C830, Telegram from Norman to the Foreign Office, 7 July 1920.
76. TNA/FO371/4907/C13609, Telegram from Norman to the Foreign Office, 11 Dec. 1920.
77. BL/MSS/Eur/E264/12 (CC), Telegram from Chelmsford to Montagu, 11 Feb. 1920.
78. TNA/FO371/3991/174799, Memorandum by Political Agent in Kabul, 17 Nov. 1919.
79. BL/IOR/L/PS/10/836, Telegram from C.G.S to D.M.I, 24 Aug. 1919.
80. Becker, *Russia's Protectorates in Central Asia: Bukhara and Khiva, 1865–1924*, pp. 288–295. For a contemporary opinion on Soviet Russia's actions towards Bokhara and Khiva see: Lobanoff-Rostovsky, 'The Soviet Muslim Republics in Central Asia', *Journal of the Royal Institute of International Affairs*, Vol. 7 (1928), pp. 241–55.
81. BL/MSS/Eur/E264/6 (CC), Letter from Chelmsford to Montagu, 4 March 1920.
82. BL/MSS/Eur/E264/12 (CC), Telegram from Chelmsford to Montagu, 11 Feb. 1920.
83. BL/MSS/Eur/E264/12 (CC), Telegram from Chelmsford to Montagu, 5 Jan. 1920.

84. BL/MSS/Eur/E264/55(l) (CC), Letter from Hamilton Grant to Dobbs, 26 Nov. 1919. In October 1919 Amanullah had sent six cannon and a number of military experts to Bokhara to aid Emir Alim against Russia. Becker, op. cit., p. 290.

85. BL/MSS/Eur/E264/12 (CC), Telegram from Montagu to Chelmsford, 7 Jan. 1920.

86. TNA/CAB23/23, Cabinet 66, 5 Dec. 1920.

87. BL/MSS/Eur/E264/55(l) (CC), Minutes on Letter from Dobbs to Chelmsford, 23 Dec. 1919 and BL/MSS/Eur/E264/12 (CC), Telegram from Chelmsford to Montagu, 5 Jan. 1920.

88. BL/MSS/Eur/E264/12 (CC), Telegram from Montagu to Chelmsford, 15 Jan. 1920.

89. BL/MSS/Eur/E264/12 (CC), Telegrams from Chelmsford to Montagu, 11 Jan. 1920.

90. BL/MSS/Eur/E264/55(l) (CC), Letter from Dobbs to Hamilton Grant, 2 Dec. 1919.

91. For full details on the meetings of the Mussoorie Conference see: MSS/Eur/E264/55(m).

92. BL/MSS/Eur/E264/12 (CC), Telegram from Chelmsford to Montagu, 30 April 1920.

93. BL/MSS/Eur/E264/55(m) (CC), Proceedings of the Ninth Meeting of the Indo-Afghan Conference, 24 June 1920.

94. BL/MSS/Eur/E264/13 (CC), Telegram from the Foreign and Political Department to Montagu, 4 Sept. 1920.

95. BL/IOR/L/PS/10/886, Telegram from Chelmsford to Montagu, 18 October 1919.

96. BL/MSS/Eur/E264/12 (CC), Telegram from Chelmsford to Montagu, 1 March 1920.

97. BL/IOR/L/PS/10/886, Telegram from Sir William Marris to All Local Governments and Administrations, 25 Nov. 1919. For further information on the Indian government's intelligence system see Popplewell, op. cit., For discussion on the effectiveness of the measure taken by the Indian government, see Chapter Five.

98. Spector, op. cit., p. 30.

99. *Ibid.*, p. 37. Cosroe Chaqueri notes that the declaration to Muslims had been carefully worded by the Bolshevik regime, it being sufficiently vague enough to leave venues open for future negotiations with the ruling elites of Turkey, Persia and Afghanistan, but at the same time was inflammatory enough to arouse the hopes of the Muslim masses. Chaqueri, *Birth of the Trauma*, p. 143.

100. Ansari, op. cit., pp. 509–37. The work by Soviet historian M.A. Persits, is also of interest for this topic, although some of the author's contentions should be approached with caution.

101. Gupta, op. cit., p. 60.
102. Marx and Engels, *On Colonialism*.
103. White, 'Colonial Revolution and the Communist International, 1919–1924', *Science and Society*, Vol. 40, No. 2 (1996), p. 173 (hereafter 'Colonial Revolution').
104. Lenin, 'Imperialism, The Highest Stage of Capitalism', in Christman, ed., *Essential Works of Lenin*, pp. 176–270.
105. In his work on the Comintern, Edward Richards has shown how the organisation's pyramidal structure placed greatest authority in the hands of the Executive Committee of the Communist International (ECCI) and its Presidium. The ECCI led all Comintern activities in the intervals between congresses, its decisions were binding for all members of the organisation, and it held the right to expel 'entire Sections, groups and individuals who violate the programme and rules of the Communist International'. Since the ECCI and its Presidium was dominated by members of the Bolshevik party, in effect the Soviet regime controlled the Comintern. See Richards, 'The Shaping of the Comintern', *American Slavic and Eastern European Review*, Vol. 18, No. 2 (1959), pp. 197–204.
106. White, 'Colonial Revolution', p. 176. On a slight aside, according to Timothy Edward O'Connor, Chicherin was one of the Bolsheviks most enthusiastic about creating revolution in Asia, and was one of the first to see the potential there. O'Connor, *Diplomacy and Revolution: G. V. Chicherin and Soviet Foreign Affairs, 1919–1930*.
107. Haithcox, 'The Roy–Lenin Debate on Colonial Policy: a New Interpretation', *The Journal of Asian Studies*, Vol. 23, No. 1 (1963), p. 94 (hereafter 'Debate').
108. *Ibid.*, p. 97. For more on Bolshevik opinion of Gandhi see: Ray, 'Changing Soviet Views on Mahatma Gandhi, *The Journal of Asian Studies*, Vol. 29 (1969), pp. 85–106.
109. Blank describes this 'conception of an alliance with the native bourgeousie' as a 'singluarly manipulative and cynical one'. Blank, op. cit., p. 184.
110. For more on the Jadids see Khalid, 'Nationalising the Revolution in Central Asia: The Transformation of Jadidism, 1917–1920', in Suny and Martin (eds), *A State of Nations: Empire and Nation-Making in the Age of Lenin and Stalin*, pp. 145–64.
111. Gupta, op. cit., p. 69.
112. BL/MSS/Eur/E264/12 (CC), Telegram from Home Department, India, to the India Office, 2 Feb. 1920.
113. Sayer, 'British Reaction to the Amritsar Massacre 1919–1920', *Past & Present*, No. 131 (1991), p. 158.
114. *Ibid.*, p. 151.

115. Gilbert, op. cit., Sir William Sutherland to David Lloyd George, 9 July 1920, pp. 1140–1.

116. BL/MSS/Eur/F112/217 (Curzon), Letter from Lord Hylton to Curzon, 21 July 1920.

117. IWM/HHW/1/35/5, Sir Henry Wilson diary, 15 May 1920.

118. Non-co-operation was a non-violent form of protest against the Indian government. It involved, among other things, encouraging Indians to withdraw from British-founded schools, renounce British honours and boycott British goods. For more detail on the movement, see Low, 'The Government of India and the First Non-Cooperation Movement – 1920–1922', *The Journal of Asian Studies*, Vol. 25 (1966), pp. 241–259 and Naeem Qureshi, op. cit., pp. 233–317.

119. *Ibid.*, p. 261.

120. Robb, *The Government of India and Reform: Policies towards Politics and the Constitution, 1916–1921*, p. 278.

121. BL/MSS/Eur/E264/6 (CC), Letter from Montagu to Chelmsford, 9 Sept. 1920.

122. BL/MSS/Eur/E264/6 (CC), Letter from Montagu to Chelmsford, 15 July 1920.

123. TNA/ADM233/15/WN408, The Diffusion of Bolshevism in the East, 21 Feb. 1920.

124. The chairman of the Tashkent Soviet, I. Kolesov, had underestimated Alim's will of resistance and been too hasty in leading troops into Bokhara. Becker, op. cit., pp. 265–9.

125. *Ibid.*, pp. 292–4.

126. Popplewell, op. cit., pp. 301–2.

127. Landau, *The Politics of Pan-Islam: Ideology and Organisation*, pp. 184–5.

128. Darwin, *Britain*, p. 173.

129. TNA/CAB23/20, Cabinet 1, 6 Jan. 1920.

130. TNA/CAB23/20, Cabinet 1, 6 Jan. 1920.

131. The Central Khilafat Committee was founded in Bombay on 20 March 1919, with regional committee also being established throughout the country. Öke, op. cit., p. 65. For more detail on the proceedings of the Caliphate movement see: Hasan and Pernau, *Regionalizing pan-Islamism: Documents on the Khilafat Movement*.

132. *The Indian Khilafat Delegation Publications* (London: 1920) and TNA/FO371/5141/E2257, Indian Khilafat Deputation, 19 March 1920.

133. TNA/FO371/5141/E2257, Indian Khilafat Deputation, 19 March 1920.

134. TNA/FO371/5141/E2257, Indian Khilafat Deputation, 19 March 1920. The delegation also met with officials from the India Office, but had just as much luck as they had with Lloyd George. Although their time in Whitehall

was ultimately fruitless, the delegation decided to stay in Europe for a while, and try to enlighten the public about the plight of the Caliph. They toured Britain, and went to France and Italy to meet politicians, journalists and intellectuals, including the pope. They finally returned to Bombay in October 1920. A. Özcan, *Pan-Islamism: Indian Muslims, the Ottomans and Britain, 1877–1924*, p. 193 and Öke, op. cit., pp. 83–92.

135. BL/MSS/Eur/E264/55(m) (CC), Proceedings of the Sixth Meeting of the Indo-Afghan Conference, 12 June 1920.
136. BL/MSS/Eur/E264/12 (CC), Report from Home Department of the Indian Government, 2 Feb. 1920.
137. TNA/FO371/5141/E2505, Minute by Crowe on telegram from Chelmsford to the Foreign Office, 12 March 1920. Since 1916, when the Muslim League and the National Indian Congress had signed the Lucknow Pact, Muslim and Hindu leaders had been in close collaboration in their activities. This was solidified on 23 November 1919 when at a meeting of the Khilafat Committee joint Muslim–Hindu action was agreed upon. Öke, op. cit., p. 67.
138. For discussion on the pan-Islamic and nationalist motives of the Caliphate agitators see: Minault, *The Khilafat Movement: Religious Symbolism and Political Mobilisation in India*. Jacob Landau contends that the Caliphat movement was definitely more than a spiritual expression of pan-Islamism, and was essentially political by nature. Landau, op. cit., pp. 213–14.
139. TNA/FO371/5142/E7376, Letter from the Nizam of Hyderabad to Chelmsford, 16 March 1920.
140. For detail on India's relationship with pan-Islamism see Naeem Qureshi, op. cit., pp. 9–88. Indian Muslims also had support from their counterparts in England. The London Muslim League, for example, worked to try to influence the Home government on the Caliphate issue. *Ibid.*, p. 417. In January 1919 South Asian Muslims submitted a petition to the British government calling for it to respect the religious integrity of Istanbul. Öke, op. cit., p. 58.
141. Reetz, op. cit., p. 21.
142. Öke, op. cit., pp. 72–3.
143. Nanda, op. cit., p. 118.
144. For example, a Caliphate day that had been declared on 17 October 1919 had met with great success as hundreds of thousands of Indians – Muslim and Hindu alike – participated in closing their businesses and gathering at meeting places in different cities. Özcan, op. cit., p. 191.
145. BL/MSS/Eur/E264/12 (CC), Telegram from Chelmsford to Montagu, 20 Jan. 1920.
146. BL/MSS/Eur/E264/12 (CC), Telegram from Chelmsford to Montagu, 28 Jan. 1920.

147. BL/MSS/Eur/E264/12 (CC), Telegram from Chelmsford to Montagu, 3 March 1920.
148. BL/MSS/Eur/E264/6 (CC), Letter from Chelmsford to Montagu, 17 March 1920.
149. TNA/FO371/5142/E5283, Minute on telegram from Chelmsford to the Foreign Office, 19 May 1920.
150. TNA/FO371/5141/E2505, Minute by Curzon on telegram from Chelmsford to the Foreign Office, 12 March 1920.
151. Particularly difficult for Turkish nationalists to accept were the terms of the treaty which gave substantial portions of eastern Anatolia to an independent Armenia and an autonomous Kurdistan. See 'Treaty of Sevres', http://wwi.lib.byu.edu/index.php/Peace_Treaty_of_Sevres, accessed 27/8/13 and Gokay, *A Clash of Empires: Turkey Between Russian Bolshevism and British Imperialism, 1918–1923.*
152. IWM/HHW/1/35/6, Sir Henry Wilson diary, 20 June 1920.
153. Gilbert, op. cit., Letter from Churchill to Lloyd George, 4 Dec. 1920, p. 1260. For more on Lloyd George's Greek policy see Montgomery, 'Lloyd George and the Greek Question, 1918–22', in Taylor, ed, *Lloyd George: Twelve Essays*, pp. 257–84.
154. BL/MSS/Eur/F112/218 (Curzon), Letter from Admiral de Robeck to Curzon, 9 March 1920.
155. BL/MSS/Eur/E264/12 (CC), Telegram from Chelmsford to Montagu, 19 May, 1920.
156. BL/MSS/Eur/E264/12 (CC), Telegram from Chelmsford to Montagu, 20 May 1920.
157. BL/MSS/Eur/E264/6 (CC), Letter from Chelmsford to Montagu, 19 May 1920.
158. BL/MSS/Eur/E264/6 (CC), Letter from Chelmsford to Montagu, 26 May 1920.
159. BL/MSS/Eur/E264/12 (CC), Telegram from Chelmsford to Montagu, 3 March 1920.
160. BL/MSS/Eur/E264/12 (CC), Telegram from Montagu to Chelmsford, 8 March 1920.
161. Öke, op. cit., p. 105.
162. Ansari, op. cit., pp. 521–2.
163. Reetz, op. cit., p. 44.
164. *Ibid.*, p. 48.
165. BL/MSS/Eur/E264/6 (CC), Letter from Chelmsford to Montagu, 11 Aug. 1920.
166. Reetz, op. cit., p. 56.
167. MSS/Eur/E264/6, Letter from Chelmsford to Montagu, 19 Aug. 1920. For more information on the social makeup and motives of the *Muhajirun* see Dierich Reetz's work *Hijrat*, pp. 41, 50–55.

168. M. Naeem Qureshi believes that the Afghan call for *hijrat* was never serious in the first place and that the emir simply wanted to embarrass the British and strengthen his position when it came to the Mussoorie talks. Naeem Qureshi, op. cit., p. 181.

169. Ansari, op. cit., p. 522.

170. Reetz, op. cit., p. 69.

171. As quoted in *Ibid.*, p. 66.

172. BL/MSS/Eur/E264/6 (CC), Letter from Chelmsford to Montagu, 25 Aug. 1920.

173. For details of the proceedings of the congress see, Riddel (ed), *To see the Dawn: Baku 1920 – First Congress of the Peoples of the East*.

174. Spector, op. cit., p. 52.

175. Carr, op. cit., p. 234.

176. Quoted in White, 'Communism and the East: The Baku Congress, 1920', *Slavic Review*, Vol. 33, No. 3 (1974), p. 492 (hereafter 'Baku Congress').

177. TNA/FO371/5435/N244, Excerpt from *Pravda*, 18 Sept. 1920.

178. Indeed, Blank argues that it was following the failure of the Baku Congress that the Bolsheviks realised the limitations of furthering the Communist cause in Asia and became even more determined to work with nationalist movements. Blank, op. cit., p. 187.

179. TNA/FO371/5178/ E13412, SIS report on proceedings of the Baku Conference, 30 Oct. 1920.

180. TNA/FO371/5435/N654, Interview with Georgian delegate in Tiflis newspaper *Slovo*, 21 Sept. 1920.

181. TNA/FO371/5435/N654, Interview with Georgian delegate in Tiflis newspaper *Slovo*, 21 Sept. 1920.

182. As quoted in White, 'Baku Congress', p. 492.

183. TNA/FO371/5178/E13412, Report by the Secret Intelligence Service on the Baku Congress, 25 Oct. 1920.

184. Spector, op. cit., pp. 56–57. Chaqueri, 'The Baku Congress', *Central Asian Survey*, Vol. 2 (1983), pp. 89–107 (hereafter 'Congress').

185. TNA/FO371/5178/E13412, Report by the Secret Intelligence Service on the Baku Congress, 25 Oct. 1920.

186. TNA/FO371/5178/E13412, Extract from 'Yangi Dunia' in Report by the Secret Intelligence Service on the Baku Congress, 25 Oct. 1920.

187. TNA/FO371/5435/N244, Excerpt from *Pravda*, 18 Sept. 1920.

188. Ansari, op. cit., p. 528.

189. BL/MSS/Eur/E264/6 (CC), Letter from Montagu to Chelmsford, 9 Sept. 1920.

190. TNA/FO371/4909/C11489, Speech by Curzon in the House of Lords, 16 Nov. 1920.

191. BL/MSS/Eur/F112/215 (Curzon), Letter from Churchill to Curzon, 27 Oct. 1920.
192. BL/MSS/Eur/E264/6 (CC), Letter from Chelmsford to Montagu, 8 Dec. 1920.
193. TWM/HHW/1/35/10, Sir Henry Wilson diary, 27 Oct. 1920.
194. TNA/FO371/5178/E851, Note by the First Lord Admiralty, 25 Dec. 1919.

Chapter 4: Making Friends, 1921

1. For more on the agreement see: Glenny, op. cit.; Ullman, *Anglo-Soviet Accord*; White, *Britain*; Debo, 'Lloyd George and the Copenhagen Conference of 1919–1920: The Initiation of Anglo-Soviet Negotiations', *The Historical Journal*, Vol. 24, No. 2 (1981), pp. 429–41 (hereafter 'Lloyd George'); McMeekin, *History's Greatest Heist: The Looting of Russia by the Bolsheviks*, pp. 168–98 (hereafter *Heist*).
2. Ullman, *Anglo-Soviet Accord*, pp. vii–x.
3. White, *Britain*, p. ix.
4. *Ibid.*, pp. 87–8.
5. Woodward, Butler, and Orde, eds. *Documents on British Foreign Policy 1919–1939, First Series, Vol. XX, No. 414:* Curzon to Hodgson, 7 Sept. 1921.
6. Soviet Russia was also instrumental in bringing about a treaty between the new Soviet republics of Armenia, Azerbaijan and Georgia and Turkey in October 1921 (the Treaty of Kars). Degras, *Soviet Documents on Foreign Policy, Vol. I, 1917–1924*, pp. 263–9.
7. TNA/FO371/6450/E8679, Speech by Lord Curzon to the House of Lords, 26 July 1921.
8. TNA/FO371/6400/E1188, Telegram from Norman to the Foreign Office, 24 Jan. 1921.
9. TNA/FO371/6401/E1985, Telegram from Curzon to Norman, 16 Feb. 1921.
10. TNA/FO371/6401/E2144, Telegram from Norman to the Foreign Office, 16 Feb. 1921.
11. TNA/FO371/6401/E1985, Telegram from Curzon to Norman, 16 Feb. 1921.
12. TNA/FO371/6401/E1985, Telegram from Norman to the Foreign Office, 11 Feb. 1921.
13. TNA/FO371/6400/E1196, Telegram from Chelmsford to the Foreign Office, 22 Jan. 1921.
14. TNA/FO371/6400/E1621, Telegram from Cox to the Foreign Office, 29 Jan. 1921.

15. 'Everyone – Norman, Gov. of India, Sir P Cox – favours us with independent views...Of course Sir P. Cox is much nearer the mark than any of the others.' TNA/FO371/6400/E1621, Curzon minute, 29 Jan. 1921.

16. Ghani, op. cit., p. 69.

17. *Ibid.*, p. 59.

18. Volodarsky, op. cit., p. 28.

19. Zia'eddin replaced Fatollah Khan Akbar on 25 February 1921.

20. TNA/FO371/6403/E4926, Declaration by Persian Prime Minister, Seyyid Zia-ud-Din, 26 Feb. 1921.

21. TNA/FO371/6402/E3438, Telegram from Norman to the Foreign Office, 18 March 1921.

22. TNA/FO371/6401/E2736, Telegram from Norman to the Foreign Office, 28 Feb. 1921.

23. TNA/FO371/6401/E2605, Telegram from Norman to the Foreign Office, 25 Feb. 1921.

24. TNA/FO371/6403/E4675, Telegram from Curzon to Norman, 18 April 1921.

25. TNA/FO371/6403/E4804, Telegram from Norman to the Foreign Office, 23 April 1921.

26. TNA/FO371/6403/E4675, Telegram from Curzon to Norman, 18 April 1921. Curzon's suspicion of Persian sincerity was not entirely unfounded; throughout the nineteenth and early twentieth centuries, many Persian officials were apt to use British and Russian rivalry for their own gain, playing one off against the other, all the while increasing their own privilege and power. Nonetheless, by 1918 Persia's rulers were certainly under more pressure than ever before to avoid being seen as pandering to foreign desires. Olson, op. cit., p. 10.

27. *Ibid.*, p. 256.

28. TNA/FO371/6403/E4804, Telegram from Norman to the Foreign Office, 23 April 1921.

29. TNA/FO371/6401/E2379, Telegram from Norman to the Foreign Office, 21 Feb. 1921. For more on the *coup* see Chaqueri, *Birth of a Trauma*, pp. 307–326. For more on Norman's alleged involvement in the *coup*, and Britain's apparent support of Reza Khan's political intrigues see Zirinsky, 'Imperial Power and Dictatorship: Britain and the Rise of Reza Shah, 1921–1926', *International Journal of Middle Eastern Studies*, Vol. 24, No. 4 (Nov., 1992), pp. 639–63.

30. Zia'eddin was overthrown on 25 May 1921. TNA/FO371/6406/E6678, Memorandum on meeting between Oliphant and Persian Minister, 11 June 1921.

31. TNA/FO371/6404/E6678, Memorandum on meeting between Oliphant and Persian Minister, 11 June 1921.

32. TNA/FO371/6404/E6678, Minute by Curzon, 12 June 1921. While it appeared that Curzon had washed his hands entirely of Persia's internal affairs,

this did not stop Norman from trying to resurrect Britain's standing in that country. The diplomat continued to try to persuade Curzon to soften his stance towards the Persian government and to abandon or amend the agreement. Indeed, in August 1920 Curzon told Norman, rather cattily, 'I think you ought to know that [the] length and frequency of your telegraphs are a source of unfavourable comment in Cabinet...it would facilitate our task by observing greater proportion and conciseness in your messages'. Ghani, op. cit., p. 95.

33. TNA/FO371/6399/E191, Telegram from Norman to the Foreign Office, 3 Jan. 1921.
34. TNA/FO371/6400/E1188, Telegram from Norman to the Foreign Office, 24 Jan. 1921.
35. The foreign secretary 'had always maintained that force was an adjunct of diplomacy'. Ghani, op. cit., p. 66.
36. TNA/FO371/6399/E406, Telegram from Norman to the Foreign Office, 8 Jan. 1921.
37. TNA/FO371/6400/E1691, Telegram from McMurray to the Foreign Office, 26 Jan. 1921.
38. TNA/FO371/6400/E1219, Telegram from Montagu to Chelmsford, 18 Jan. 1921.
39. BL/MSS/Eur/F112/199 (Curzon), Letter from Hardinge to Curzon, 15 Jan. 1921.
40. TNA/FO371/6400/E1196, Telegram from Chelmsford to Montagu, 22 Jan. 1921.
41. TNA/FO371/6400/E1219, Letter from the India Office to the Foreign Office, 25 Jan. 1921.
42. TNA/FO371/6401/E1985, Memorandum by Armitage-Smith, 14 Feb. 1921.
43. Gilbert, op. cit., Letter from Churchill to Curzon, Laming Worthington Evans and Montagu, 18 Feb. 1921, p. 1394.
44. TNA/FO371/6399/E26, Memorandum by the Admiralty, 24 Dec. 1920. The issue of oil has not been really discussed in this work since it is not much mentioned in the sources that have been studied. Others, however, have written on the matter, including Fatemi, *Oil Diplomacy* and Ewalt, 'The Fight for Oil', *History Today*, Vol. 31 (1981), pp. 11–15.
45. TNA/FO371/6405/E9260, Memorandum by W.A. Smart, 21 June 1921. While the Soviet Republic that had been established in Gilan had been short-lived – ultimately disintegrating in late 1920 – the north of Persia remained the main base for the Persian Communist Party and generally where more revolutionaries of all ilk were to be found. Hence the British belief that this was now a 'Bolshevik' area. See White, 'Soviet Russia', pp. 223–5.
46. TNA/FO371/6401/E1985, Memorandum by Armitage-Smith, 14 Feb. 1921.
47. TNA/FO371/6400/E1226, Telegram from Curzon to Norman, 21 Jan. 1921.

48. TNA/FO371/6400/E1196, Telegram from Chelmsford to Montagu, 22 Jan. 1921.

49. Given that the Indian government was used to working with the various tribal leaders who controlled the south of Persia, it also did not have much sympathy for attempts to bolster what it saw as a weak Shah. That being said, this was not simply a matter of Delhi's preference for a decentralised Persia versus London's desire for centralisation. Instead, the argument centred on *how far* British interference in Persia should go, not *where* it should concentrate its attention.

50. TNA/FO371/6403/E4805, Telegram from Norman to the Foreign Office, 23 April 1921.

51. Debo, *Survival*, p. 370. Tapp, 'The Soviet–Persian Treaty of 1921', *International Law Quarterly*, Vol. 4 (1951), pp. 511–14 provides a brief look at some of the details of the treaty.

52. TNA/FO371/6399/E717, Telegram from Norman to the Foreign Office, 14 Jan. 1921.

53. TNA/FO371/6404/E8648, Telegram from Norman to the Foreign Office, 7 May 1921.

54. TNA/FO317/6402/E3493, Telegram from Moshaver ul Mamalek to Persian Prime Minister, 21 Dec. 1920.

55. Volodarsky, op. cit., p. 55.

56. TNA/FO371/6399/E545, Telegram from Persian Consul-General, Tiflis, to Persian Minister for Foreign Affairs, 28 Oct. 1920.

57. TNA/FO371/6403/E4805, Telegram from Norman to the Foreign Office, 23 April 1921.

58. Quoted in Volodarsky, op. cit., p. 60.

59. TNA/FO371/6403/E4270, Oliphant minute on article in the 'Manchester Guardian', 31 March 1921.

60. TNA/FO371/6403/E4270, Memorandum by G.P. Churchill, 9 April 1921.

61. Pearce, *Staroselsky Problem*, pp. 81–2.

62. TNA/FO371/6403/E4805, Minute by Oliphant, 24 April 1921.

63. TNA/FO371/6404/E8648, Telegram from Norman to the Foreign Office, 7 May 1921.

64. TNA/FO371/6405/E8679, Speech by Lord Curzon to the House of Lords, 26 July 1921.

65. TNA/FO371/6404/E8341, Minute by Lindsay, 15 July 1921. In the aftermath of the failed Bolshevik *coup* in Tiflis in March 1920 and distracted by the Polish invasion of Ukraine the following month, the Soviet government had put on hold its plans to invade the independent Georgian republic and instead signed a treaty granting it official recognition (the Treaty of Moscow, 7 May 1920). Once a settlement with Poland had been reached, the Red Army invaded Georgia in February 1921.

66. TNA/FO371/6407/E13131, Telegram from Bridgeman to the Foreign Office, 29 Nov. 1921.

67. TNA/F0371/6407/E13177, Telegram from Bridgeman to the Foreign Office, 30 Nov. 1921.

68. TNA/FO371/6407/E13131, Telegram from Bridgeman to the Foreign Office, 29 Nov. 1921.

69. Kapur, *Soviet Russia*, p. 233. Also Bairathi, *Communism and Nationalism in India: A Study in Inter-Relationship, 1919–1947*, pp. 29–32.

70. The Soviet–Afghan Treaty of Friendship was duly signed in Moscow on 28 February 1921. Degras, op. cit., pp. 233–5. However, it would take a number of months for Afghanistan to ratify it, during which time Delhi and Kabul wrangled over both this and their own treaty.

71. BL/MSS/Eur/E264/13 (CC), Telegram from Montagu to Chelmsford, 8 Dec. 1920.

72. BL/MSS/Eur/E264/13 (CC), Telegram from Chelmsford to Montagu, 10 Dec. 1920.

73. TNA/FO371/6746/N2932, Telegram from Montagu to Chelmsford, 4 March 1921.

74. Degras, op. cit.: 'Treaty between the RSFSR and Afghanistan', 38 Feb, 1921, p. 234.

75. TNA/CAB23/24, Cabinet 10, 3 March 1921.

76. Indeed, the British government was well aware of the details of the treaty through its intercepts of Bolshevik telegrams: TNA/FO371/WO106/5186, Soviet–Afghan Treaty, 28 Feb. 1921.

77. TNA/FO371/6746/N2932, Telegram from Montagu to Chelmsford, 4 March 1921.

78. Gregorian, op. cit., p. 233–4.

79. TNA/FO371/6746/N2645, Memorandum by Dobbs, 18 Jan. 1921.

80. TNA/FO371/6746/N2645, Memorandum by Dobbs, 18 Jan. 1921.

81. TNA/FO371/6746/N2645, Memorandum by Dobbs, 18 Jan. 1921.

82. BL/MSS/Eur/E264/13 (CC), Telegram from Chelmsford to Montagu, 19 Oct. 1920.

83. TNA/FO371/6746/N2827, Telegram from Chelmsford to Montagu, 1 March 1921.

84. TNA/FO371/6746/N7365, Telegram from Montagu to Chelmsford, 23 Feb. 1921.

85. TNA/FO371/6746/N5060, Telegram from Chelmsford to Montagu, 15 March 1921.

86. TNA/FO371/6746/N5060, Telegram from Chelmsford to Montagu, 15 March 1921.

87. TNA/CAB23/24, Cabinet 10, 3 March 1921.

88. TNA/CAB23/24, Cabinet 10, 3 March 1921.

89. TNA/FO371/N3517, Telegram from Chelmsford to Montagu, 15 March 1921.

90. BL/MSS/Eur/E264/6 (CC), Letter from Chelmsford to Montagu, 16 March 1921.

91. BL/MSS/Eur/D523/12 (MC), Letter from Montagu to Reading, 20 April 1921.

92. Waley, *Edwin Montagu: A Memoir and an Account of his Visits to India*, p. 223.

93. BL/MSS/Eur/E264/4 (CC), Letter from Chelmsford to Montagu, 22 April 1918.

94. For example, in March 1919 Montagu complained that he was 'still much worried by the antagonism which exists between your Government and my Office', while in October he lamented further about the general lack of accord which existed between the two, feeling that they disagreed on so much. He also complained of a lack of communication between him and Chelmsford, and that the viceroy was always rejecting his proposals and, when forced to accept them, publicly announced his dissent. BL/MSS/Eur/D523/3 (MC), Letter from Montagu to Chelmsford, 4 March 1919 and Letter from Montagu to Chelmsford, 2 Oct., 1919

95. Waley, op. cit., p. 252.

96. Robb, op. cit., p. 4.

97. Ghose, *Lord Chelmsford's Viceroyalty: A Critical Survey*, p. 81.

98. Tinker, op. cit., p. 79.

99. *Ibid.*, pp. 4, 71–91.

100. Robb, op. cit., p. 5.

101. BL/MSS/Eur/D523/14 (MC), Letter from Reading to Montagu, 12 May 1921.

102. BL/MSS/Eur/E264/4 (CC), Letter from Chelmsford to Montagu, 28 April 1918.

103. Robb, op. cit., p. 20.

104. *Ibid.*, p. 5.

105. BL/MSS/Eur/D523/12 and 13 (MC).

106. '…with the change in viceroyalty there was no obvious change in policy'. Naeem Qureshi, *Indian Politics*, p. 283. For more on Reading's career see: Judd, *Lord Reading: Rufus Isaacs, First Marquess of Reading, Lord Chief Justice, and Viceroy of India, 1860–1935*.

107. These intercepts included Soviet discussion on the overthrow of the emir of Bokhara, and their hesitation about arming the Afghans among other things. TNA/FO371/6746/N4365, Telegram from Dobbs to the Indian Chief of General Staff, 3 March 1921.

108. Popplewell, op. cit., p. 310.

109. TNA/FO371/6746/N4581, Telegram from Reading to Montagu, 12 April 1921.
110. TNA/FO371/6746/N6234, Telegram from Dobbs to Reading, 14 April 1921.
111. Gregorian, op. cit., p. 232.
112. Becker, op. cit., p. 297.
113. Particularly with the provision of munitions and telegraph facilities, which the Soviet government had promised and which his government would therefore otherwise lose. TNA/FO371/6746/N4887, Telegram from Reading to Montagu, 20 April 1921.
114. TNA/FO371/6746/N6235, Telegram from Reading to Dobbs, 22 April 1921.
115. TNA/FO317/6747/N5504, Telegram from Montagu to Reading, 29 April 1921. [Emphasis mine].
116. TNA/FO371/6746/N4887, Telegram from Reading to Montagu, 20 April 1921.
117. TNA/FO371/6747/N5173, Telegram from Reading to Montagu, 27 April 1921.
118. TNA/FO371/6747/N5504, Telegram from Reading to Montagu, 5 May 1921.
119. TNA/FO371/6747/N6933, Telegram from Montagu to Reading, 12 May 1921.
120. TNA/CAB/23/25/Cab37, Cabinet meeting, 10 May 1921.
121. TNA/FO371/6747/N6669, Telegram from Reading to Montagu, 6 June 1921.
122. TNA/FO371/6747/N6927, Telegram from Reading to Montagu, 12 June 1921.
123. TNA/FO371/6748/N8170, Telegram from Reading to Montagu, 12 July 1921.
124. TNA/FO371/6748/N8170, Telegram from Reading to Montagu, 13 July 1921.
125. TNA/FO371/6747/N7459, Telegram from Reading to Montagu, 25 June 1921.
126. TNA/FO371/6748/N8906, Telegram from Reading to Montagu, 30 July 1921.
127. TNA/FO371/6748/N8906, Telegram from Reading to Montagu, 30 July 1921.
128. TNA/CAB23/26, Cabinet 63, 5 Aug. 1921.
129. TNA/CAB23/26, Cabinet 63, 5 Aug. 1921.
130. TNA/FO371/6748/N9963, Telegram from Reading to Montagu, 25 Aug. 1921.
131. TNA/FO371/6748/N10093, Telegram from Montagu to Reading, 2 Sept. 1921.

132. TNA/FO371/6768/N10112, Telegram from Reading to Montagu, 30 Aug. 1921.
133. TNA/FO371/6749/N11732, Telegram from Reading to Montagu, 17 Oct. 1921.
134. TNA/FO371/6749/N12229, Telegram from Reading to Montagu, 1 Nov. 1921.
135. TNA/FO371/6749/N11920, Telegram from Maffey to Reading, 23 Oct. 1921.
136. TNA/FO371/6769/N12212, Telegram from Montagu to Reading, 28 Oct. 1921.
137. TNA/CAB23/27, Cabinet 85, 3 Nov. 1921.
138. MSS/Eur/D523/14, Letter from Reading to Montagu, 11 Aug. 1921.
139. This was the Treaty of Moscow (16 March 1921), also known as the 'Treaty of Brotherhood', the terms of which were extremely generous to Turkey (in particular with the delineation of its border with Soviet Armenia): Degras, op. cit., pp. 237–42.
140. The Interdepartmental Committee on Bolshevism as a Menace to the British Empire produced two lengthy reports based on information supplied by SIS, Special Branch and the India Office, detailing Soviet violations of the trade agreement. Fisher, 'Interdepartmental Committee', pp. 2–3.
141. Degras, op. cit., Reply from Litvinov to Curzon's Note, 27 Sept. 1921, pp. 257–62.
142. Victor Madeira explains some of the flaws with the intelligence on Bolshevism, including the lack of a grading system for information and the attention paid to rumour. Madeira, op. cit., pp. 31–6.
143. Since it had been Montagu who had made the first draft of the note of protest, Curzon could more easily distance himself from the responsibility of its failure: White, *Britain*, pp. 104–9. A quick reply to the Soviet government was made, re-affirming the original accusations but not pushing the case any further: Woodward, op. cit., No. 437, Curzon to the Cabinet, 27 Oct. 1921.
144. The *Times*, 1 Sept 1921.
145. TNA/CAB23/23, Cabinet 82, 31 Dec. 1920.
146. Gilbert, op. cit., Letter from Curzon to his wife, 14 Feb. 1921, p. 1349.
147. *Ibid.*, Letter from Churchill to Clementine Churchill, 16 Feb. 1921, p. 1355.
148. Ibid., Letter from Curzon to Lloyd George, 13 June 1921, p. 1502.
149. *Ibid.*, Letter from Lloyd George to Curzon, 14 June 1921, p. 1506.
150. *Ibid.*, Letter from Curzon to Churchill, 13 June 1921, p. 1503.
151. *Ibid.*, Letter from Churchill to Curzon, 13 June 1921, p. 1504.
152. *Ibid.*, Letter from Curzon to Churchill, 15 June 1921, p. 1509.
153. *Ibid.*, Letter from Curzon to Churchill, 9 Nov. 1921, p. 1665.

154. TNA/FO371/6450/E8679, Speech by Lord Curzon to the House of Lords, 16 July 1921.
155. As quoted in Pearce, *Staroselsky Problem*, p. 86.
156. TNA/FO371/6749/N12799, Telegram from Dobbs to Reading, 17 Nov. 1921 and TNA/FO371/6750/N14188, Anglo-Afghan Treaty, 29 Dec. 1921.
157. In an exchange of letters in December 1921 between the two departments, it was agreed that all written communication between Kabul and the Foreign Office was to be forwarded to the India Office and that any decisions regarding Afghan policy was to be subject to India Office approval first. The India Office was also to be notified of any verbal communication between the Afghan minister in London and the Foreign Office and Foreign Office officials were to refrain from any important discussions with the Afghan minister before seeking India Office permission. TNA/FO371/6750/N13766, Letter from the India Office to the Foreign Office, 15 Dec. 1921; letter from the Foreign Office to the Indian Office, 21 Dec. 1921.
158. TNA/FO371/6748/N8906, Telegram from Reading to Montagu, 30 July 1921.

Chapter 5: A Gigantic Drum, 1922–1923

1. White, 'Baku Congress', pp. 506–13.
2. White, 'Colonial Revolution', pp. 177–8.
3. Spector, op. cit., p. 101.
4. Von Laue, op. cit., p. 241.
5. White, 'Soviet Russia', pp. 221–2.
6. In the opinion of Spector 'as yet, inadequate recognition has been given to the role of Turkey, Iran and Afghanistan, weak and divided though they were, in stemming the tide of communism in the Muslim world'. Spector, op. cit., p. 102.
7. Zirinsky, op. cit., p. 650.
8. Ghani, op. cit., pp. 253–4. Loraine was to become one of Britain's greatest diplomats, serving under seven Foreign Ministers and in a variety of highly important posts.
9. 'You are a brick and I know you will realise from his [Curzon's] letter of some time ago how completely you enjoy his confidence.' TNA/FO1011/10, Letter from Oliphant to Loraine, 28 Sept. 1922.
10. TNA/FO1011/44, Letter from Curzon to Loraine, 30 May 1922.
11. TNA/FO1011/124, Letter from Loraine to Gertrude Bell, 1 Dec. 1922.
12. White, 'Soviet Russia', p. 221.
13. TNA/FO371/7802, Telegram from Loraine to the Foreign Office, 16 Jan. 1922.

14. Threatening to withhold royalties which the Anglo–Persian Oil Company owed to the Persian government had in the past been a useful tool of persuasion for the British government. TNA/FO1011/124, Letter from Loraine to Arnold Wilson, 1 Dec. 1922.
15. Ghani, op. cit., p. 44.
16. TNA/FO371/7811, Telegram from Loraine, 28 Nov. 1922.
17. TNA/FO1011/124, Letter from Loraine to Gertrude Bell, 1 Dec. 1922.
18. Volodarsky, op. cit., p. 60.
19. Chaqueri, *Birth of the Trauma*, p. 332 and Volodarsky, op. cit., pp. 56–7.
20. Burke, 'Theodore Rothstein, Russian Emigré and British Socialist', *Immigrants and Minorities*, Vol. 2 (1983), pp. 80–99.
21. Ghani, op. cit., p. 210.
22. TNA/FO371/7802/E449, Memorandum by Lieutenant-Colonel Saunders, 8 Nov. 1921.
23. TNA/FO371/7806/E6425, Report by Major Bray on Bolshevik and Kemalist Activity in Persia, 23 June 1922. Major Bray was a special intelligence officer at the India Office from August 1920 to May 1923, authored a number of memorandum on Asian and Middle Eastern affairs and was involved in the work of the Interdepartmental Committee on Bolshevism as a Menace to the British Empire. Fisher, 'Major Norman Bray and Eastern Unrest in the Aftermath of World War I', *Asian Affairs*, Vol. 31 (2010), pp. 189–97 (hereafter 'Bray').
24. Spector, op. cit., p. 95.
25. TNA/FO1011/124, Letter from Loraine to Lieutenant-Colonel Prideaux, 16 Jan 1922.
26. TNA/FO371/7802/E233, Minute by Oliphant, 9 Jan. 1922.
27. Indeed, by 1925 Reza Khan would have deposed the Shah and set himself upon the throne of Persia.
28. TNA/FO371/6404/E6040, Telegram from Norman, 25 May 1921 and Ghani, op. cit., p. 217.
29. TNA/FO371/7802/E102, Memorandum by Oliphant on Interview with Armitage-Smith, 2 Jan. 1922.
30. TNA/FO371/7804/E3079, Telegram from Loraine, 31 March 1922.
31. Zirinsky, op. cit., p. 653.
32. TNA/FO371/7804/E3079, Memorandum by W.A. Smart, 22 Jan. 1922.
33. Zirinsky, op. cit., p. 658. For more information on Loraine's relationship with Reza Shah and his involvement in helping the minister's ascendance to the Persian crown see *ibid.*, pp. 649–57.
34. TNA/FO371/7802/E909, Telegram from Loraine, 24 Jan. 1922. TNA/FO371/7804/E3079, Memorandum by W.A. Smart, 22 Jan. 1922.

35. Once he had later become ruler of Persia, Reza Khan would in fact break up the small Persian Communist Party and arrest its members. White, 'Soviet Russia', p. 228.
36. TNA/FO371/7805/E4712, Telegram from Loraine, 20 Feb. 1922.
37. TNA/FO371/7806/E6588, Report on Persian Situation by Loraine, 7 May 1922.
38. TNA/FO1011/124, Letter from Loraine to Lindsay, 7 Dec. 1922. Again, Loraine identifies that tradition of Persian officials to try and use Britain's and Russia's interests in their country for their own ends.
39. TNA/FO371/7802/E1172, Telegram from Loraine, 1 Feb. 1922.
40. TNA/FO371/7802/E1172, Foreign Office telegram to Loraine, 4 Feb. 1922.
41. TNA/FO371/7805/E5237, Telegram from Curzon to Loraine, 24 May 1922.
42. TNA/FO1011/127, Letter from Loraine to Gregory, 30 Nov. 1923.
43. Although in its typical paranoid fashion the committee also warned that Persia still needed to be watched carefully for Bolshevik intrigue. Fisher, 'Interdepartmental Committee', p. 12.
44. TNA/FO371/7802/E362, Telegram from His Majesty's Consul in Dazap to the Viceroy, 6 Nov. 1921.
45. TNA/FO371/7802/E449, Memorandum by Lieutenant-Colonel Saunders, 8 Nov. 1921.
46. TNA/FO371/7802/E449, Telegram from Bridgeman, 18 Nov. 1921. Emphasis added.
47. TNA/FO371/7803/E2427, Telegram from Reading, 17 Dec. 1921.
48. In 1921 treaties had been concluded between Russia and Afghanistan, Russia and Turkey, and Turkey and Afghanistan. See Kapur, op. cit., p. 103 and Spector, op. cit., pp. 99–100.
49. TNA/FO371/7803/E2517, Telegram from Lieutenant-Colonel Saunders to Loraine, 28 Dec. 1921.
50. TNA/FO371/7806/E6425, Report by Major Bray on Bolshevik and Kemalist Activity in Persia, 23 June 1922.
51. TNA/FO371/7803/E2517, Telegram from Loraine, 30 Dec. 1921.
52. Curzon could not help making a dig in his reply 'that this union was inevitable when the decision had been taken to abandon the Caucasus. He had foreseen it at the time'. TNA/CAB/23/29, Cabinet 19, 20 March 1922.
53. It is also worth noting that Britain had traditionally been a supporter of the Ottomans and had actually encouraged the affiliation of Indian Muslims with the Caliph; during the 1857 revolt the Indian government had procured a proclamation from the Sultan advising Indian Muslims to remain loyal to his British allies. Naeem Qureshi, op. cit., pp. 18–20.

54. It was agreed by the treaty that Batum would go to the Soviet government and the districts of Kars and Ardahan of Armenia would go to the Ankaran government. For more on Turko–Soviet relations see: Kapur, *op. cit.*; Gokay, op. cit., and Davison, 'Turkish Diplomacy from Mudros to Lausanne', in Craig, op. cit., pp. 172–209.

55. TNA/FO1011/123, Letter from Lord D'Abernon (Ambassador to Berlin) to Loraine, 29 Oct. 1922.

56. Woodward, op. cit., No. 10, Memorandum respecting Co-operation of Moslem Countries and Russia, 26 Jan. 1923.

57. For example, in March 1922 two British fishing vessels were arrested off the northern coast of Russia, while a steam trawler was also detained in February 1923. White, *Britain*, pp. 155–6.

58. *Ibid.*, pp. 158–9.

59. Woodward, op. cit., No. 53, Telegram from Curzon to Hodgson, 2 May 1923.

60. Bennett, *Curzon Period*, p. 73.

61. Andrew, 'The British Secret Service and Anglo-Soviet Relations in the 1920s. Part I: From the Trade Agreement to the Zinoviev Letter', *The Historical Journal*, Vol. 20 (1977), p. 693. Victor Madeira notes how with the Curzon Note, 'for the first time ever, a government had protested to another while acknowledging that the message relied on intercepted communications of the recipient nation'. Madeira, op. cit., p. 41.

62. Woodward, op. cit., No. 67, Telegram from Hodgson to Curzon, 13 May 1923; No. 72, Minutes of a Meeting between Curzon and Krassin, 17 May 1923; No. 78, Letter from Krassin to Curzon, 23 May 1923; No. 80, Letter from Gregory to Krassin, 29 May 1923; No. 94, Letter from Krassin to Curzon, 9 June 1923; No. 100, Letter from Curzon to Krassin, 13 June 1923.

63. TNA/CAB/23/46, Cabinet 30, 11 June 1923.

64. As quoted in White, *Britain*, p. 168.

65. Shumiatskii later became head of the Soviet film industry and in the 1930s planned to build a 'Soviet Hollywood' in the Crimea.

66. TNA/FO1011/50, Letter from Loraine to Curzon, 7 Feb. 1923.

67. Woodward, op. cit., No. 132, Telegram from Preston to Peters, 18 July 1923.

68. TNA/FO371/7804/E4076, Minute by Lindsay and Curzon on Telegram from Loraine, 18 April 1922.

69. The Conference of London had taken place in February–March 1921 but had broken down partly over the issue of Thrace and Smyrna. For more on the course of the conflict between Turkey and Greece see Cooper-Busch, *Mudros to Lausanne: Britain's Frontier in West Asia, 1918–1923*, pp. 269–358 (hereafter *Mudros*).

70. BL/MSS/Eur/E238/11 (RC), Telegram from Reading to Montagu, 28 Feb. 1922.

71. BL/MSS/Eur/E238/11 (RC), Telegram from Montagu to Reading, 6 March 1922.
72. Lloyd George as quoted in Waley, op. cit., p. 276.
73. BL/MSS/Eur/E238/16 (RC), Telegram from Montagu to Reading, 9 March 1922.
74. BL/MSS/Eur/E238/16 (RC), Excerpts from Montagu's speech in Telegram from Chamberlain to Reading, 15 March 1922.
75. BL/MSS/Eur/E238/16 (RC), Telegram from Reading to Lloyd George, 13 March 1922.
76. BL/MSS/Eur/D523/13 (MC), Letter from Montagu to Reading, 1 Sept. 1921.
77. Anti-Semitism is clear in some of the reports on Montagu's speech: 'Under interruption, Montagu got excited when making his speech and became more racial and more Yiddish in screaming tone and gesture, and a strong anti-Jewish sentiment was shown by shouts and excitement among normally placid Tories...' Gilbert, op. cit., Letter from Sir William Sutherland to Lloyd George, 9 July 1920, pp. 1140–1; 'Mr Montagu, patriotic and sincere English Liberal as he is, is also a Jew, and in excitement has the mental idiom of the East', the *Times*, 9 July 1920. See also Sayer, op. cit., p. 157.
78. Darwin, *Britain*, p. 22.
79. TNA/CAB/23/39, Conclusion of Conference of Ministers, 13 Feb. 1922.
80. BL/MSS/Eur/D523/13 (MC), Letter from Montagu to Reading, 1 Feb. 1922.
81. Cooper-Busch, *Mudros*, p. 333.
82. Indian Muslims themselves were shocked at Montagu's departure and unhappy to see him leave, believing as they did that he was their sole sympathiser in the London government. Naeem Qureshi, op. cit., p. 319.
83. BL/MSS/Eur/E238/16 (RC), Telegram from Chamberlain to Reading, 15 March 1922.
84. Robb, op. cit., p. 286.
85. *Ibid.*, p. 286.
86. BL/MSS/Eur/E238/16 (RC), Statement by Curzon to the House of Lords as quoted in Telegram from Chamberlain to Reading, 15 March 1922.
87. Cooper-Busch, *Mudros*, p. 333.
88. Nanda, op. cit., p. 104.
89. Cooper-Busch, *Mudros*, p. 329.
90. In August 1922 the Kemalist forces had launched a counter attack against the Greeks, and by 9 September had captured Smyrna and were advancing on Constantinople. On 15 September the British Cabinet decided that it would stand its ground at Chanak, and the following day sent a communiqué to the Turkish nationalist forces threatening a declaration of war on the grounds that the Treaty of Sèvres had been violated. However, without support from France

and the dominions, Lloyd George was forced to back down from his position. Although war was averted, the whole affair proved fatal for Lloyd George's political careers. For more detail on the Chanak Crisis see Macfie, 'The Chanak Affair (September–October 1922)', *Balkan Studies*, Vol. 20 (1979), pp. 309–341; Psomiades, *The Eastern Question, the Last Phase: A Study in Greek–Turkish Diplomacy* and Darwin, 'The Chanak Crisis and the British Cabinet', *History*, Vol. 65 (1980), pp. 32–48.

91. White, *Britain*.
92. TNA/FO1011/123, Letter from Gregory to Loraine, 21 Oct. 1922.
93. TNA/FO1011/124, Letter from Lindsay to Loraine, 7 Dec. 1922.
94. Much to the consternation of the Soviet government. For any resolution of the problems between Turkey and the Allies would inevitably leave Ataturk and his regime less dependent upon Russia. Kapur, op. cit., p. 116.
95. Gilmour, op. cit., p. 579. With Turkish support, the Soviet government also managed to attend the conference, but only to participate in the issue of the Straits. Kapur, op. cit., pp. 119–28.
96. 'Treaty of Lausanne', http://wwi.lib.byu.edu/index.php/Treaty_of_Lausanne, accessed 27/8/13. See also Cooper-Busch, *Mudros*, pp. 359–389 and Davison, op. cit., pp. 199–209. For a contemporary opinion on the conference see Brown, 'The Lausanne Conference', *The American Journal of International Law*, Vol. 17 (1923), pp. 290–6.
97. Öke, op. cit., p. 140. 'There were flag bearing processions, illuminations, displays of fireworks and special prayers in mosques, *gurdwaras* and temples.' Naeem Qureshi, op. cit., p. 362.
98. By March 1924 the assembly had completely abolished the Caliphate: *Ibid.*, pp. 124–31 and p. 174.
99. As one Foreign Office official observed, 'By kicking out the Caliph, they [the Turks] have deprived themselves of a means of squeezing us whenever it stood them to do so and have effectually knocked the bottom out of a Caliphate agitation in India.' Quoted in Ferris, 'Muslim Menace', p. 71.
100. BL/MSS/Eur/E238/11 (RC), Telegram from Reading to Peel, 5 Dec. 1922.
101. Naeem Qureshi, op. cit., p. 336.
102. Özcan, op. cit., p. 198.
103. Öke, op. cit., p. 132.
104. BL/MSS/Eur/E238/12 (RC), Telegram from Reading to Peel, 6 Feb. 1923.
105. Cooper-Busch, *Mudros*, p. 364.
106. Öke, op. cit., p. 133.
107. See, for example, Crowe's quote, Chapter Three.
108. BL/MSS/Eur/E238/12 (RC), Telegram from Reading to Peel, 12 Jan. 1923 and BL/MSS/Eur/E238/12 (RC), Telegram from Reading to Peel, 6 Feb. 1923.

109. Öke, op. cit., p. 182.
110. Naeem Qureshi, op. cit., pp. 316 and 345
111. Reetz, op. cit., p. 19.
112. BL/MSS/Eur/D523/14 (MC), Letter from Reading to Montagu, 19 May 1921.
113. Aziz, op. cit., p. 89.
114. BL/MSS/Eur/D523/14 (MC), Letter from Reading to Montagu, 25 Oct. 1921.
115. BL/MSS/Eur/E238/11 (MC), Telegram from Reading to Montagu, 12 Jan. 1922.
116. The call for Indians to boycott government-aided schools and universities, for example, had been a grand failure, with only a small percentage of students participating. Naeem Qureshi, op. cit., pp. 266–9.
117. Low, op. cit., pp. 247–8.
118. *Ibid.*, p. 252.
119. TNA/CAB/23/29, Cabinet 8, 6 Feb. 1922.
120. BL/MSS/Eur/E238/11 (RC), Telegram from Montagu to Reading, 6 Feb. 1922.
121. BL/MSS/Eur/E238/11 (RC), Telegram from Reading to Montagu, 8 Feb. 1922.
122. BL/MSS/Eur/E238/16 (RC), Telegram from Montagu to Reading, 26 Jan. 1922.
123. BL/MSS/Eur/D523/14 (RC), Letter from Reading to Montagu, 5 Jan. 1922.
124. For a detailed account of the Indian government's dealings with Gandhi and the non-co-operation movement see Low, op. cit., pp. 241–59 and Naeem Qureshi, op. cit., pp. 233–317.
125. BL/MSS/Eur/D523/14 (MC), Letter from Reading to Montagu, 23 Feb. 1922.
126. BL/MSS/Eur/E238/11 (RC), Telegram from Reading to Montagu, 8 Feb. 1922.
127. BL/MSS/Eur/E238/16 (RC), Telegram from Reading to Montagu, 14 Feb. 1922.
128. BL/MSS/Eur/E238/11 (RC), Telegram from Reading to Montagu, 27 Feb. 1922.
129. Low, op. cit., pp. 254–55.
130. BL/MSS/Eur/E238/11 (RC), Telegram from Reading to Montagu, 25 March 1922. Low, op. cit., p. 255.
131. Reed, 'The Governance of India', *Journal of the Royal Institute of International Affairs*, Vol.6 (1927), p. 317.
132. BL/MSS/Eur/E238/11 (RC), Telegram from Reading to Peel, 5 Dec. 1922.

133. Naeem Qureshi, op. cit., p. 420.

134. Andrew, op. cit., p. 692.

135. For more on the Genoa Conference see White, *The Origins of Detente: the Genoa Conference and Soviet-Western relations, 1921–1922.*

136. Speech by Lloyd George in 'The Genoa Conference and Britain's Part', *Advocate of Peace Through Justice*, Vol. 84 (1922), p. 135. The New Economic Policy (NEP) brought an end to the War Communism that had characterised Russia's economy since the outbreak of the Russian Revolution. It saw the introduction of a mixed economy which allowed from some freedom of individual commercial activity.

137. The Rapallo Treaty was signed on 16 April 1922 and normalised relations between Soviet Russia and Germany.

138. Woodward, op. cit., No. 481, Memorandum by Gregory on the Soviet Government and Genoa, 12 Feb. 1922.

139. Andrew, op. cit., p. 692.

140. Ansari, op. cit., p. 528 and Ullman, *Accord*, p. 44.

141. Gupta, op. cit., p. 73. For a description of the training the students of the KUTV received, see Ansari, op. cit., pp. 533–6.

142. BL/MSS/Eur/E238/11 (RC), Telegram from Peel to Reading, 12 Dec. 1922.

143. For a very detailed account of M.N. Roy's activities see Kaye, *Communism in India*. Kaye was Director of the Central Intelligence Bureau in India from 1920 to 1925, and published this work upon his retirement. A brief summary of Kaye's work is also found in that of his successor at the Bureau, Sir David Petrie, *Communism in India, 1924–1927* [first published in 1927]. Also, Roy, *Memoirs*.

144. It would appear that Roy and other Indian revolutionaries abroad were often referred to as 'Bolsheviks' by the British authorities. BL/MSS/Eur/E238/11 (RC), Telegram from Peel to Reading, 2 Dec. 1922.

145. BL/MSS/Eur/E238/11 (RC), Telegram from Reading to Peel, 21 Dec. 1922.

146. Popplewell, op. cit., p. 306.

147. *Ibid.*, p. 309.

148. Kaye, op. cit., p. 239.

149. Report in the *Times*, quoted in White, 'Soviet Russia', p. 226.

150. Popplewell, op. cit., p. 312.

151. Andrews, op. cit., p. 684.

152. Popplewell, op. cit., p. 310.

153. *Ibid.*, pp. 312–14.

154. *Ibid.*, p. 316.

155. Sanat Bose discusses some of the reasons why the likes of Roy failed to establish Communism in India. Bose, 'Communist International and Indian

Trade Union Movement (1919–1923)', *Social Scientist*, Vol. 8 (1979), pp. 23–36.

156. Popplewell, op. cit., pp. 314–15.
157. Fisher, 'Interdepartmental Committee', pp. 1–34.
158. Madeira, op. cit., p. 30 and 38.
159. BL/MSS/Eur/E238/12 (RC), Telegram from Reading to Montagu, 23 Feb. 1922.
160. Adamec, *Afghanistan's Foreign Affairs to the Mid-Twentieth Century: Relations With the USSR, Germany and Britain*, pp. 67–82 and Reetz, op. cit., p. 33.
161. TNA/FO371/8076/N1450, Report by Dobbs on Negotiations in Kabul, 15 Feb. 1922.
162. Indeed, the 'Great Russian chauvinism' which had been displayed by the Tashkent officials had been of concern to Moscow, and telegrams had been sent as soon as communications had been re-established in 1919, with orders for the Soviet to work more with the Turkestan population. Mawdsley, op. cit., p. 238 and Carrére D' Encausse, op. cit., pp. 151–3.
163. For more on the Basmachi see: Olcott, 'The Basmachi or Freemen's revolt in Turkestan 1918–24', *Europe–Asia Studies*, Vol. 33 (1981), pp. 352–69; Chokaev, 'The Basmaji Movement in Turkestan', *Asiatic Review*, Vol. 24 (1928), pp. 273–88 and Broxup, 'The Basmachi', *Central Asian Survey*, Vol. 2 (1983), pp. 57–81.
164. Carrére D' Encausse, op. cit., pp. 177–8.
165. TNA/FO371/8077/N8664, Telegram from Humphrys to Curzon, 17 Aug. 1922.
166. TNA/FO371/8076/N1450, Report by Dobbs on Negotiations in Kabul, 15 Feb. 1922.
167. TNA/FO371/8079/N4909, Telegram from Humphrys to Curzon, 30 March 1922.
168. TNA/FO371/8079/N4909, Telegram from Humphrys to Curzon, 30 March 1922.
169. White, 'Baku Congress', pp. 508–9.
170. For details on this see Sonyel, 'Enver Pasha and the Basmaji Movement in Central Asia', *Middle Eastern Studies*, Vol. 26 (1990), pp. 52–64.
171. Kapur, op. cit., pp. 234–35.
172. BL/MSS/Eur/E238/11 (RC), Telegram from Reading to Peel, 24 April 1922.
173. BL/MSS/Eur/E238/11 (RC), Telegram from Reading to Peel, 27 April 1922.
174. TNA/FO371/8079/N3527, North-West Frontier Province Intelligence Bureau Diary, 23 Feb. 1922.
175. Gregorian, op. cit., p. 237.

176. TNA/FO371/8079/N2819, North-West Frontier Province Intelligence Bureau Diary, 9 Feb. 1922.
177. Woodward, op. cit., No. 99, Telegram from Hodgson to Curzon, 11 June 1923.
178. BL/MSS/Eur/E238/12 (RC), Telegram from Peel to Reading, 13 Nov. 1923.
179. Poullada, op. cit., pp. 251–5.
180. TNA/FO1011/44, Letter from Curzon to Loraine, 30 May 1922.

The End of An Epoch

1. BL/MSS/Eur/D523/3 (MC), Letters from Mr. Montagu to Lord Chelmsford, 22 Jan. 1919. [Emphasis added].
2. Hence why events in South and Central Asia during this time cannot simply be characterised as a revival of the Great Game. If the premise is accepted that the Great Game was a mentality then we see that for the likes of Curzon the Great Game never ended, while for the Indian government it did not exist in this period. The game could not be revived if it a) had not ended for some and b) did not exist for others. A matter of semantics perhaps but an important point for demonstrating the complexity of British foreign policy during this period.
3. Andrew, 'The British Secret Service and Anglo-Soviet relations in the 1920s: Part I, From Trade Negotiations to the Zinoviev Letter', *The Historical Journal*, Vol. 20 (1977), p. 673.
4. Crowe, 'The Zinoviev Letter', *Journal of Contemporary History*, Vol. 10 (1975), pp. 407–32.
5. Bennett, *'A Most Extraordinary and Mysterious Business': The Zinoviev Letter of 1924.*
6. Nicolson, op. cit., p. 19.
7. Ronaldshay, op. cit., p. 383.
8. Aziz, op. cit., p. 104.
9. The reason given to Curzon was that it was not possible to have a prime minister who sat in the House of Lords. However, the fact was that not many of his colleagues appeared comfortable with Curzon in the premiership, while apparently King George V greatly disliked the ex-foreign secretary. Gilmour, op. cit., pp. 580–5.
10. '...I really cannot allow the tendency you have sometimes shown in your telegrams that if things do not go as you wish you will declare your disagreement in public'. BL/MSS/Eur/D523/3 (MC), Letter from Montagu to Chelmsford, 29 Aug. 1919.

11. For example: 'I have felt the difficulty of my position more keenly than I can say...I have isolated myself from my colleagues...I wonder whether the sun will ever shine again'. BL/MSS/Eur/E264/6 (CC), Letter from Montagu to Chelmsford, 20 May 1920.
12. Mawdsley, op. cit., p. 239.
13. Bullard, 'The Power of Menace: Soviet Relations with South Asia, 1917–1974', *British Journal of International Studies*, Vol. 2 (1976), p. 56.
14. *Ibid.*, p. 57.
15. Carrére D' Encausse, op. cit., p. 159.
16. Woodward, op. cit., Telegram from MacDonald to Hodgson, 1 Feb. 1924 and *No. 208:* Telegram from MacDonald to Hodgson, 1 Feb. 1924.
17. White, *Britain*, pp. 204–33.
18. Gilmour, op. cit., pp. 585–6.
19. Mosley, *Curzon: The End of an Epoch*, p. xii.
20. *Ibid.*, p. 288.

Bibliography Reference Works

I. Jennings, *Cabinet Government* (Cambridge: Cambridge University Press, 1959), 3rd Edition.

J.P. Mackintosh, *The British Cabinet* (London: Stevens and Sons Ltd, 1977), 3rd Edition.

M. Moir, *A General Guide to the India Office Records* (London: The British Library, 1988).

S. de Mowbray, *Key Facts in Soviet History, Vol. 1, 1917 to 22 June 1941* (London: Pinter, 1990).

J.G. Parker, *Lord Curzon 1859–1925: A Bibliography. Bibliographies of British Statesmen, No. 5* (Westport: Greenwood Press, 1991).

Public Records Office Handbooks, No. 13, *The Records of the Foreign Office, 1782–1939* (London: HMSO, 1969).

J. Smele, *The Russian Revolution and Civil War 1917–1921: An Annotated Bibliography* (London: Continuum International Publishing Group, 2006).

Primary Sources

Archival Sources

The National Archives

FO371	General Correspondence – Persia, Afghanistan, Russia and Turkey
FO1011	Loraine Papers
WO106/157,	Director of Military Intelligence (DMI) 5186, 6274
CAB23	Cabinet Minutes and Conclusions
CAB24	Cabinet Papers and Memorandum
CAB27	Cabinet Committees
ADM 233	'Wireless News' (Decrypts)

The British Library

IOR/L/PS/10	India Office Records, Political and Secret Department, Subject Files

IOR/L/PS/11	India Office Records, Political and Secret Department, Subject Files
MSS/Eur/E264	Chelmsford Collection MSS/Eur/D523 Montagu Collection
MSS/Eur/E238	Reading Collection
MSS/Eur/F112	Curzon Collection

The Imperial War Museum

| HHW/1/35 | Sir Henry Wilson Diary, 1920 |
| HHW/2/20 | Sir Henry Wilson Correspondence with Lord Curzon, May 1920–Feb. 1922 |

Newspapers

The *Times*
Daily Telegraph
Manchester Guardian

Published Documents

A Collection of Reports on Bolshevism in Russia (London: HMSO, 1919).

J. Bunyan and H.H. Fisher, *The Bolshevik Revolution, 1917–1918: Documents and Materials* (Stanford: Stanford University Press, 1934).

J. Degras, *Soviet Documents on Foreign Policy, Vol. I, 1917–1924* (London: Oxford University Press, 1951).

M. Gilbert, *Winston S. Churchill. Volume IV, Companion, Parts 2 and 3* (London: Heinemann, 1977).

G.P. Gooch and H. Temperley, eds, *British Documents on the Origins of the War, Vol. III* (London: HMSO, 1928).

G.P. Gooch and H. Temperley, eds, *British Documents on the Origins of the War, Vol. IV* (London: HMSO, 1929).

Hansard Parliamentary Debates, 4th Series, Vol. 183, 29 Jan. – 11 Feb. 1908.

Hansard Parliamentary Debates, 4th Series, Vol. 184, 12 Feb. – 26 Feb. 1908.

The Turkish settlement and the Muslim and Indian attitude: the address presented by the Indian Khilafat deputation to the Viceroy at Delhi, on January 19th, 1920: and the manifesto of the All-India Khilafat Conference passed at its Bombay session, held on February 15th, 16th and 17th, 1920 (London: Indian Khilafat Delegation, 1920).

Report (Political and Economic) of the Committee to Collect Information on Russia (London: HMSO, 1921).

Report of the British Labour Delegation to Russia, 1920 (London: Trades Union Congress, 1920).

Russia: the Official Report of the British Trades Union Delegation to Russia and Caucasia, Nov. and Dec., 1924 (London: Trades Union Congress, 1925).

'Treaty of Lausanne', http://wwi.lib.byu.edu/index.php/Treaty_of_Lausanne.

'Treaty of Sèvres', http://wwi.lib.byu.edu/index.php/Peace_Treaty_of_Sèvres.

E.L. Woodward, R. Butler, and A. Orde, eds, *Documents on British Foreign Policy 1919–1939* (London: HMSO, 1968).

Memoirs, Diaries and Contemporary Writings

Z. Avalov and J.E.S. Cooper, 'The Caucasus since 1918', *The Slavonic Review*, Vol. 3, No. 8 (1924), pp. 320–336.

P.M. Brown, 'The Lausanne Conference', *The American Journal of International Law*, Vol. 17 (1923), pp. 290–296.

Sir G. Buchanan, *My Mission to Russia and Other Diplomatic Memories* (Boston: Brown, 1923).

G. Chicherin, *Two Years of Foreign Policy: The Relations of the Russian Socialist Federal Soviet Republic with Foreign Nations, from November 7, 1917, to November 7, 1919* (Russian Soviet Government Bureau, 1920).

V. Chirol, 'The Downfall of the Khalifate', *Foreign Affairs*, Vol. 2 (1924), pp. 571–582.

M. Chokaev, 'The Basmaji Movement in Turkestan', *Asiatic Review*, Vol. 24 (1928), pp. 273–288.

G.N. Curzon, *Russia in Central Asia in 1889 and the Anglo-Russian Question* (London: Elibron Classics, 2006 reprint).

G.N. Curzon, *Persia and the Persian Question* (London: Longmans, Green and Co., 1892).

W.T. Goode, *Is Intervention in Russia a Myth?* (London: Williams & Norgate Ltd., 1931).

J.D. Gregory, *On the Edge of Diplomacy* (London: Hutchinson, 1929).

Viscount Grey of Fallodon, *Twenty Five Years, 1812–1916* (London, 1925).

Lord Hardinge of Penhurst, *Old Diplomacy* (London: John Murray, 1947).

C. Kaye, *Communism in India* (Calcutta: Editions India, 1971).

Col. G. de Lacy Evans, *On the Practicability of an Invasion of British India* (London: J.M Richardson, 1829).

Prince Lobanoff-Rostovsky, 'The Soviet Muslim Republics in Central Asia', *Journal of the Royal Institute of International Affairs*, Vol. 7 (1928), pp. 241–255.

D. Lloyd George, 'The Genoa Conference and Britain's Part', *Advocate of Peace through Justice*, Vol. 84 (1922), pp. 131–137.

K. Marx and F. Engels, *On Colonialism* (London: Lawrence and Wishart Ltd, 1968).

H. Nicolson, *Curzon: The Last Phase, 1919–1925. A Study in Post-War Diplomacy* (London: Constable, 1934).

H. Nicolson, *Sir Arthur Nicolson Bart, First Lord Carnock: A Study in the Old Diplomacy* (London: Constable, 1930).

L. Oliphant, *An Ambassador in Bonds* (London: Putnam and Co., 1946).

D. Petrie, *Communism in India, 1924–1927* (Calcutta: Editions India, 1972).

Earl of Ronaldshay, *The Life of Lord Curzon, 3 Vols.* (London: Stanhope Press, 1928).

M.N. Roy, *Memoirs* (Bombay: Allied Publishers, 1964).

S. Sazonov, *Fateful Years 1909-1916. The Reminiscences of Serge Sazonov* (London: John Cape, 1928).

C. L. Seeger, ed., *Memoirs of Alexander Iswolsky* (London: Hesperides Press, 2006).

S.I.A. Shah, 'The Bolshevist Menace in the Middle East', *Contemporary Review,* Vol. 20 (1921), pp. 500–506.

W.M. Shuster, *The Strangling of Persia* (London: The Century Co., 1912).

Gen. Sir A. Skeen, *Lessons in Imperial Rule: Instructions for British Infantrymen on the Indian Frontier* (Barnsley: Pen and Swords Books, 2008), 5th Edition.

P. Sykes, 'South Persia and the Great War', *The Geographical Journal*, Vol. 58, No. 2 (1921), pp. 101–116.

J. William Kaye, *A History of War in Afghanistan* (London: R. Bentley, 1851).

Secondary Sources

Unpublished Works

C.N.B. Ross, 'Lord Curzon, the "Persian Question", and Geopolitics, 1888–1921', PhD (July, 2012; University of Cambridge).

Published Works

L.W. Adamec, *Afghanistan's Foreign Affairs to the Mid-Twentieth Century: Relations With the USSR, Germany and Britain* (Arizona: The University of Arizona Press, 1974).

C. Andrew, 'The British Secret Service and Anglo-Soviet relations in the 1920s: Part I, From Trade Negotiations to the Zinoviev Letter', *The Historical Journal,* Vol. 20 (1977), pp. 673–706.

K.H. Ansari, 'Pan-Islam and the Making of the Early Indian Muslim Socialists', *Modern Asian Studies,* Vol. 20, No. 3 (1986), pp. 509–537.

A.A. Arghandawi, *British Imperialism and Afghanistan's Struggle for Independence, 1914–21* (New Delhi: Munshiram Manoharlal, 1989).

R.P. Arnot, *The Impact of the Russian Revolution in Britain* (London: Lawrence and Wishart, 1967).

A.H. Arslanian, 'The British Decision to Intervene in Transcaucasia during World War I', *Armenian Review,* Vol. 27 (1974), pp. 146–159.

A.H. Arslanian, 'Dunsterville's Adventures: A Reappraisal', *International Journal of Middle East Studies*, Vol.12 (1980), pp. 199–216.

S.R. Ashton, *British Policy Towards the Indian States, 1905–1939* (London: Curzon Press, 1982).

K.K. Aziz, *Britain and Muslim India: A Study of British Public Opinion vis-a-'vis the Development of Muslim Nationalism in India, 1857–1947* (London: Heinemann, 1963).

S. Bairathi, *Communism and Nationalism in India: A Study in Inter-Relationship, 1919–1947* (Delhi: Pooja Press, 1987).

V. Baskakov, trans., *A History of Afghanistan* (Moscow: Progress Publishers, 1985).

R.F. Baumann, *Russian and Soviet Unconventional Wars in the Caucasus–Central, Asia–Afghanistan* (Milton Keynes: Military Press, 2001).

Lord Beaverbrook, *The Decline and Fall of Lloyd George* (London: Collins, 1963).

S. Becker, *Russia's Protectorates in Central Asia: Bukhara and Khiva, 1865–1924* (Cambridge: Harvard University Press, 1968).

G.H. Bennett, *British Foreign Policy in the Curzon Period, 1919–1924* (New York: St. Martin's Press, 1995).

G.H. Bennett, 'Lloyd George, Curzon and the Control of British Foreign Policy 1919–1922', *Australian Journal of Politics and History*, Vol. 4 (1999), pp. 467–482.

G. Bennett, *'A Most Extraordinary and Mysterious Business': The Zinoviev Letter of 1924* (London: HMSO, 1999).

D.G. Bishop, *The Administration of British Foreign Relations* (New York: Syracuse University Press, 1961).

C.E. Black, *Rewriting Russian History: Soviet Interpretations of Russia's Past* (New York: Frederick A. Praeger, 1956).

S. Blank, 'Soviet Politics and the Iranian Revolution of 1919–1921', *Cahiers du Monde russe et soviétique*, Vol. 21 (1980), pp. 173–194.

S. Bose, 'Communist International and Indian Trade Union Movement – 1919–1923', *Social Scientist*, Vol. 8 (1979), pp. 23–36.

C.E. Bosworth, 'The Hon. George Nathaniel Curzon's Travels in Russian Central Asia and Persia', *Iran*, Vol. 31, (1993), pp. 127–136.

C.F. Brand, 'British Labour and Soviet Russia', *South Atlantic Quarterly*, Vol. 48 (1949), pp. 327–340.

M. Broxup, 'The Basmachi', *Central Asian Survey*, Vol. 2 (1983), pp. 57–81.

J.M. Brown, 'Imperial Facade: Some Constraints upon and Contradictions in the British Position in India, 1919–35', *Transactions of the Royal Historical Society*, Vol. 26, (1976), pp. 35–52.

G. Bullard, 'The Power of Menace: Soviet Relations with South Asia, 1917–1974', *British Journal of International Studies*, Vol. 2 (1976), pp. 51–66.

R. Bullen, ed., *The Foreign Office, 1782–1982* (Frederick MD: University Publications of America, 1984).

D. Burke, 'Theodore Rothstein, Russian Emigré and British Socialist', *Immigrants and Minorities*, Vol. 2 (1983), pp. 80–99.

L. Cahill, *Forgotten Revolution: Limerick Soviet, 1919* (Dublin: O'Brian Press, 1990).

P.J. Cain and A.G. Hopkins, *British Imperialism: Crisis and Deconstruction 1914–1990* (London: Longman, 1993).

E.H. Carr, *The Bolshevik Revolution, 1917–1923* (London: Macmillan, 1950–78).

H. Carrère d'Encausse, *Islam and the Russian Empire: Reform and Revolution in Central Asia* (Berkeley: University of California Press, 1988).

J. Castagné, 'Soviet Imperialism in Afghanistan', *Foreign Affairs*, Vol. 13 (1935), pp. 698–703.

R. Challinor, *The Origins of British Bolshevism* (London: Croom Helm, 1977).

C. Chaqueri, 'The Baku Congress', *Central Asian Survey*, Vol. 2 (1983), pp. 89–107.

C. Chaqueri, *The Soviet Socialist Republic of Iran, 1920–1921: Birth of the Trauma* (Pittsburgh: University of Pittsburgh Press, 1995).

S. Chattopadhyay, 'The Bolshevik Menace: Colonial Surveillance and the Origins of Socialist Politics in Calcutta', *South Asia Research*, Vol. 26 (2006), pp. 165–179.

D.N. Chester and F.M.G. Wilson, *The Organisation of British Central Government, 1914–1964* (London: George Allen and Unwin, 1957).

H.M. Christman, ed., *Essential Works of Lenin* (New York: Bantam Books, 1966).

R.P. Churchill, *The Anglo-Russian Convention of 1907* (Iowa: Torch Press, 1939).

P. Clarke and C. Trebilcock, eds, *Understanding Decline: Perceptions and Realities of British Economic Performance* (Cambridge: Cambridge University Press, 1997).

W.P. Coates and Z.K. Coates, *Armed Intervention in Russia, 1918–1922* (London: Gollancz, 1935).

W.P. Coates and Z.K. Coates, *Soviets in Central Asia* (New York: Philosophical Library, 1951).

J. Connell, *The 'Office': A Study of British Foreign Policy and its Makers, 1919–1951* (London: Allan Wingate, 1958).

B. Cooper-Busch, *Britain and the Persian Gulf, 1894–1914* (Berkeley: University of California Press, 1967).

B. Cooper-Busch, *Mudros to Lausanne: Britain's Frontier in West Asia, 1918–1923* (New York: University of New York Press, 1976).

M.H. Cowden, *Russian Bolshevism and British Labour, 1917–1921* (Boulder CO: East European Monographs, 1984).

G.A. Craig and F. Gilbert, eds, *The Diplomats, 1919–1939* (Princeton: Princeton University Press, 1953).

C. Cross, *The Fall of the British Empire, 1918–1968* (London: Hodder and Stoughton, 1968).

S. Crowe, 'The Zinoviev Letter', *Journal of Contemporary History*, Vol. 10 (1975), pp. 407–432.

P. Dailami, 'The Bolsheviks and the Jangali Revolutionary Movement, 1915–1920', *Cahiers du monde russe et sovietique*, Vol. 31 (1990), pp. 43–60.

P. Dailami, 'Bravin in Tehran and the Origins of Soviet Policy in Iran', *Revolutionary Russia*, Vol. 12 (1999), pp. 63–82.

P. Dailami, 'The Bolshevik Revolution and the Genesis of Communism in Iran, 1917 – 1920', *Central Asian Survey*, Vol. 11 (1992), pp. 51–82.

J.G. Darwin, *Britain, Egypt and the Middle East: Imperial Policy in the Aftermath of War, 1918–1922* (London: Macmillan Press, 1981).

J.G. Darwin, 'Imperialism in Decline? Tendencies in British Imperial Policy between the Wars', *Historical Journal*, Vol. 23, No. 3 (1980), pp. 657–79.

J.G. Darwin, 'The Fear of Falling: British Politics and Imperial Decline Since 1900', *Transactions of the Royal Historical Society* (1986), pp. 27–43.

J.G. Darwin, 'The Chanak Crisis and the British Cabinet', *History*, Vol. 65 (1980), pp. 32–48.

R.K. Debo, *Survival and Consolidation: The Foreign Policy of Soviet Russia, 1918–1921* (London: McGill-Queen's University Press, 1992).

R.K. Debo, *Revolution and Survival: the Foreign Policy of Soviet Russia, 1917–1918* (Buffalo: University of Toronto Press, 1978).

R.K. Debo, 'Lloyd George and the Copenhagen Conference of 1919–1920: The Initiation of Anglo–Soviet Negotiations', *The Historical Journal*, Vol. 24 (1981), pp. 429–441.

D. Dilks, *Curzon in India, Vols. I–II* (London: Rupert-Hart Davis, 1969–70).

D. Dilks, ed., *Retreat from Power: Studies in Britain's Foreign Policy of the Twentieth Century, Vol. I, 1906–1939* (London: Macmillan, 1981).

S. ud-Din, *Afghanistan and Central Asia in the New Great Game* (New Delhi: Lancer's Books, 2003).

C. Dobson and J. Miller, *The Day We Almost Bombed Moscow* (London: Hodder and Stoughton, 1986).

M.L. Dockrill and B.J.C McKercher, eds, *Diplomacy and World Power: Studies in British Foreign Policy, 1890–1951* (Cambridge: Cambridge University Press, 1996).

D.N. Druhe, *Soviet Russia and Indian Communism, 1917–1949* (New York: Bookman Associates, 1959).

P. Dukes, *October and the World: Perspectives on the Russian Revolution* (London: St. Martin's Press, 1979).

G. Egerton, ed, *Political Memoir: Essays on the Politics of Memory* (London: Frank Cass, 1994).

C.H. Ellis, *The Transcaspian Episode, 1918–1919* (London: Hutchinson, 1963).

C.H. Ellis, 'Operations in Transcaspia, 1918–1919, and the 26 Commissars Case', *St. Anony's Papers*, No. 6 (1959), pp. 131–150.

D. Ewalt, 'The Fight for Oil', *History Today*, Vol. 31 (1981), pp. 11–15.

M. Ewans, *The Great Game: Britain and Russia in Central Asia 1880–1907* (London: Routledge, 2004).

N.S. Fatemi, *Diplomatic History of Persia 1917–1923: Anglo-Russian Power Politics in Iran* (New York: R.F. Moore Co., 1952).

N.S. Fatemi, *Oil Diplomacy* (New York: Whittier Books, 1954).

J.R. Ferris, '"The Greatest Power on Earth": Great Britain in the 1920s', *The International History Review*, Vol. 13 (1991), pp. 726–750.

J.R. Ferris, '"The Internationalism of Islam": The British Perception of a Muslim Menace, 1840–1951', *Intelligence and National Security*, Vol. 24 (2009), pp. 57–77.

J.R. Ferris, *The Evolution of British Strategic Policy, 1919–1926* (London: MacMillan Press, 1989).

L. Fischer, *The Soviets in World Affairs, Vol. I* (London: Jonathan Cape, 1930).

J. Fisher, '"On the Glacis of India": Lord Curzon and British Policy in the Caucasus, 1919', *Diplomacy and Statecraft*, Vol. 8 (1997), pp. 50–82.

J. Fisher, 'The Interdepartmental Committee on Eastern Unrest and British Responses to Bolshevik and Other Intrigues Against the Empire During the 1920s', *Journal of Asian History*, Vol. 34 (2000), pp. 1–34.

J. Fisher and A. Best, eds, *On the Fringes of Diplomacy: Influences on British Foreign Policy, 1800–1945* (Farnham: Ashgate, 2011).

J. Fisher, *Curzon and British Imperialism in the Middle East, 1916–1919* (London: Frank Cass Publishers, 1999).

P. Fleming, *Bayonets to Lhasa* (London: Rupert Hart Davis, 1962).

M.G. Fry, 'Britain, the Allies and the Problem of Russia, 1918–1919', *Canadian Journal of History*, Vol. 2, No. 2 (1967), pp. 62–84.

J. Gallagher and A. Seal, 'Britain and India between the Wars', *Modern Asian Studies*, Vol. 15 (1981), pp. 387–414.

J. Gallagher, 'Nationalisms and the Crisis of Empire, 1919–1922', *Modern Asian Studies*, Vol. 15 (1981), pp. 355–368.

J. Gallagher, *The Decline, Revival and Fall of the British Empire* (Cambridge: Cambridge University Press, 1982).

C. Ghani, *Iran and the Rise of Reza Shah: From Qajar Collapse to Pahlavi Power* (London: I.B. Tauris, 2000).

A.K. Ghose, *Lord Chelmsford's Viceroyalty: A Critical Survey* (Madras: Ganesh and Co., 1921).

D. Gilmour, *Curzon* (London: John Murray, 1994).

J.H. Gleason, *The Genesis of Russophobia in Great Britain* (London: Oxford University Press, 1950).

M.V. Glenny 'The Anglo-Soviet Trade Agreement, March 1921', *Journal of Contemporary History*, Vol. 5, No. 2 (1970), pp. 63–82.

B. Gokaky, *A Clash of Empires: Turkey Between Russian Bolshevism and British Imperialism, 1918–1923* (London: IB Tauris, 1997).

E. Goldstein, 'British Peace Aims and the Eastern Question: The Political Intelligence Department and the Eastern Committee, 1918', *Middle Eastern Studies*, Vol. 23 (1987), pp. 419–436.

E. Goldstein, 'The British Official Mind and the Lausanne Conference, 1922–1923', *Diplomacy and Statecraft*, Vol. 14 (2003), pp. 185–206.

D. Goold, 'Lord Hardinge and the Mesopotamia Expedition and Inquiry, 1914–1917', *The Historical Journal*, Vol. 19 (1976), pp. 919–945.

N.F. Grant, ed., *The Kaiser's Letters to the Tsar* (London: Hodder and Stoughton, 1920).

S.R. Graubard, *British Labour and the Russian Revolution, 1917–1924* (Cambridge, MA: Harvard University Press, 1956).

P. Graves, *The Life of Sir Percy Cox* (London: Hutchinson and Co., 1941).

R.L. Greaves, 'Some Aspects of the Anglo-Russian Convention and Its Working in Persia, 1907–1914', *Bulletin of the School of Oriental and African Studies, University of London*, Vol. 13 (1968), pp. 69–91.

V. Gregorian, *The Emergence of Modern Afghanistan: Politics of Reform and Modernization, 1880–1946* (Stanford: Stanford University Press, 1969).

S.D. Gupta, *Comintern and the Destiny of Communism in India, 1919–1943* (Kolkata: Seribaan, 2006).

W. Habberton, *Anglo-Russian Relations Concerning Afghanistan, 1837–1907* (Illinois: Illinois Studies in the Social Sciences, 1937).

J.P. Haithcox, 'The Roy–Lenin Debate on Colonial Policy: a New Interpretation', *The Journal of Asian Studies*, Vol. 23 (1963), pp. 93–101.

J.P. Haithcox, *Communism and Nationalism in India. M.N. Roy and Comintern Policy, 1920–1939* (Princeton: Princeton University Press, 1971).

M. Hasan, ed., *Communal and pan-Islamic Trends in Colonial India* (New Delhi: Manohar, 1981).

T.A. Heathcote, *The Afghan Wars, 1839–1919* (London: Osprey, 1980).

J. Hiden ed. *Contact or Isolation? Soviet-Western Relations in the Interwar Period* (Stockholm: Almquest, 1991).

F.H. Hinsley, ed., *British Foreign Policy under Sir Edward Grey* (Cambridge: Cambridge University Press, 1977).

P. Hopkirk, *Setting the East Ablaze: Lenin's Dream of an Empire in Asia* (Oxford: Oxford University, 1986).

P. Hopkirk, *On Secret Service East of Constantinople: The Plot to Bring Down the British Empire* (London: John Murray, 1994).

P. Hopkirk, *The Great Game: On Secret Service in High Asia* (London: John Murray, 2006 edition).

M. Hughes, *Diplomacy before the Russian Revolution: Britain, Russia and the Old Diplomacy, 1894–1917* (New York: St. Martin's Press, 2000).

M. Hughes, *British Foreign Secretaries in an Uncertain World, 1919–1939* (London: Routledge, 2004).

M. Hughes, *Inside the Enigma: British Officials in Russia, 1900–1939* (London: Hambledon Press, 1997).

M. Hughes, 'Searching for the Soul of Russia: British Perceptions of Russia during the First World War', *Twentieth Century British History*, Vol. 20, No. 2 (2009), pp. 198–226.

R. Hyam, *Britain's Imperial Century 1815–1914* (London: Macmillan, 1993).

Z. Imam, *Colonialism in East–West Relations: A Study of Soviet Policy Towards India and Anglo-Soviet Relations* (New Delhi: Eastman Publications, 1969).

Z. Imam, 'The Effects of the Russian Revolution in India, 1917–1920', *St. Antony's Papers*, No. 18 (1966), pp. 74–97.

E. Ingram, 'Great Britain's Great Game: An Introduction', *The International History Review*, Vol. 2 (1980), pp. 160–171.

E. Ingram, 'Review Article: Approaches to the Great Game in Asia', *Middle Eastern Studies*, Vol. 18 (1982), pp. 449–457.

E. Ingram, *The Beginning of the Great Game in Asia, 1828–1834* (Oxford: Oxford University Press, 1979).

E. Ingram, *Commitment to Empire: Prophecies of the Great Game in Asia, 1797–1800* (London: Clarendon Press, 1981).

A. Jalal and A. Seal, 'Alternative to Partition: Muslim Politics between the Wars', *Modern Asian Studies*, Vol. 15 (1981), pp. 415–454.

K. Jeffrey, 'Sir Henry Wilson and the Defence of the British Empire, 1918–22', *The Journal of Imperial and Commonwealth History*, Vol. 5 (1977), pp. 270–293.

K. Jeffrey, *The British Army and the Crisis of Empire, 1918–1922* (Manchester: Manchester University Press, 1984).

K. Jeffrey, '"An English Barrack in the Oriental Seas"? India in the Aftermath of the First World War', *Modern Asian Studies*, Vol. 15 (1981), pp. 369–386.

G. Johnson, ed., *The Foreign Office and the British Diplomacy in the Twentieth Century* (New York: Routledge, 2005).

J. Joll, *1914: The Unspöken Assumptions* (London: Weidenfeld and Nicolson, 1968).

C. Jones, 'Lord Curzon of Kedleston, 1859–1925: An Appreciation', *International Affairs*, Vol. 37, No. 3 (1961), pp. 332–338.

D. Judd, *Lord Reading: Rufus Isaacs, First Marquess of Reading, Lord Chief Justice, and Viceroy of India, 1860–1935* (London: Weidenfeld and Nicolson, 1982).

H. Kapur, *Soviet Russia and Asia, 1917–1927: A Study of Soviet Policy Towards Turkey, Iran and Afghanistan* (Geneva: Victor Chevalier, 1965).

H. Katouzian, 'The Campaign against the Anglo-Iranian Agreement of 1919', *British Journal of Middle Eastern Studies*, Vol. 25 (1998), pp. 5–46.

F. Kazemzadeh, *Russia and Britain in Persia. A Study in Imperialism, 1864–1914* (Yale: Yale University Press, 1968).

F. Kazemzadeh, 'The Origin and Early Development of the Persian Cossack Brigade', *American Slavice and Eastern European Review*, Vol. 15 (1956), pp. 351–363.

E. Kedourie and S.G. Haim, eds, *Towards a Modern Iran: Studies in Thought, Politics and Society* (London: Frank Cass, 1980).

J.B. Kelly, 'The Legal and Historical Basis of the British Position in the Persian Gulf', *St. Antony's Papers* (1958), pp. 119–140.

G.F. Kennan, *Russia and the West under Lenin and Stalin* (New York: New American Library, 1961).

G.F. Kennan, *Soviet-American Relations, 1917–1920:*
Vol. 1. Russia Leaves the War (London: Faber and Faber, 1956).
Vol. 2. The Decision to Intervene (London: Faber and Faber, 1958).
Vol. 3. Intervention and the Peace Conference (London: Faber and Faber, 1959).

P. Kennedy, *The Realities Behind Diplomacy: Backround Influences on British External Policy, 1865–1980* (London: George Allen and Unwin, 1981).

C. Kinvig, *Churchill's Crusade: the British Invasion of Russia, 1918–1920* (London: Hambledon Continuum, 2006).

I. Klein, 'The Anglo-Russian Convention and the Problem of Central Asia, 1907–1914', *The Journal of British Studies*, Vol. 11 (1971), pp.126–147.

I. Klein, 'British Intervention in the Persian Revolution, 1905–1909', *The Historical Journal*, Vol. 15 (1972), pp. 731–752

L. Kleveman, *The New Great Game: Blood and Oil in Central Asia* (London: Atlantic, 2003).

J.M. Landau, *The Politics of Pan-Islam: Ideology and Organisation* (Oxford: Clarendon Press, 1994).

C. Larner, 'The Amalgamation of the Diplomatic Service with the Foreign Office', *Journal of Contemporary History*, Vol. 7 (1972), pp. 107–126.

I.J. Lederer, ed., *Russian Foreign Policy. Essays in Political Perspective* (New Haven: Yale University Press, 1967).

D.E. Lee, 'The Origins of Pan-Islamism', *The American Historical Review*, Vol. 47 (1942), pp. 278–287.

G. Lenczowski, *Russia and the West in Iran, 1918–1948: A Study in Big-Power Rivalry* (New York: Cornell University Press, 1949).

D.C.B. Lieven, *Russia and the Origins of the First World War* (London: St. Martin's Press, 1983).

D.A. Low, 'The Government of India and the First Non-Cooperation Movement – 1920–1922', *The Journal of Asian Studies*, Vol. 25 (1966), pp. 241–259.

C.J. Lowe and M.L. Dockrill, *The Mirage of Power: British Foreign Policy 1902–1922* (London: Routledge and Kegan Paul, 1972).

L.J. Macfarlane, 'Hands off Russia: British Labour and Russo-Polish War, 1920', *Past and Present*, Vol. 38 (1967), pp. 126–152.

A.L. Macfie, 'The British Decision Regarding the Future of Constantinople, November 1918–January 1920', *The Historical Journal*, Vol. 18 (1975), pp. 391–400.

A.L. Macfie, 'The Chanak Affair (September–October 1922)', *Balkan Studies*, Vol. 20 (1979), pp. 309–341.

M. Macmillan, *Peacemakers: The Paris Conference of 1919 and its Attempt to End War* (London: John Murray, 2003).

V. Madeira, '"Because I Don't Trust Him, We are Friends": Signals Intelligence and the Reluctant Anglo-Soviet Embrace, 1917–1924', *Intelligence and National Security*, Vol. 19 (2004), pp. 29–51.

E. Maisel, *The Foreign Office and Foreign Policy, 1919–1926* (Brighton: Sussex Academic Press, 1994).

E. Mawdsley, *The Russian Civil War* (London: Unwin Hyman, 1987).

B.J.C. McKercher and D.J. Moss, eds, *Shadow and Substance in British Foreign Policy, 1895–1939* (Alberta: The University of Alberta Press, 1984).

D. McLean, 'English Radicals, Russia and the Fate of Persia 1907–1913', *The English Historical Review*, Vol. 93 (1978), pp. 338–352.

D. McLean, *Britain and Her Buffer State. The Collapse of the Persian Empire, 1890–1914* (London: Royal Historical Society, 1979).

S. McMeekin, *History's Greatest Heist: The Looting of Russia by the Bolsheviks* (Yale: Yale University Press, 2009).

S. McMeekin, *The Berlin-Baghdad Express: The Ottoman Empire and Germany's Bid for World Power, 1898–1918* (London: Penguin, 2011).

H. Mejcher, 'British Middle East Policy 1917–21: The Inter-Departmental Level', *Journal of Contemporary History*, Vol. 8, No. 4 (1973), pp. 81–101.

K.E. Meyer and S.B. Brysac, *Tournament of Shadows: The Great Game and the Race for Empire in Central Asia* (Washington DC: Counterpoint, 1999).

K.W.B. Middleton, *Britain and Russia. An Historical Essay* (New York: Kennikat Press, 1971).

B. Millman, 'The Problem with Generals: Military Observers and the Origins of Intervention in Russia and Persia, 1917–1918', *Journal of Contemporary History*, Vol. 33, No. 2 (1998), pp. 291–320.

G. Minault, *The Khilafat Movement: Religious Symbolism and Political Mobilization in India* (New York: Columbia University Press, 1982).

P. Mishra, *From the Ruins of Empire: the Revolt against the West and the Remaking of Asia* (London: Allen Lane, 2012).

L.V. Mitrovkin, *Failure of Three Missions: British Diplomacy and Intelligence in the Efforts to Overthrow Soviet Government in Central Asia* (Moscow: Progress Publishers, 1987).

F.J. Moberly, *Operations in Persia 1914–1919* (London: HMSO, 1987).

G.N. Molesworth, *Afghanistan, 1919: An Account of Operations in the Third Afghan War* (London: Asia Publishing House, 1963).

E. Monroe, *Britain's Moment in the Middle East, 1914–1971* (London: Chatto & Windus, 1981).

R.J. Moore, 'Curzon and Indian Reform', *Modern Asian Studies*, Vol. 27, No. 4 (1993), pp. 719–740.

K.O. Morgan, 'Lloyd George's Premiership: A Study in 'Prime Ministerial Government", *The Historical Journal*, Vol. 13 (1970), pp. 130–157.

L. Mosley, *Curzon: The End of an Epoch* (London: Longmans, 1960).

C.L. Mowat, *Britain Between the Wars, 1918–1940* (London: Methuen, 1968).

M. Naeem Qureshi, *Pan-Islam in British Indian Politics: A Study of the Khilafat Movement, 1918–1924* (Leiden: Brill, 1999).

B.R. Nanda, *Gandhi, Pan-Islamism, Imperialism and Nationalism in India* (Oxford: Oxford University Press, 1989).

J.F. Naylor, *A Man and an Institution: Sir Maurice Hankey, the Cabinet Secretariat and the Custody of Cabinet Secrecy* (Cambridge: Cambridge University Press, 1984).

K. Neilson, *Britain, Soviet Russia and the Collapse of the Versailles Order, 1919–1939* (Cambridge: Cambridge University Press, 2009).

K. Neilson, *Britain and the Last Tsar: British Policy and Russia, 1894–1917* (Oxford: Clarendon Press, 1995).

K. Neilson and T.G. Otte, eds, *The Permanent Under-Secretary for Foreign Affairs, 1854–1946* (London: Routledge, 2009).

F.S. Northedge, '1917–1919: The Implications for Britain', *Journal of Contemporary History*, Vol. 3 (1968), pp. 191–209.

T.E. O'Connor, *Diplomacy and Revolution: G.V. Chicherin and Soviet Foreign Affairs, 1918–1930* (Ames: Iowa State University Press, 1988).

M.K. Öke, *The Turkish War of Independence and the Independence Struggle of the South Asian Muslims: 'The Khilafat Movement', 1919–1924* (Ankara: Ministry of Culture, 1991).

M.B. Olcott, 'The Basmachi or Freemen's revolt in Turkestan 1918–24', *Europe–Asia Studies*, Vol. 33 (1981), pp. 352–369.

W.J. Olson, *Anglo-Iranian Relations During World War I* (London: Frank Cass, 1984).

T.G. Otte and C.A. Pagedas, eds, *Personalities, War and Diplomacy* (London: Frank Cass, 1997).

T.G. Otte, *The Foreign Office Mind: The Making of British Foreign Policy, 1865–1914* (Cambridge: Cambridge University Press, 2011).

A. Özcan, *Pan-Islamism: Indian Muslims, the Ottomans and Britain, 1877–1924* (New York: Brill, 1997).

B. Pearce, 'A Falsifier of History', *Revolutionary Russia*, Vol.1 (1988), pp. 20–23.

B. Pearce, 'The 26 Commissars', *Sbornik* (1981), pp. 54–66.

B. Pearce, *The Staroselsky Problem 1918–1920: An Episode in British-Russian Relations in Persia* (London: School of Slavonic and Eastern European Studies, 1994).

M.A. Persits, *Revolutionaires of India in Soviet Russia. Mainsprings of the Communist Movement in the East* (Moscow: Progress Publishers, 1973).

R. Pipes, *The Russian Revolution, 1899–1919* (London: Harvill, 1990).

R. Pipes, *Russia Under the Bolshevik Regime, 1919–1924* (London: Harvill, 1994).

A.J. Plotke, *Imperial Spies Invade Russia: The British Intelligence Interventions, 1918* (London: Greenwood Press, 1993).

R.J. Popplewell, *Intelligence and Imperial Defence: British Intelligence and the Defence of the Indian Empire, 1904–1924* (London: Frank Cass, 1995).

B. Porter, *The Lion's Share* (London: Longman, 2004).

L.B. Poullada, *Reform and Rebellion in Afghanistan, 1919–1929* (New York: Cornell University Press, 1973).

A. Prestona, 'Sir Charles MacGregor and the Defence of India, 1857–1887', *The Historical Journal*, Vol. 12, No. 1 (1969), pp. 58–77.

H.J. Psomiades, *The Eastern Question, the Last Phase: A Study in Greek–Turkish Diplomacy* (New York: Pella, 2000).

J. Ramsden, *The Age of Balfour and Baldwin* (London: Longman, 1978).

A. Rashid, *Taliban: Islam, Oil and the New Great Game in Central Asia* (New York: I.B. Tauris, 2008).

H. Ray, 'Changing Soviet Views on Mahatma Gandhi', *The Journal of Asian Studies*, Vol. 29, No. 1 (1969), pp. 85–106.

S. Reed, 'The Governance of India', *Journal of the Royal Institute of International Affairs*, Vol. 6 (1927), pp. 314–326.

D. Reetz, *Hijrat: The Flight of the Faithful: a British File on the Exodus of Muslim Peasants from North India to Afghanistan in 1920* (Berlin: Verlag Das Arabische Buch, 1995).

E.B. Richards, 'The Shaping of the Comintern', *American Slavic and East European Review*, Vol. 18, No. 2 (1959), pp. 197–204.

W.L. Richter and B. Ramusack, 'The Chamber and the Consultation: Changing Forms of Princely Association in India', *The Journal of Asian Studies*, Vol. 34, No. 3 (1975), pp. 755–776.

J. Riddel, ed, *To see the Dawn: Baku 1920 – First Congress of the Peoples of the East* (New York: Pathfinder Press, 1993).

P.G. Robb, *The Government of India and Reform: Policies towards Politics and the Constitution, 1916–1921* (Oxford: Oxford University Press, 1976).

K. Robbins and G.S. Holmes, *The Eclipse of a Great Power: Modern Britain, 1870-1992* (London: Longman, 1994).

P.E. Roberts, *British Rule in India, Volume II: India Under the British Crown, 1856–1947* (New Delhi: Reprint Publication, 2006 Edition).

J.D. Rose, 'Batum as Domino, 1919–1920: The Defence of India in Transcaucasia', *The International History Review*, Vol. 2, No. 2 (1980), pp. 266–287.

C.N.B. Ross, 'Lord Curzon and E.G. Browne Confront the 'Persian Question'', *The Historical Journal*, Vol. 52, No. 2 (2009), pp. 385–411.

H. Sabahi, *British Policy in Persia, 1918–1925* (London: Frank Cass, 1990).

B. Sakhawaz, *The Role of Afghan Intellectuals in Modernisation and Independence from Britain*, http://www.goftaman.com/daten/en/articles/article47.htm.

C.S. Samra, *India and Anglo-Soviet Relations, 1917–1947* (Bombay: Asia Publishing House, 1959).

T.R. Sareen, *British Intervention in Central Asia and Trans-Caucasia* (New Delhi: Anmol Publications, 1989).

A. Sareen, *India and Afghanistan: British Imperialism vs. Afghan Nationalism, 1907–1921* (Delhi: Seema Publications, 1981).

D. Sayer, 'British Reaction to the Amritsar Massacre 1919–1920', *Past & Present*, No. 131 (1991), pp. 130–164.

B. Schwarz, 'Divided Attention: Britain's Perception of a German Threat to her Eastern Position in 1918', *Journal of Contemporary History*, Vol. 28, No. 1 (1993), pp. 103–122.

R. Service, *Spies and Commissars: Bolshevik Russia and the West* (London: Macmillan, 2012).

A. Sharp, 'The Foreign Office in Eclispe, 1919–1922', *History*, Vol. 61, No. 2 (1976), pp. 198–218.

J. Siegel, *Endgame: Britain, Russia and the Final Struggle for Central Asia* (London: I. B. Tauris, 2002).

J. Siegel, 'British Intelligence on the Russian Revolution and Civil War – A Breach at the Source', *Intelligence and National Security*, Vol. 10 (1995), pp. 468–485.

U. Sims-Williams, 'The Afghan Newspaper Siraj al-Akhbar', *Bulletin (British Society for Middle Eastern Studies)*, Vol. 7, No. 2 (1980), pp. 118–122.

S.R. Sonyel, 'Enver Pasha and the Basmaji Movement in Central Asia', *Middle Eastern Studies*, Vol. 26 (1990), pp. 52–64.

I. Spector, *The Soviet Union and the Muslim World, 1917–1958* (Seattle: University of Washington Press, 1959).

D.W. Spring, 'The Trans-Persian Railway Project and Anglo-Russian Relations, 1909–14', *The Slavonic and Eastern European Review*, Vol. 54, No. 1 (1976), pp. 60–82.

F. Stanwood, *War, Revolution and British Imperialism in Central Asia* (London: Ithaca Press, 1983).

F. Stanwood, 'Revolution and the "Old Reactionary Policy": Britain in Persia, 1917', *Journal of Imperial and Commonwealth History*, Vol. 6 (1978) pp. 144–165.

Z. Steiner, *The Foreign Office and Foreign Policy, 1898–1914* (London: Cambridge University Press, 1969).

Z. Steiner and M.L. Dockrill, 'The Foreign Office Reforms, 1919–21', *The Historical Journal*, Vol. 17, No. 1 (1974), pp. 131–156.

R.G. Suny and T. Martin, eds, *A State of Nations: Empire and Nation-Making in the Age of Lenin and Stalin* (Oxford: Oxford University Press, 2001).

G. Swain, *Russia's Civil War* (Stroud: The History Press, 2008).

M. Swartz, *The Union of Democratic Control in British Politics During the First World War* (Oxford: Clarendon Press, 1971).

P. Sykes, *A History of Afghanistan* (London: Macmillan, 1940).

J. Tapp, 'The Soviet-Persian Treaty of 1921', *International Law Quarterly*, Vol. 4 (1951), pp. 511–514.

A.J.P Taylor, ed., *Lloyd George: Twelve Essays* (London: Hamilton, 1971).

R. Teague-Jones, *The Spy Who Disappeared: Diary of a Secret Mission to Russian Central Asia in 1918* (London: Victor Gollancz, 1991).

I.D. Thatcher, ed, *Reinterpreting Revolutionary Russia* (London: Palgrave Macmillan, 2006).

J.M. Thompson, 'Lenin's Analysis of Intervention', *American Slavic and Eastern European Review*, Vol. 17, No. 2 (1958), pp. 151–160.

H. Tinker, *Viceroy: Curzon to Mounbatten* (Oxford: Oxford University Press, 1997).

J. Tomes, *Balfour and Foreign Policy: The International thought of a Conservative Statesman* (Cambridge: University Press Cambridge, 1997).

J. Townsend, *Proconsul to the Middle East: Sir Percy Cox and the End of Empire* (London; I.B. Tauris, 2010).

T.J. Uldricks, *Diplomacy and Ideology: Origins of Soviet Foreign Relations, 1917–1930* (London: Sage Publications, 1979).

R.H. Ullman, *Anglo-Soviet Relations, 1917–1921*:

Volume One, Intervention and the War (London: Oxford University Press, 1961).

Volume Two, Britain and the Russian Civil War, November 1918–February 1920 (London: Oxford University Press, 1968).

Volume Three, The Anglo-Soviet Accord (London: Oxford University Press, 1972).

M. Volodarsky, *The Soviet Union and its Southern Neighbours Iran and Afghanistan, 1917–1933* (Ilford: Frank Cass, 1994).

R. Warman, 'The Erosion of Foreign Office Influence in the Making of Foreign Policy, 1916–1918', *The Historical Journal,* Vol. 15, No.1 (1972), pp. 133–159.

D.C. Watt, *Personalities and Policies: Studies in the Formulation of British Foreign Policy in the Twentieth Century* (London: Longmans, 1965).

S.D. Waley, *Edwin Montagu: A Memoir and an Account of his Visits to India* (London: Asia Publishing House, 1964).

S. White, 'Communism and the East: The Baku Congress, 1920', *Slavic Review*, Vol. 33, No. 3 (1974), pp. 492–514.

S. White, *Britain and the Bolshevik Revolution: A Study in the Politics of Diplomacy, 1920–1924* (London: Macmillan, 1979).

S. White, 'Soviet Russia and the Asian Revolution, 1917–1924', *Review of International Studies*, Vol. 10, No. 3 (1984), pp. 219–232.

S. White, 'British Labour in Soviet Russia, 1920', *The English Historical Review*, Vol. 109, No. 432 (1994), pp. 621–640.

S. White, 'Colonial Revolution and the Communist International, 1919–1924', *Science and Society,* Vol. 40, No. 2 (1996), pp. 173–193.

S. White, *The Origins of Detente: the Genoa Conference and Soviet-Western relations, 1921–1922* (Cambridge: Cambridge University Press, 2002).

B.J. Williams, 'The Strategic Backround to the Anglo-Russian Entente of August 1907', *The Historical Journal,* Vol. 9, No. 3 (1966), pp. 360–373.

D.R. Woodward, 'British Intervention in Russia during the First World War', *Military Affairs*, Vol. 41 (1977), pp. 171–175.

D. Wright, *The English among the Persians, 1787–1921* (London: Heinemann, 1977).

A. Wynn, *Persia in the Great Game: Sir Percy Sykes Explorer, Consul, Soldier, Spy* (London: John Murray, 2003).

M.A. Yapp, 'British Perceptions of the Russian Threat to India', *Modern Asian Studies,* Vol. 21, No. 4 (1987), pp. 647–665.

M.E. Yapp, *Strategies of British India: Britain, Iran and Afghanistan 1798–1850* (Oxford: Clarendon Press, 1980).

G.M. Young, *Victorian England: Portrait of an Age* (Oxford: Oxford University Press, 1977).

M.P. Zirinsky, 'Imperial Power and Dictatorship: Britain and the Rise of Reza Shah, 1921–1926', *International Journal of Middle Eastern Studies*, Vol. 24, No. 4 (Nov., 1992), pp. 639–663.

Index

Afghanistan
  encouragement of Hijrat, 69–70
  relations with Bolsheviks, 39, 40, 59,
    89, 93, 124–5
Allied Intervention, xx
  Dunsterforce, xx, 23
  Malleson mission, xx, 23, 28, 32, 39
Amanullah, Emir, 38–41, 59–60,
  69–70, 93, 95, 122–5
Amritsar Massacre, 39, 42, 64
Anglo-Afghan Treaty, 100
Anglo-Persian Agreement, viii, 35,
  54–5, 78–80, 83, 85, 98, 108
Anglo-Russian Convention, 3–8, 20, 85
Anglo-Soviet Trade Agreement, 76–7,
  86, 97, 135
Armistice of Mudanya, 116
Asian nationalism, 27–8, 46, 65, 71, 81,
  123, 129
Ataturk, Kemal, viii, 27, 67, 103, 110,
  116, 124

Baku, xx, 50, 70, 120
  26 Commissars, case of, vii
Baku Congress
  See First Congress of the Peoples
    of the East
Baldwin, Stanley, xi, 136
Balfour, Arthur, ix, xiii, xv, 18–9, 25,
  38, 204
Basmachi, 123–4
Bolsheviks

Appeal to the Working Moslems
  of Russia and the East, viii
Commissariat for Muslim
  Affairs, 62
Enzeli, invasion of, 52
foreign policy, 29, 41, 103, 120
New Economic Policy (NEP), 120
Red Army, 50–1
relations with Afghanistan,
  39, 102
relations with Indian
  revolutionaries, 39
relations with Persia, 51, 102,
  105–106
Bonar Law, Andrew, xi
Bravin, Karl, 28–9, 39, 59, 60, 106
Brest-Litovsk, Treaty of, xxi
British Empire
  decline, xvii–xix
  economic performance, xvii
  power, xvii–xviii, 10, 22, 47
  prestige, 76, 88, 97, 101
British government (Home)
  anti-Bolshevik, xx–xxi, 109, 129
  domestic turmoil, 49
  intelligence, 122
  military expenditure, 49–50
  policy towards Persia, 104, 109
  Russophobia, 6–12
British Raj, 10
Browne, E.G., 6, 16, 31, 78, 146
Bukhara, 12, 59, 65, 93, 123–25

Cabinet Secretariat, x–xii
Caliphate issue, 65–8, 116–17, 123
  See also Pan-Islamism
Cecil, Robert, xiii, 8, 25–6, 30, 35
Chauri Chaura riots, 118
Chelmsford, Lord, 31–47, 55, 64,
  67–9, 71, 79, 82–4, 88, 91–2,
  128, 154
  opinions on, 91–2
  See also Montagu-Chelmsford
    reforms
Churchill, Winston, xi, xiii, 49–54, 65,
  73, 84–5, 98–9, 109, 131
Comintern, viii, 62–3, 103, 122
  See also Second Congress of
    the Comintern
Communist University of the Toilers
  of the East, 120
Conolly, Arthur, 1
Cossack Division, 7, 32, 37, 56–7, 129
Cox, Percy, 26–9, 32–3, 36–7, 56, 73,
  79–80
Crowe, Eyre, x–xii, xv, 25, 34, 66,
  131, 195
Curzon, George Nathaniel
  anti-Bolshevik, 36, 105,
    129, 130
  dispute with Kitchener, 19
  dominance, xvi, 17–8, 46, 72–3,
    98–9, 128
  expertise, 14, 16, 19, 132
  Great Game mentality, 20, 26,
    130, 134
  Lord President of the Council, 136
  note, 110
  opinions on, 13–4
  publications, 11, 16
  Russophobia, 14–5, 21, 129
  travels, 11, 16
  viceroy of India, 17–9
  Younghusband expedition, 18

Denikin, General, 37, 50, 53
Dobbs, H.R.C., 40–1, 60–1, 66, 89,
  90–6, 100, 123–24
Dyer, General
  See Amritsar Massacre

Eastern Committee, xiii, 13, 19, 24–6,
  29, 31, 37–8, 52–3, 83, 105, 132

First Anglo-Afghan War, 2
First Congress of the Peoples of
  the East, 70–1, 102, 124
Foreign Office
  conflict with War Office, 54
  control of information, xii
  criticism of, xiv
  influence, ix, 98–9
  'mind', xv–xvi
  recruitment to, xiv
  relationship to other
    deptartments, xi
  remit, ix, x, xii, 115

Gandamak, Treaty of, 3
Gandhi, Mahatma
  See Non-cooperation movement
Germany
  Berlin-Baghdad railway, 4, 6
Grant, Hamilton, 30–1, 40–4, 59–60,
  69–70, 131
Great Game, 2–3, 41, 103, 108
  mentality, xxi–xxiii, 1, 8–9, 20, 101,
    128, 130–1

Habibullah, Emir, 34–8, 43
Hands off Russia, 49
Hankey, Maurice, xi
Hardinge, Charles, x, xii, xv,
  xvi, 6, 14, 17, 25, 65, 82,
  115, 131
Hirtzel, Arthur, 22, 25

Humphrys, Colonel, 123–5
Hunter Commission
   See Amritsar Massacre

India Office
   See British government (Home)
Indian government
   and Afghanistan, 41, 44, 60, 88–9,
      95, 125–6
   and Bolsheviks, xxi, 27, 41, 61,
      74, 120–1, 130–1
   and Persia, 31, 46, 83–4
   anti-Bolshevik measures, 62
   control of Afghanistan's foreign
      affairs, 43–4, 100
   disagreement with Home
      government, 41, 44, 88, 90–1,
      96, 133
   expertise, 34
   finances, 23, 34, 51
   foreign relations, xix
   Gandhi
      See Non-cooperation
         movement
   intelligence network, 121–2
   jurisdiction, 24, 115
   reaction to Caliphate issue, 68
   reaction to Hijrat, 69
Interdepartmental Conference on the
   Middle East, 25

Jangalis, 36–7, 53

Kerr, Philip, x–xi
Khan, Reza, viii, 3, 29, 36–8, 50, 53,
   57, 63, 81, 93, 103, 107
Khiva, 59, 93, 123–4

Lloyd George, David, x, xi, xiii, 66,
   113, 115
Loraine, Percy, 104–109, 111

Marling, Charles, 26, 30, 31, 33
Mesopotamia Administration
   Committee
   See Eastern Committee
Mesopotamia Commission, 34
Middle Eastern Department, xiii,
   25–6, 98
Minto, Lord, xviii
Montagu, Edwin, xix, 24, 29–30, 33–5,
   38, 41, 44–5, 56, 65–73, 82, 89,
   90–8, 128
   and Curzon, 13, 114
   opinions on, 64, 113
   resignation, 111–3
Montagu-Chelmsford reforms,
   xvii, 113
Moplah rebellion, 118
Mussoorie Conference
   See Indian government: and
      Afghanistan

Niedermayer Mission, 155
Non-cooperation movement, 64,
   118–9
Norman, Herman, 54–8, 78–82, 85–6,
   99, 104, 107
Norperforce, 57, 82, 84

Oliphant, Lancelot, 29, 33, 81, 86,
   104, 106

Pan-Islamism, 27–8, 46, 64, 67, 71, 95,
   104, 109, 116–7, 122–3, 129
Pasha, Enver, 124–5
Peel, Lord, 120–1
Persia
   reaction to Anglo-Russian
      Convention, 8
   relations with Bolsheviks, 107
   relations with Britain, 7–8, 29, 56,
      78–9, 81, 85, 108

Reading, Lord, 91–7, 112, 115, 118, 121, 125
Red Terror
  See British government (Home): anti-Bolshevik
Roos-Keppel, George, 43–4
Rothstein, Theodore, 105–109
Rowlatt Bill, 39
Roy, M.N., 63, 71, 88, 120–2
Russia
  fear of Germany, 4
  role in Persia, 7
  Russian Legation in Tehran, 32, 36
  White Russians, 36–7, 50
Russo-Japanese War, 4

Second Anglo-Afghan War, 2–3, 37
Second Congress of the Comintern, 62–3, 106, 123
Shuster, W.M., 8, 81
South Persia Rifles, 23, 83
Soviet foreign policy
  See Bolsheviks: foreign policy
Soviet Republic of Iran, 53
Soviet-Afghan Treaty, 93–6

Soviet-Persian Treaty, 85–7
Staroselskii, Colonel, 32–7, 57–8
Sykes, Mark, xiii, 22–3, 140

Tarzi, Muhammad, 38, 43, 94, 96, 125
The Battle of George Square
  See British government (Home): domestic turmoil
Third Anglo-Afghan War, 38–9, 42
Tibet, 18
Tournament of Shadows
  See Great Game
Treaty of Lausanne, 116
Treaty of Sèvres, 69, 72, 110, 112, 117
Turkey, 109–112, 117

Wilson, Henry, 37, 43, 49, 50–4, 68, 73

Younghusband expedition
  See Curzon, George Nathaniel: Younghusband expedition

Zinoviev Letter, 129, 135
Zinoviev, Grigory, 63, 70–1, 129